Making the Special Schools Ordinary?

Making the Special Schools Ordinary?

Volume 1 – Models for the Developing Special School

Edited by
Derek Baker and Keith Bovair

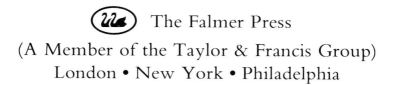 The Falmer Press

(A Member of the Taylor & Francis Group)
London • New York • Philadelphia

UK   The Falmer Press, Falmer House, Barcombe, Lewes, East Sussex. BN8 5DL

USA   The Falmer Press, Taylor & Francis Inc., 242 Cherry Street, Philadelphia, PA 19106–1906

First published 1989

British Library Cataloguing in Publication Data

Making the Special Schools Ordinary?: Volume
1. Models for the Developing Special School.
1. Great Britain. Special Schools. Education.
I. Title. II. Bovair, Keith.
317.9
ISBN 1-85000-436-6
ISBN 1-85000-437-4 (pbk.)

Typeset in Bembo by
David John Services Limited, Slough, Berks.

Printed in Great Britain by Taylor & Francis (Printers) Ltd, Basingstoke

Contents

Contents

Acknowledgments

We chose to collaborate on this project because of our varied experiences in Special Education, and our work with children, parents, fellow teachers, psychologists, and administrators in Great Britain, Canada, and the United States.

We would like to acknowledge the stimulus and inspiration given to us by our many colleagues in Haringey and Cambridgeshire, and in particular the staffs of The Moselle School and The Lady Adrian School. We are deeply grateful to Mel Ainscow and Tony Dessent for their guidance and support, and to Christine Cox for her faith in our idea.

Last but not least special thanks are due to our wives, Jane and Maggie, our children — Debra, James and Clare, and Christian, Simone and Dominic and Nicole — for their tolerance and understanding during the completion of this project.

List of Abbreviations

ACE	Advisory Council for Education
AEO	Assistant or Area Education Officer
CDT	Craft Design & Technology
CPVE	Certificate of Pre-Vocational Education
CSE	Certificate of Secondary Education
DES	Department of Education and Science
EBD	Emotional and Behavioural Difficulties
ELSA	Early Learning Skills Analysis
ESG	Education Support Grant
FE	Further Eduation
GCSE	General Certificate of Secondary Education
GERBIL	(Great) Education Reform Bill
GRIST	Grant Related In-Service Training
HMI	Her Majesty's Inspectorate
HSC	Home-School Council
ILEA	Inner London Education Authority
INSET	In-Service Training
IST	Integration Support Teacher(s)
LEA	Local Education Authority
MLD	Moderate Learning Difficulties
MSC	Manpower Services Commission
NFER	National Foundation for Education Research
PE	Physical Education
PMLD	Profound and Multiple Learning Difficulties
PSE	Personal and Social Education
PTA	Parent-Teacher Association
RSA	Royal Society of Arts
SEC	Secondary Examinations Council
SEN	Special Educational Needs

SERC	Special Education Resource Centre
SLD	Severe Learning Difficulties
SNAP	Special Needs Action Programme
SPS	Schools Psychological Service
TRIST	Technical and Vocational Related In-Service Training
TVEI	Technical and Vocational Education Initiative
YTS	Youth Training Scheme

Foreword
John Fish

Special schools, not necessarily in their present form, will continue to play an important role, in this country, in the range of provision to meet special educational needs. Whether one's viewpoint is that of the integrationist or that of the traditionalist this represents reality. Because of inadequate policies and resources together with the inability of primary and secondary schools to be infinitely flexible, in the one view, or because there is no acceptable alternative and such schools have an absolute right to exist, in the other, a future is secure.

Among the rich array of information, opinion and argument in this book there are still echoes of uncertainty and of self-justification among the impressive evidence of innovation and development. There are still mis-understandings and uncertainties about integration among the descriptions of positive links between special schools and other schools.

Nevertheless, children with and without special educational needs are sharing more social and educational activities. Special schools through their growing work with primary and secondary schools are becoming part of the school system. Expertise and experience is flowing both ways: for example, the management of learning from special schools and curriculum knowledge and breadth from primary and secondary schools.

It is as well that different approaches are described and analysed here because new legislation may make it increasingly difficult for primary and secondary schools to cooperate in the future. Implementing the National Curriculum may result in many children with special educational needs being excluded from what it offers. It may also force special schools without strong links to become more isolated from the primary and secondary school system.

In such circumstances how can schools, particularly those with small staffs, maintain a high level of knowledge and skills in a wide range of curriculum areas, a wide range of aspects of teaching and a wide range of specialisms? Contributors outline many additional skills, for example in consultancy work, for which training is also necessary.

Current methods of determining and funding in-service education threaten the maintenance of a teaching force trained and experienced to work with particular disabilities and learning difficulties in special schools and classes.

In an era of emphasis on management it is important to recognize that many of the things to be managed in special schools are not unique to them. Special schools have many common concerns with other schools as well as their additional responsibilities. They do not have different concerns. Hence much of what this book is about matters to all schools and teachers.

The 1990s are going to see radical changes in the education system as new legislation is understood and implemented. It is essential that we should take stock of special educational provision. We need to know where special schools are in their development, what they have accomplished and what are their most effective practices. Only by being clear about the contributions of special schools and services can we ensure that they support other schools as part of the education service as a whole.

This book exemplifies the thinking that has taken place and needs to take place in the continued development of special schools. It is important to maintain a positive image in the minds of parents and colleagues in the education service. Special schools must not be seen as places to which failures go but as schools offering something of value which is additional. *Making the Special Schools Ordinary?* is a major contribution to this process.

Introduction
Derek Baker and Keith Bovair

Following the Warnock Report and the 1981 Education Act much informed speculation ensued regarding the probable structure of provision for pupils with special educational needs. This book examines how special schools have responded, and describes ways in which special schools can adapt now for the future.

Recent books quite properly address the ways in which ordinary schools may respond to current legislation and educational orthodoxy. However, it is by no means clear that all special schools will cease to exist; in fact it is likely that most will continue to operate for the foreseeable future. Moreover, they will continue in a climate that is uncertain, if not hostile.

Much of the good practice now being adopted by ordinary schools first developed in special schools. In recent years many special schools have continued to innovate.

The fundamental principles underlying special education have been seriously questioned. Few sections of the education service could have responded to the challenge so swiftly and professionally as the special school, and in the process created such a stimulating and far-sighted environment.

Current literature now largely ignores special schools except to dismiss them. They have become unfashionable and many people say that they are no longer necessary. That assumes, however, that ordinary schools have adapted to fulfil the role previously held by special schools and indeed that few children now attend special schools. Nothing could be farther from reality.

This book is neither an apology nor a justification for special schools. It presents examples of ways in which special schools have adapted, and are continuing to adapt, in a way that will be of interest to those working in both ordinary and special schools.

Volume 1 brings together the views of some of the most respected and influential writers in the field of special education and special needs, as well as experienced practitioners who are at the forefront of current developments.

Volume 2 presents a series of case studies written by teachers and other educational practitioners which represent models of interesting and innovative good practice for other schools to examine.

Contributions to the first volume have been set out under five themes: The Context for Change; Working with Ordinary Schools; Special Schools: A Positive Response; The Wider Context; and Specialized Views.

In the first section Mel Ainscow examines developments in special school curricula and makes recommendations for future developments in light of the National Curriculum. Derek Baker discusses the role of the headteacher in a time of rapid change, and proposes a positive strategy for meeting both external demands for change and the development needs of an institution.

The second section presents the views of three practitioners, Eileen Tombs, Maggie Balshaw, and Allan Day, who have each experienced the positive nature of working with ordinary schools, through practice and research.

The third section deals with two special schools that have attempted to be responsive to the current climate of change. Keith Bovair, Andrew Hinchcliff and Carmen Renwick draw from their experience of taking an isolated special school with a limited curriculum and expanding that curriculum while working in close partnership with ordinary schools in their community. Barry Carpenter and Ann Lewis describe patterns of integration of children with severe and profound and multiple learning difficulties into an ordinary setting.

Section 4 begins with Ian Galletley putting forward a curriculum for post-16 provision, while Sheila Wolfendale examines the parental role in special needs provision. Mike Wright describes a whole authority approach to in-service training and the role of the special school. Morag Styles and Catherine Pearce show the benefits to be gained from initial teacher training occurring in a special school setting.

Jim Muncey opens section 5 by highlighting the role of the special school in a whole authority response to special educational needs. Tom Peryer writes from the perspective of an education officer who is dealing daily with the increased pressures of the changing climate in special education. Tony Dessent identifies the dilemmas that still face the special school in a period dominated by theories of non-segregation.

It is intended that this book should be of particular value to those involved in initial training, teachers of children with special needs in both special and ordinary schools, headteachers, and those following further or advanced courses of training. It brings together a wealth of experience and practical expertise, and fulfils the need for a companion volume to recent publications in providing an insight into the response of individual schools and authorities to both recent trends and legislation.

Section 1
The Context for Change

Chapter 1

Developing the Special School Curriculum: Where Next?

Mel Ainscow

In Tolstoy's great novel *Anna Karenina*, Anna, a woman who has experienced deep shame as a result of an extra-marital relationship, commits suicide by throwing herself in front of an on-coming train. It is said that Tolstoy wrote a number of different versions of his story but in each case the outcome was the same, Anna ended up on the railway line.

It seems to me that we can look at the future of special schools in this country in the same way. No matter what happens in the meantime, sooner or later special schools as we have known them will disappear.

Accepting this to be the case, it has to be recognised that their demise is likely to take place over a period of many years. Consequently it is important that every effort is made to ensure that during these 'many years' the pupils who receive all or part of their education in special schools should have the best possible experience that can be provided.

In this chapter I examine the state of the art as far as the curriculum in special schools is concerned, and make some recommendations for future developments. My analysis leads me to make reference to wider matters concerning the curriculum in schools generally, not least the current debate about the introduction of a National Curriculum.

I should add that by its very nature the chapter consists of broad generalizations which, when applied to a school system that is by tradition so diverse, do not always apply. Nevertheless I believe that the points I make are reasonably typical of the situation in special schools across the country.

THE PAST

The last ten years or so have seen a significant increase of interest in the nature of the curriculum in special schools. Previously it was an issue that seemed to be rarely considered. The emphasis on care and protection that had been the major feature of such schools had meant that what actually happened in the classrooms was of no great concern. Consequently the curriculum tended to be constructed largely around the interests of individual teachers used as a means of maintaining the attention of the pupils.

During the late 1970s, however, there was evidence of a new interest in the curriculum of special schools. This was in part an element of a wider community concern about the purpose of schooling, leading to demands for greater accountability. There were, in addition, other more specific pressures that seemed to draw attention to the need for an examination of what happens in special schools.

Certainly a number of significant publications had the effect of raising concern. In particular the Warnock Report suggested that the quality of education offered to pupils with special educational needs was in some respects unsatisfactory, and that the evidence gathered by the authors of the report indicated that many special schools underestimated their pupils' capabilities (DES, 1978). Other publications (e.g. Brennan, 1979; Tomlinson, 1982) were also critical of existing practice.

The 1981 Education Act added further to the debate about the nature of special schooling and its relationship with the curriculum of ordinary primary and secondary schools. It also gave encouragement to those parents who wished to have a greater say in the curriculum offered to their children.

The reaction of teachers in many special schools to this new focus of attention on their work was to become more interested in the theoretical basis of their practice. In particular they became interested in the theory of curriculum development. In their search for guidance in this respect many special school teachers were influenced by the literature on planning with objectives, sometimes referred to as rational curriculum planning. This approach to planning, which was by no means new in the field of curriculum studies, had become very popular in special education in North America, probably because of the strong influence of behavioural psychologists. In this country many of us working at that time in special schools found the approach helpful as we sought ways of planning our teaching in a more systematic manner.

Consequently a new literature emerged providing suggestions and guidelines as to how teachers in special schools might plan the curriculum using behavioural objectives and task analysis techniques (e.g. Ainscow and Tweddle, 1979; Brennan, 1979; Gardner, Murphy and Crawford, 1983). Also, in-service courses for teachers began to include sessions which dealt with this approach.

Undoubtedly this focus on rational curriculum planning has had a major impact on the curriculum in special schools, particularly those for pupils with severe and moderate learning difficulties. In the main this influence has been a positive one. It has, for example, given many teachers a means of talking about the purposes of their work. It has raised teacher expectations about what some of their pupils may achieve. On the other hand it is increasingly recognised that as an approach to curriculum planning it has significant limitations and possible dangers (Ainscow and Tweddle, 1988).

THE PRESENT

How, then, might we characterise the current scene as far as the curriculum in special schools is concerned? What has been placed on curriculum planning in many special schools during recent years?

In considering these issues I will present a balance sheet, indicating areas of strength and weakness. The areas of strength are aspects of current practice which need to be maintained and developed; the areas of weakness, on the other hand, should be examined and ameliorated.

First, the areas of strength. It seems to me that the attention that has been given to curriculum planning in many special schools has led to a greater sense of purpose. The holiday camp ambience that so characterised special schools in the past is much less apparent these days. Instead there is an emphasis on the achievement of objectives which tends to inject purpose and urgency into the classroom encounters that take place.

The process of curriculum review that is now apparent in many special schools can also be powerful in achieving a *common* sense of purpose within which members of staff have come to a reasonable agreement about the overall intentions of their work. Indeed it may well be that the *process* of discussing the curriculum is more significant than the actual decisions that are made. Certainly a noticeable feature of successful schools (of any type) is an overall feeling amongst staff that they are working towards an agreed set of aims.

Associated with this emphasis on a sense of purpose in many special schools is a policy for monitoring and recording pupil progress. In effect the definition of objectives within the curriculum has raised questions about how achievement of these objectives can be measured. Where special schools have developed more sensitive recording systems this can also have a positive effect on teacher expectations. Recording and celebrating achievement tends to be good for teacher morale, which in turn yields benefits in terms of confidence and ambition.

Inevitably the form of recording used in special schools varies, but in general there is a tendency to use various forms of checklist which are intended to be used to indicate objectives that have been achieved. Accepting that there are obvious limitations in this type of approach, it can have a further positive influence in that it encourages teachers to pay greater attention to pupils as individuals. What it provides is a relatively simple format that can be used by teachers to observe and record the positive achievements of each pupil. This positive orientation is very different to so much traditional special education practice which tended to focus attention on pupils' deficits and areas of difficulty.

To sum up, the strengths of current practice in the curriculum of special schools are to a large extent as a result of the process of review and development that has become a feature of many such establishments in recent years. In particular this has had a postive effect on the professional confidence of members of staff and has led to a greater sense of purpose. In addition, the process of discussion has provided the basis of a significant staff development programme. In saying this I am reminded of Lawrence Stenhouse's words, 'Curriculum development must rest on teacher development...'.

What then of the areas of weakness in current practice? In my view these are all to do with the range of experiences provided for the pupils in such schools. By the very nature of their size, resources and populations, special schools provide a curriculum which is narrow, restricted and, at times, restricting. For some, this narrowness has been seen as a positive feature. Essentially the idea was to bring together pupils perceived as sharing similar areas of educational difficulty with a view to providing them with a form of curriculum that would help them to overcome their difficulties. Thus pupils who experienced significant problems in learning in ordinary schools were offered a programme that attempted to achieve objectives that were felt to be of particular importance to their future welfare.

The traditionally narrow focus of special schools may have been further encouraged in some cases by the emphasis that has been placed on determining precise objectives in so-called basic skill areas of the curriculum. Certainly in many schools for pupils with severe learning difficulties a great deal of attention has been paid to the planning of sequences of objectives in areas of social competence, such as dressing and feeding. Similarly in schools that cater for pupils with behaviour difficulties, objectives which are to do with social conduct may be emphasised.

Planning with objectives fits rather nicely in these situations. By and large it is relatively easy to agree detailed statements of intention in areas of rudimentary learning. Unfortunately if this line is followed rigidly it leads to the production of lists of objectives which define in detail those aspects of the curriculum which are most easily measured. Other aspects of learning, which in themselves may be of greater importance, are left unrecorded and, by implication, defined as requiring less attention.

My argument is that all children in a democratic society have the right to participate in broadly the same range of educational experiences. If the presence of a child in a special school effectively rules out this possibility because of the decisions made by the staff, such a pupil is disadvantaged. Furthermore, if the curriculum of a school becomes so narrow that it is detached from experiences that have meaning for the pupils, their interest in learning is likely to be diminished.

A further aspect of this narrowness which characterizes the work of many special schools is the tendency to engage pupils in an extensive diet of individual activity. Once again this may in part be an outcome of the emphasis that is placed on planning objectives for each pupil. Despite the value that this provides in terms of pupils working on tasks which are matched to their existing skills and knowledge, if this means that they spend large parts of each day working in isolation this is again to their disadvantage. Most of us learn most successfully when we are engaged in activities with other people. Apart from the intellectual stimulation that this can provide, there is also the confidence that comes from having other people to provide support and help as we work. If special school pupils are working alone for most of their time in school, none of these benefits can accrue.

In considering this issue there is a further argument that is worthy of consideration. It concerns personal and social development. It is not uncommon for pupils to be placed in special schools partly, at least, because of difficulties they have in relating to other children in school. In other words, their special educational needs are to do with their limited skills in working and playing with others. If the special school curriculum does not require them to engage with their peers in completing tasks it is, in effect, helping them to avoid their areas of need.

The final aspect of narrowness which characterizes the work of some special schools is to do with pupil-teacher relationships. Again partly as a result of the emphasis on predetermined curriculum objectives, pupils are regarded as having little or no role to play in taking responsibility for their own learning. Their role in school is largely a passive one. They are there to follow the directions provided by the teachers. As a consequence they gain little experience of decision-making. Yet most of these youngsters when they leave school will be expected to make all sorts of decisions and live with the consequences.

I am afraid that this description of passivity is still a feature of many of the special schools I have visited recently. It is, for example, noticeable in some special schools that cater for pupils with physical disabilities, where the hidden message of the curriculum seems to be that they must learn not to make too many demands of society.

To summarize, despite the undoubted progress that has been made in terms of the quality of curriculum experience provided for pupils in special schools in recent years, there is still a tendency to narrowness which is to the disadvantage of these pupils. This narrowness is characterized by limitations of content, experience and relationships.

THE FUTURE

My review of existing practice suggests that the developments in the special school curriculum that have occurred in recent years have had positive effects on teacher expectations. Nevertheless they are still characterized by a narrowness which is inevitably a source of restriction for the pupils. In considering future developments, therefore, my recommendations take account of this analysis. I am wanting to start from where we are at the moment. This being the case the curriculum question that I would want colleagues in special schools to address is:

> How can we provide a suitably broad range of curriculum experiences for our pupils?

Continuing my argument at the level of broad generalization I will look at four areas that seem to me to be of particular importance. These are:

1. Links with mainstream schools;
2. Pupil involvement;
3. Cooperative learning; and
4. Recording and evaluation.

1. Links with mainstream schools

One fairly obvious way in which the experience of pupils in special schools can be broadened is by seeking to develop closer links with neighbouring primary and secondary schools. It is encouraging to report that recent years have seen an increase in examples of this type of initiative, some of which are reported elsewhere in this book.

During the immediate post-Warnock period the nature of these links tended to grow out of an assumption that special schools should develop a new role in providing support to pupils in local schools. Special schools were to become area resource centres for meeting special needs or, more ambitiously, 'centres of expertise'.

The limitations of this type of approach, and the potential hazards, have gradually become more apparent. The idea that a particular school is a centre of expertise can set up all sorts of expectations which may backfire, not least of which is that somebody may question the authenticity of the expertise that is said to be available. Also, many special school teachers have, as a result of their new links with primary and secondary schools, come to a realization that expertise is spread fairly evenly across the education service. Consequently relationships between schools from different sectors of the service should be developed in the belief that colleagues from each will benefit from the experience.

Certainly where special schools have developed closer links with neighbouring schools there seems to be a range of ways in which curriculum opportunities can be extended. Sharing teachers, resources and facilities, exchanging staff and pupils, planning joint projects or option schemes, are all strategies which can benefit all the participants and can be seen as part of a 'whole community' approach to providing education. They can also be helpful in overcoming the prejudice that both pupils and teachers from special schools have experienced in the past.

What is the nature of the curriculum benefits that may result from such ventures? Most obviously they can facilitate opportunities for special school pupils to take part in subjects which hitherto have not been possible because of lack of specialist staff and facilities. In addition, the enrichment that pupils from different types of school can gain through their interactions can be a positive benefit in both an academic and a social sense.

2. Pupil involvement

One of the trends that is so influential in curriculum development in ordinary schools at present is towards greater pupil involvement in decision-making. It is based on a belief that schools should be helping pupils to become more autonomous learners. This is reflected particularly in new forms of examination at the secondary stage, including GCSE and the introduction of records of achievement.

I have argued that the tendency to see pupils as having a passive role in special schools is part of the narrowness of experience to which they are exposed. A potential benefit of closer links with ordinary schools is that these will encourage the introduction into special education of approaches to teaching and learning which recognise the importance of pupil involvement. Certainly my experience has been that where secondary schools have introduced forms of assessment and recording which emphasize the role of pupils in self-assessment this can have a significant effect on the nature of the classroom encounters that occur. The negotiations between teacher and pupils that this necessitates creates a new relationship within which the teaching role is less one of instructor and more one of facilitator of learning. It also encourages a much less dependent relationship between pupils and their teachers.

If pupils are to become more actively involved in their own learning and development they will need help in:

- understanding the purposes of particular lessons or activities;
- defining personal objectives within the overall aims of an activity;
- seeing links between different learning experiences;
- planning ahead to achieve their objectives;
- assessing their own progress;
- appreciating their own strengths and weaknesses in the learning situation.

All of this assures a flexible and cooperative working relationship between teacher and pupils within which these issues can be discussed. Such relationships are often a feature of special schools and represent a strength if used to give pupils greater responsibility in a planned way.

It would, of course, be naive to argue that such approaches are easy to introduce with pupils in special schools, particularly those who have severe and complex disabilities which limit their ability to communicate. My argument is simply that the traditions of special education have been such that attempts are rarely made. It is assumed that the pupils would not be able to cope.

3. Cooperative learning

Related to the need to find ways of encouraging greater pupil involvement in decisions about their learning is the argument for a greater use of approaches which require pupils to learn together. In any classroom there are two major resources for helping pupils to learn, the teacher and the other members of the class. Much of traditional thinking and practice in special schools, with its emphasis on carefully planned, teacher-directed individual programmes, has tended to underestimate if not dismiss the benefits that can be gained as a result of pupils working cooperatively. As I have said, it is not uncommon to see pupils in special schools working alone for large parts of the school day.

Whilst working alone on individualized tasks is an important and legitimate approach for all children, used excessively it is a limited and limiting form of learning. This has been recognized in many ordinary schools, where attempts are being made to encourage pupils to become more skilful in learning cooperatively. This is not an easy task since it requires a sophistication of curriculum planning and implementation for which many teachers feel ill-prepared.

Where pupils are to be introduced to cooperative ways of working this has to be planned and introduced in a systematic way, as with any other new learning experience. Effectively it involves the introduction of an additional series of demands, requiring pupils to work towards objectives associated with the content of the curriculum at the same time as achieving new objectives to do with their skills in collaboration.

When this works well, the benefits are enormous. Cooperative learning that is successful can have a positive effect on academic outcomes, self-esteem, social relationships and personal development (Johnson and Johnson, 1986). Furthermore it has the potential to free teacher time as a result of making pupils less dependent on the teacher for help and support.

I wish to argue, therefore, that one significant way in which the curriculum of special schools might be broadened and enriched is to introduce a planned policy to encourage pupils to work cooperatively. I must stress, however, that such a policy will require the staff involved to have appropriate in-service training and support. Put simply, cooperation amongst teachers is likely to be helpful as they try to introduce greater cooperation to their pupils.

4. Recording and evaluation

My final recommendation is to do with evaluation of the curriculum in special schools. I believe that widening the range and perspective of the forms of evaluation used can have a positive influence on the range of curriculum experiences offered to the pupils.

In recent years the forms of evaluation used in special schools have tended to be guided by the question:

– Are the pupils achieving their objectives?

In schools where the planned objectives have been narrowly conceived this has meant that the forms of evaluation used have also been narrow — one leads to the other.

A broader perspective on evaluation can be achieved by creating an agenda which recognises the complexity of classroom life; the need to reflect on the value of particular learning activities; the potential importance of events that are unplanned; and the interpretations that different participants may place on the same encounter. With this in mind I would suggest that evaluation needs to focus on three further questions. These are:

– Are the objectives worthwhile?
– What else is happening?
– How do people feel?

Given all of these questions, evaluation becomes a continuous process of gathering information about the curriculum as it is enacted with a view to make improvements as seems necessary. A commitment to such an approach is more to do with attitude of mind rather than actual techniques. What is needed is a desire to involve all members of a school community, staff, pupils and parents, in a continuous dialogue about the purpose, nature and effectiveness of the curriculum that is offered. Such an orientation represents a concerted effort to ensure that the curriculum of a school remains responsive to the individual needs of pupils and the community of which they are members.

IMPLICATIONS OF A NATIONAL CURRICULUM

At the time of writing the above analysis and recommendations about the curriculum in special schools there is considerable debate about the government's proposals to introduce a National Curriculum, including associated procedures for assessing pupil progress. A very small part of this debate has focused on the future role of special schools within an education system which is geared to the delivery of such a curriculum.

So far the main argument seems to be that the process of writing a statement of special educational need will be a means of excluding pupils from all or part of the National Curriculum. It is assumed, I suppose, that such an exclusion will be in the best interests of these pupils.

My fear is that rather than being in their interests it may have the effect of retarding some of the interesting developments in the special school curriculum that are currently under way. As we have seen, the aspects of the special school curriculum that need developing either require or can be enhanced by the establishment of closer links with mainstream education. A policy for a National Curriculum which endorses the entitlement of *all* pupils to take part in the same broad range of experiences would be helpful in this respect. If, on the other hand, the procedure of writing statements becomes a facility to exclude pupils from these experiences this may well encourage a return to a special school scene which is characterized by separation and limited opportunity.

Whilst supporting the idea of a National Curriculum in principle, therefore, I hope that it will take the form of a statement of curriculum entitlement which will encourage the development of closer links between special and ordinary schools. Indeed the logical extension of such a trend must surely be the eventual amalgamation of the two sectors into a genuinely comprehensive education service.

CONCLUSION

The argument presented in this chapter assumes that sooner or later special schools as we have known them will disappear. Indeed the trends in curriculum practice that I recommend represent a case for the gradual amalgamation of special schools into the mainstream of the education service.

Put in this way I trust that it will be seen that my case is not intended to be damaging to what exists at present. Rather my idea would be to build on the strengths of the current situation. Consequently the disappearance of special schools should not be resisted but should be seen as a goal to be achieved. Perhaps instead of jumping in front of the train, as Anna Karenina did, teachers in special schools should buy a ticket and get on board.

Chapter 2

Headteacher: Architect of Change or Victim of Events?
Derek Baker

> As long as we have schools and headteachers, if the headteacher does not lead the development of an effective organisational process or if he or she leaves it to others, it will normally not get done. That is, change will not happen. [Fullen (1982: 146)]

Such a responsibility is a daunting prospect for any headteacher, and at a time of increasing demands when new regulations and curriculum initiatives seem to arrive almost daily, it can seem impossible to fulfil.

If we believe all that we read then headteachers are to be the salvation of the education system. Not only are they to continue to perform their already legion tasks, but they are also to manage all the school finances, sort out industrial relations problems for the Local Education Authority, implement and monitor the government's new National Curriculum, develop a totally new relationship with governors, compete against other schools for students, introduce records of achievement, etc. They can be the victims of events: few managers are asked to adopt so many new schemes and undertake such a variety of new tasks in addition to their primary roles.

Surely it is impossible for any headteacher to contemplate, let alone achieve meaningful change in their school. What if they happen to be the headteacher of a special school? Add to the above list: dealing with the 1981 Education Act, losing support from speech therapists, the threat of closure or change of role, maintaining morale of staff who see their career plan ended. Implement change?...contemplate change?...very unlikely.

This chapter is about taking up the challenge, about what is possible considering all the constraints noted above. It stresses that it is possible to initiate and manage change, in fact it is essential!

In this chapter change is seen as being synonymous with growth, both of the organisation and of the individuals within it. We are not concerned with change for change's sake but a normal and healthy process. Growth is essential for any organisation. Growth is a change process; schools should never be static. What must be remembered is that change (growth) often takes a long time, that it must be planned, and is invariably painful.

CHAPTER OVERVIEW

This chapter will contain a discussion of the developing role of the headteacher; the specific demands on special school administrators (the challenges facing special schools, possible directions for special schools), an examination of theory concerning the management of change, and practical guidance for special school administrators in responding to the challenges facing them, and taking their schools into an uncertain future. At all times a major concern is the degree to which headteachers are able to initiate change, or are merely responding to outside pressures over which they may feel they have little or no control or influence.

The intention in this chapter is at all times to be positive and practical, to offer alternatives relevant in any school. Much of what is contained in this chapter may seem 'obvious', 'common sense'; this is of course true of most education texts, little is new or original, the intention is to present ideas in a way that will be of interest and use to colleagues in a variety of educational settings.

PRESSURES FOR CHANGE FACING SPECIAL EDUCATION

Many recent trends, as well as government legislation and the actions of individual local education authorities, have produced pressures for change that affect not only special education as a whole, but every special school headteacher. Figure 2.1 is an attempt to draw together some of these influences.

WHAT EXACTLY DOES A HEADTEACHER DO? WHAT QUALITIES ARE NEEDED?

It depends who you ask! There are as many different views as there are people willing to give one, and there is certainly no shortage of them at the

	PRESSURE FOR CHANGE	CHALLENGE FOR SPECIAL SCHOOL HEADTEACHER
GENERAL	Rights Issue Falling Rolls Attitude to Special Education	annual reviews/13+ re-assessments 16–19 provision, how to justify? response to National Curriculum?
LEA	Review of provision Re-organisation of support Attention to ordinary schools Clusters	where is special school in plans? are you planning for a new role? does LEA know your plans? what support will you get? could you resource a cluster?
ORDINARY SCHOOL	Special needs departments Special needs coordinators Curriculum initiatives	do you know what is happening in ordinary schools? do they know what you can offer? are two-way links in place? do you offer GCSE, CPVE? are you part of TVEI?
SPECIAL SCHOOL	Numbers down Changing ability range Low morale Outreach links	what will be your roll? what will be your ability range? what will be your age range? what support are you giving to staff? what plans are there for using staff elsewhere?
INSET	GRIST School based	do you provide INSET? what could you offer to other staff?

Figure 2.1: Pressures for change in Special Education

present time! These views range from ignorance, through suspicion, to admiration. As a special school headteacher I have no hesitation in stressing that a headteacher requires above all else a sense of humour and of proportion. What is clear is that no two headteachers can be said to have the same job, or to approach it in the same way; and that their job has become more difficult, challenging, complex and stressful in the last few years.

Numerous texts list the 'role of the headteacher' or the 'qualities required for headship'. Bunnell (1987) suggests that the qualities demanded of the good head are daunting: outstanding teacher, manager, public relations officer, leader, inspirer and supporter. Mason (1987) adds exemplar, initiator, facilitator, counsellor.

There is no shortage of descriptions as to the various qualities required by a headteacher, e.g. oral and written communication, the ability to give a clear presentation of facts to many different types of audience, parents, governors, colleagues, the local authority. Sensitivity, leadership, decisiveness, organisational ability, planning, judgement, managerial skills and knowledge, problem analysis, delegation, motivation.

Even if we could establish exactly what a headteacher is expected to do, or does, we are not even halfway there, the more crucial element is... how they do it. Therein lies another dilemma: even if we knew what we were expected to do, who is going to tell us how to do it? Training for headship is a rare luxury and while most of us will be satisfied with the way in which we have evolved into headteachers, surely it would have been preferable for us to have had some initial training. Ask most headteachers and they will say that their most useful training and support has come from fellow, but more experienced headteacher colleagues. How is that expertise and advice channelled? In most areas it is on the basis of informal networks. Most headteachers do a very hard job very well, despite the lack of initial training or in-post support.

How many times have you heard headteachers say that they simply struggle from one crisis to another, that there is never time to do anything useful or to do with education? They are weighed down by trivia, buried under a pile of paperwork and forever trying to sort out other people's problems. The fact is that a headteacher has too many roles to play. S/he is an administrator/manager, but surely most importantly the head teacher. Unfortunately s/he is also something quite different to each member of staff, parents, pupils, governors, local authority officers, support staff, the local community, etc. Furthermore, in all these roles his/her credibility and effectiveness is dependant also on ability to select and/or motivate staff.

Headship has, or should, become concerned with settling priorities. A headteacher simply cannot fulfil the expectations of every individual or group, and should not be reduced to crisis management. Where is the time for thinking, planning a strategy, developing ideas, brainstorming with senior colleagues, for developing an overall view? For most headteachers, particularly in the days of directed time, union disputes, and decreasing resources, these things are all luxuries belonging to some long forgotten golden age. More disturbing still is the fact that in the last few years headteachers have been appointed thinking that this is the norm.

Headteachers must be ruthless when it comes to priority setting and time-management. There is much to be learned from the industrial experience in this area. Monitor one of your normal days... how much was actually planned and allowed for? More importantly, how much would you consider to be of educational value?

HEADTEACHER IN SPECIAL EDUCATION...
A HARD JOB MADE HARDER

Considering the difficulties of role, new pressures, expectations, etc. faced by headteachers, those who choose to make their career within special education are brave indeed. Following the Warnock Report and the 1981 Education Act there has been much informed (and uninformed) speculation regarding the probable structure of special education in the future.

Special school headteachers are in a position where they are on the one hand expected to be the guardians of all that is good about their special school, while at the same time possibly planning its closure, or at the other extreme, helping to make it into the area's principal support service. Such pressures are being experienced when teacher morale is arguably at its lowest ebb for a good many years.

Warnock and the 1981 Education Act did not herald the demise of special schools. It is true that some have closed, but the vast majority have continued to exist and to evolve. Moreover they exist in what is for many special schools a distinctly hostile atmosphere. Special schools live with uncertainty, but at the same time are expected to initiate new responses to a changing situation, Since the Warnock Report it is possible to identify a number of factors affecting special schools, many of which appear contradictory. These are shown in Figure 2.2.

The fact that the list given in Figure 2.2 presents apparent contradictions is an indicator of the variable and uncertain situation facing special schools. It was always hard to generalize about special schools, now it is near impossible.

The purpose of this chapter is to argue that headteachers should react to this uncertainty by rising above it and creating with their staff a vision for the school's future. This argument is more fully developed in Baker (1989).

Special school headteachers are currently working within a context where Local Education Authorities are diverting funds to ordinary schools, there are re-organizations of support services, and reviews of special needs provision.

More than ever before headteachers are dealing with externally imposed changes, for example the National Curriculum, GCSE and TVEI, precisely at a time when staff morale is low and scope for school initiated change seems more limited than ever before. It would be easy to forgive special school headteachers for withdrawing into concern only with their own

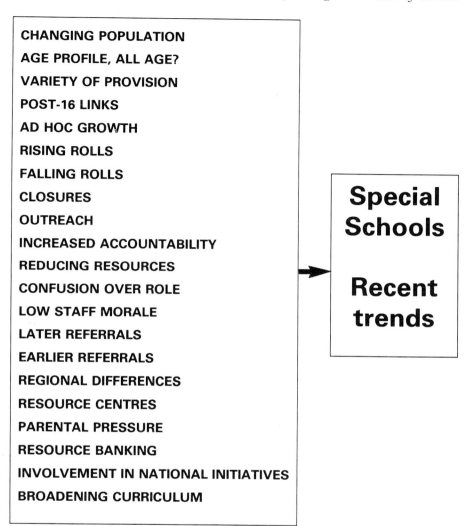

Figure 2.2: Special Schools, Recent Trends

establishment and a concentration on the needs of their own pupils and the use of only their existing resources.

This is not what is happening in an increasing number of special schools.

WHERE ARE SPECIAL SCHOOLS GOING?

Special Schools do not have a right to exist. They exist because of the limitations of ordinary schools in providing for the full range of abilities and disabilities among children (Dessent, 1987).

To a certain extent, then, the future of special schools is dependent on ordinary schools adapting to meet individual differences, but it also depends on the willingness and ability of individual special schools to adapt to a changing situation. It is most unlikely that in the near future we shall see the end of special schools. They will exist, but in a new form evolved from the strengths of the past and an awareness of future needs. Fish (1984) argues that the question is not whether special schools should continue to exist but what should be their contribution within a range of special educational arrangements. The process of change has already begun in many areas.

It would be difficult, indeed dangerous, to attempt to produce a definitive statement of the directions in which special schools are developing. It is possible, however, to discern certain trends: special schools appear all to be moving in the same direction but by different routes and at different speeds. These trends are: a clearly defined role; a wider range of ability; a curriculum related and linked to ordinary schools; to be part of a continuum of provision; resource and support centre; INSET centre; flexibility to change to meet developing needs of individuals and the special needs service.

An example of recent planned change that has occurred in many special schools is 'outreach'. Figure 2.3 is an attempt to explain why and how outreach projects have developed (this theme is more fully developed by Day, in chapter 5).

Having asked the question, where are special schools going?, it is then necessary to address the issue of what impact a headteacher can have on those changes. In many special schools staff are working to promote the development of pupils who are pro-active, and self-actualize. Why not the headteachers themselves? As Dessent points out, special school headteachers can help to make what we now consider special to be normal.

Moreover, when change is taking place in other areas of the education system can we wait until it reaches special education? We are at a major choice point, special schools are in a position of potential leadership.

Changing a Special School

Whether a special school is changing as a result of external pressures of school-generated growth it is crucial that this process is carefully planned, in much the same way as one would plan the curriculum. Special schools have in many cases pioneered the 'objectives approach' to curriculum planning following the lead of successful practitioners such an Ainscow and Tweddle (1979). Where are we now? Where do we want to get to? How will we get there? As a curriculum development the final destination often differs from that which you originally identified, but the process of getting there was all-important.

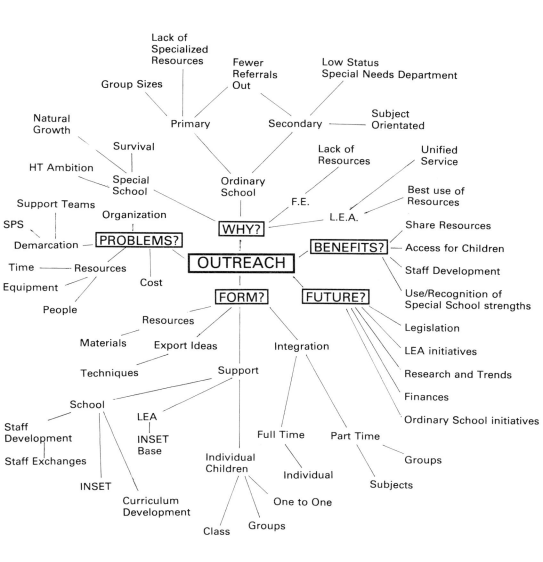

Figure 2.3: The Outreach Web

Special schools have to change, they have no choice.

Planned change in any school is dependent on the headteacher — often for initiation and support, but always for leadership. The next section examines theory relating to leadership, administration and change. It draws on literature and experience from both the educational and commercial worlds. These practices and theories are then used, in conjunction with a consideration of the realities faced by special schools and their developments in recent years, to construct some suggestions for the process of change.

LEADERSHIP AND CHANGE

Leadership and the role of the headteacher

Numerous texts have examined the nature of leadership, and the particular role of the headteacher. It is not my intention in this chapter to present a detailed examination of these theories, but rather to briefly examine those key aspects that will make possible some proposals as to how special school headteachers could respond to uncertainty and the far-reaching changes now affecting all sectors of the education service.

Esp (1987) has said that the power and responsibility of the British headteacher has no parallel in the world:

the single most important factor in a good school is the quality of leadership of the headteacher. They have imagination, vision tempered by realism of the current situation but also attainable future goals. Sympathetic understanding of staff and pupils, accessibility, good humour, sense of proportion, dedication to task.

Craig (1987) suggests that it is the role of the headteacher to provide the most stimulating environment possible — management is the organisation of that environment. In such an environment it is crucial that everyone knows what is expected of them. Sandbrook (1987) emphasises that the headteacher should ensure that the aims of the school are understood by all, that the school continually moves forward, there are no doubts about areas of responsibility, and that potential is recognized and developed.

In educational administration theory much is made of the effect of individuals on institutions, but the most elaborate theories in existence tell us little about why people will do things for one headteacher and not another. Sergiovanni and Carver (1973) note the importance of self-fulfilling prophecy, the fact that people respond to the expectations that important others hold for them. Motivation is a key concept of leadership theory. The work of Maslow, McGregor, and Herzberg (see Owens 1970, ch.2) highlighted the factors contributing to motivation, the needs hierarchy. It is possible to identify a move away from task-oriented authoritarian leadership to relationship-oriented participatory leadership. Turner (1984) stresses the need for everyone in the school to be involved in planning.

A headteacher's position is an amalgam of professional, bureaucratic, and charismatic authority; to a certain extent, however, they also inherit the role of their predecessor. How often has a newly appointed headteacher been haunted by cries of 'we didn't do things this way when X was here'? In addition, over recent years the traditional role of the headteacher, states Clerkin (1987), had been modified from determining policy to leading the policy formulation process.

Amongst the leadership/administrative qualities required by the modern headteacher could be included technical, human, and conceptual skills. Technical skills are those concerned with the methods, processes, procedures, and techniques of education. Human skills concern the ability to work in groups, one to one, empathy, and consideration, as well as motivation and human resource skills. The conceptual skills are those associated with seeing the school as a whole and an ability to map the environment.

Corporate decision-making, i.e. that which involves the whole staff, while desirable, is also the most difficult to achieve. It presupposes a large degree of trust, and is often the result of many years of development; training for staff will often speed up this process. There are however many ocassions when either a quick decision is required, or when only the headteacher can make the decision – for example, about closing the school. At times like this even the most participative headteacher must be prepared to be unpopular, and possibly wrong. All manner of theories cannot protect a headteacher from the reality of exposed decision-making. It is at these times when sometime the veneer of participation is stripped away from many managers and their true style is revealed. These are the occasions when it is possible to observe the difference between directive and decisive, tell or sell.

Often 'good' headteachers can be identified by their degree of organisation. With such a vast array of duties and responsibilities, time-management becomes a crucial skill. Craig (1987) goes as far as to suggest that 'it is only by the systematic management of time that a headteacher will achieve their full potential and thus manage their schools more effectively'.

Once again there is a valuable analogy to curriculum development: objectives are set and priorities established. Care should be taken to ensure that time is allocated for planning. Various authors suggest that an essential first step in better use of time is to establish a 'time log': what were you doing, how long did it take, who was it with, where, etc. An evaluation is then made as to the actual use of time as against an ideal view as to what are the established priorities for the time. Time saved from, say, administrative tasks, may then be used on planned, high-value activities.

One method of creating time is delegation — low priority tasks can often be delegated. The administrative skill lies in the initial judgment about to whom the task can be delegated. In addition to time savings there are many benefits of delegation, for example in terms of staff professional development and organisational health. As Mason (1987) says, real delegation is trusting someone to do the job well and giving them all the back-up they need to do it.

There need be no conflict between the desire of a headteacher to inspire professional respect and loyalty, and the desire for full staff participation in the running of the school. It is the way decisions are arrived at that is crucial, and the extent to which the headteacher is willing and able to allow staff growth. Below is listed a selection of statements from Maslow's (1965) Eupsychian management, an interesting starting point for headteachers!

Assume everyone is to be trusted

Assume everyone is to be informed as completely as possible of as many facts and truths as possible

Assume in all your people the impulse to achieve

Assume good will among all the members of the organisation rather than rivalry or jealousy

Assume an active trend towards self-actualisation

Assume that everyone can enjoy good team work, friendship, good group spirit, good group harmony

Assume that everyone prefers or perhaps even needs to love his/her boss

Assume everyone prefers to be a prime mover rather than a passive receiver

Assume a tendency to improve things, to put things right, make things better, to do things better

Assume the preference for working rather than being idle

Assume that fairly well-developed people would rather be interested than destroy

Assume that everyone prefers to feel important, needed, useful, successful, proud, respected rather than unimportant, interchangable, anonymous, wasted, unused, expendable, disrespected.

Change theory

Effecting change in many schools is, and is likely to continue to be, achieved by intuition, knowledge of the school, pupils and staff, and hope. If the desired change is achieved then who is to say that the methods were not correct?

The management of change is a subject dealt with in great detail in numerous texts, e.g. Fullan (1982), Havelock (1973), Alfonso, Firth and Neville (1975) and Owens (1970). In this short section I shall address topics that may be of particular concern to headteachers.

The problem with educational change lies in the fact that, as Fullan (1982) points out, planned change attempts rarely succeed as intended. True, the outcome may be acceptable, but was it the best possible? Fullan goes on to question the conditions under which educational change improves schools; 'change for change's sake will not help. New programmes either make no difference, help improve the situation, or make it worse'.

Change, however initiated and supported, is invariably slow, difficult to measure, and the cause of conflict, tension, and pain. The effect of the change process cannot be accurately predicted because each situation is unique. Despite this, as Bowers (1984) points out, schools must adapt to the demands of the system in which they operate if they are to remain effective.

Certain questions arise when considering educational change. Who benefits from the change? On what basis are decisions to change made? What do we mean when we say that something has changed? Is change necessarily progress?

The headteacher has a central role in the change process — the headteacher must either leave change in his/her school pretty much to chance or deliberately map out a strategy to foster change. Mason (1987) adds that 'however many ideas people have, however much they want to initiate, it is the headteacher whose interest and support puts the seal of success upon that innovation'.

In order to facilitate change headteachers may employ a number of strategies, which are largely dependant on their leadership style: their prevailing style, which may be authoritarian, democratic, laissez-faire, bureaucratic or charismatic, will determine whether they use methods such as force, paternalism, bargaining, or mutual means. Owens (1970) warns that school administrators are rarely endowed with the personal charm and inner spiritualness that is usually associated with charismatic leadership. The organisational climate in which change takes place is reliant on the behaviour of the headteacher, his/her skill in assessing teachers, and their perceptions of him/her.

The reasons why people decide to change things are many and varied. They include the desire for personal prestige, political responsiveness, and concern for solving an unmet need. Whatever the reason, schools should strengthen their ability to do more than survive the changes and pressures to which they are being subjected by their environment. They must increase their effectiveness in anticipating change, and also in creating change.

How and why decisions about change are made strongly influences what will happen when they are implemented, as will the extent to which those affected by the decision are involved in the formulation of a strategy. Alfonso, Firth and Neville (1975) note that significant change will only take place if those expected to change participate in deciding what the change shall be and how it will be implemented. Effective headteachers seek more information and clarification of responses, and seek the opinions of others. Innovators work out the effects of the changes and forget that those upon whom they will impose it have to do so also. Ainscow (1984) stresses that headteachers should seek to create a cooperative working atmosphere in which mutual support, professional debate, and group problem-solving are part of everyday life.

Headteachers should never assume that what they see is what others see! Moreover, from their vantage point they can at best view only some portions of whatever is happening. The management of change demands sensitive understanding of teachers' attitudes and psychology as well as management expertise.

The process of change is as stated earlier a very similar one to that of curriculum development: define the problem — identify possible alternatives — predict consequences of each alternative — choose alternative — implement — review. It also borrows from the computer world in that at every stage the question asked is 'what if?' in much the same way as a spreadsheet operates. The process of change is crucial. Gipps, Gross and Goldstein (1987) stress that many local authorities, in curriculum innovation, have concentrated on the changes they wish to make and have not considered the process of change.

Educational planning is a vague concept. Those involved tend to import structures and techniques that are inappropriate, borrowing uncritically. Planning is a continuous process concerned not only with where to go but with how to get there and by what route. Planning is preparing sets of decisions for future action. Miklos, Bourgette and Cowley (1972) point out that planning must be continuous, the process must be recognised as being complex and multi-dimensional, it must be directed towards increasing rather than decreasing the range of possible future options, and the approaches and techniques must be appropriate to current policies and goals.

However well thought out and planned, there are numerous reasons why an attempted innovation may fail. Leaving the tried and tested and trying the new, forsaking the familiar and comfortable in favour of an unknown quantity leads to resistance and insecurity. Change attempts can fail due to lack of resources, lack of appropriate skills or experience in staff, lack of clarity, an incompatible organization, etc., but most of all because of people. Staff are under pressure, they often need time to assimilate new ideas — they may simply lack motivation. All of these reasons could of course stem from lack of preparation or insight on the part of the headteacher. They could be the result of deliberate attempts to block change — why should this be?

What could be more frustrating for a headteacher who believes in a particular innovation than to face a campaign against it? There will of course, however well planned the innovation, however much all staff are involved, be some who simply work against it. That is a fact of life, an uncomfortable fact of life that headteachers learn at an early stage: simply because you are the headteacher many of your suggestions, plans, changes will be unacceptable. Havelock (1973) in his classic text on change in education described a group of staff who could be called the 'resisters'. Knowing that there will always be resisters in one way makes the headteacher's task that much easier; surely the ultimate good must be to create a situation that is win–win. Alfonso (1975) indicates that teachers are by training and experience sensitive to the hidden agenda present, in every discussion group and decision-making gathering. Teachers are autonomous professionals; we must avoid creating situations of resentment which result in a subversion of change proposals by teachers at best simply going through the motions of conformity while ignoring the spirit of the proposals. This is often the result, suggests Bowers (1984), due to the tendency of the proponents of change:

> to ignore, override or dismiss as irrational anyone who emerges as an opponent. The cost of such a policy will often be to transform the process of change into a conflict in which energy is devoted to winning rather than achieving the initially desired outcome.

The problems associated with the implementation of change often result in nothing happening, a type of organisational drift. The scale of changes necessary and the probable demands that changes will place on them could be too great; another unintended outcome could be re-organisation, often a substitute for or an illusion of real change.

Fullen (1982) believes that implementing effective change is just as much a matter of good common sense as of fancy theories, and warns that the more committed an individual is to a specific form of change the less effective he/she will be in getting others to implement it. Innovative schools are characterised by acceptance of aims, openness, cohesiveness, high morale, and the ability of all staff to influence policy.

THE HEADTEACHER AS ARCHITECT OF CHANGE

> It is a good deal easier to think about something and do nothing than it is to do something. (McPherson, Crowson and Pitner, 1986).

Faced with increasing responsibilities, external demands for change, and the uncertainty regarding the future fuelled by the Warnock Report, the 1981

Education Act, and the National Curriculum, special school headteachers might be excused for hesitancy or inaction. However, it is the author's view that headteachers have been, and are currently, too passive; recent legislation and educational trends should not be viewed as obstacles to the continued development of special schools, rather as opportunities for growth, albeit in new ways. The re-organisation of services in many authorities and the integration movement have given special school headteachers a wider role than ever before, they are now intricately associated with ordinary schools and in many cases have entered the world of local politics as a result of threatened closure or re-allocation of resources. Many headteachers have learned important lessons about how to influence and affect decisions made at higher levels. This has been added to the traditional influence of special school headteachers on parents, governors, voluntary agencies, and the local press, politicians and community. Traditional annual negotiations with local officers regarding numbers, curriculum statements and staffing have been enhanced by discussion of age range and support for ordinary schools.

Drawing on the work of Baker (1989), comments made earlier in this chapter and the theory of planned change, Table 2.1 is designed to provide suggestions for headteachers who wish to be architects of change and not merely victims of events. As this table indicates, there are many ways in which headteachers can adapt their behaviour in order to create and realise a vision for their school. Of course, none of this takes place in a vacuum; in many ways the future for special schools is dependent on what happens elsewhere, and the climate in which change takes place. In recent years special schools have been under siege, and many have closed, amalgamated, or undergone major organisational changes. They have been years of doubt and uncertainty. Sculley (1987) argues that the real test of any organisation is how well it works in the worst of times, and also that the time to take the biggest risks is when you face your biggest obstacles.

As has been stated earlier, change, or at least real change that will endure, is unlikely to occur unless the staff who work in the school have been part of the development of that change. However, the responsibility of the headteacher in creating and making change happen is paramount.

Often headteachers at some stage in a planned change will feel isolated and experience a loss of faith in themselves and possibly the quality of their judgment. It may be a situation in which staff have been asked to alter long-established working practices, they are angry and become resistant to a number of other innovations, and the easiest and least painful course is to back off, to re-think and salvage some change. All headteachers must experience these situations at some time. Of course it is desirable to take all the staff with you on decisions, but it is not always possible to do so. We are paid to make decisions/exercise judgment, however uncomfortable the

Table 2.1: Guidelines for Headteachers Managing Change

adopt a pro-active attitude
create a vision
anticipate developments
establish a core mission
adopt a consistant style
map the environment
network widely
build support among the like-minded
establish a team
have a clear understanding of how as well as what to change
involve everyone in planning change
identify the blockages to change
identify the costs of change
don't be afraid to be unpopular
delegate wisely and widely
know your weaknesses
guard your thinking time
don't make up your mind too quickly
deliberately manage time
make every meeting useful
allow time to consolidate changes
know your LEA, how it works, and how to manipulate it
be clear about what your school has to offer
write papers about every development
market the school and its innovations
enrich the school through federation/links with other education establishments
seek partnership with local commerce/industry
enhance image by use of the latest technology
strictly monitor the quality of all documents produced
use complaints as a springboard for further growth

results may be. As my adviser always said, 'you are not there to be cuddly!' If a headteacher has a vision then they must be prepared to see it through. It takes a passionate belief in the power of your own ideas and the conviction to see them through to the end. It can sometimes be a lonely, difficult journey. Those who wish to change schools are constantly fighting conventional wisdom, they see the world ahead in terms of what it can be, not what it is.

Self-confidence is critical, there are never any guarantees that you will make it through. However, it is critical that headteachers realise early on that making mistakes is essential as well as inevitable; making mistakes is an important part of succeeding.

The warning of John Sculley, writing from the perspective of chief executive of a large company in a time of crisis, applies equally to headteachers at a time of great change in special education: 'My natural instincts were to be authoritative, cool, and distant. I was too consumed with solving a problem instead of building for the future'.

It is too easy to adopt a reactive posture, accept what seems to be inevitable and drift towards it. Headteachers have a responsibility to be pro-active, to continue the advances made in special education over recent years, to preserve and build on the best practice, to create an interface with ordinary schools that will lead eventually to a system where it is possible for all children's needs to be met in ordinary schools. Headteachers are in a unique and powerful position.

They can help invent the future.

Section 2
Working with Ordinary Schools

Chapter 3

The Transferability of Good Practice from Special to Ordinary Schools
Eileen Tombs

INTRODUCTION

The aim of this chapter is to provide for teachers a clearer understanding of why some teaching methodology can successfully be applied in teaching children with special educational needs within one teaching context and yet be unsuccessful in another.

It has been prompted by a desire to respond to criticisms directed at special schools in recent years which direct attention to the weaknesses of such schools, for example, didactive, prescriptive, insular curriculum and styles. It is not intended to be a defensive paper but to suggest a constructive and practical way forward which may lead teachers to a better understanding of the strengths each has to offer children with special educational needs. Indeed, one would not wish to defend any schools exhibiting poor educational practice, but at the same time attention should be drawn to those techniques which have been employed successfully.

The intention is to provide an understanding of why such skill sharing has not been more successful; provide a model which could identify good practice; and identify principles which might be applied which would ensure the success of such transfer.

OVERVIEW

It is my firm belief that one of the major contributing factors to the problems that many teachers highlight in their attempts to involve pupils with special educational needs in the ordinary classroom is the lack of real evidence and research from practitioners in the field.

The concept of special educational needs and integration is dominated by educational psychologists and professional researchers. There is a plethora of articles and studies which emphasize the identification of, and appropriate provision for children with special educational needs. There is a tremendous lack of well documented evidence which tells practising teachers how ordinary teachers (whether in special or mainstream schools) manage their teaching of children with learning difficulties on a daily basis. The gap between a child responding in an experimental learning situation and one learning within the reality of the classroom is enormous.

The key to the transferability of any skill in teaching — and by this I mean improving teaching efficiency by sharing ideas — is through in-service training. But the form of such in-service training is crucial if the changes we look for are to be real, thoroughly understood and permanent. The in-service training format must have its base in the principles of action research. In this way there can be improved practice to change skills and attitudes and provide well constructed research to be used in other teaching situations. Class teachers become researchers: a concept which does not receive nearly enough attention.

Amidst the uncertainty and obvious dichotomy that currently exists between special educational needs and the National Curriculum there may well be a thread of hope. If the statement made by Swann (1987) is to be accepted, that is that numbers in special schools will not reduce unless ordinary schools are willing to change their curricula, there follows the need for some agreement with regard to curricula and learning styles.

If closer collaboration between schools as to the content of curricula can be achieved and initiatives like TVEI, Records of Achievement, CPVE and Education 2000 can influence the teaching/learning style within all schools, it follows that some of the disagreements voiced to date may well disappear.

The concept of special schools housing children with similar problems has, through necessity, encouraged the selection of innovative responses. Good special schools have been at the forefront of change in many areas. Perhaps the most obvious is the introduction of well planned leavers' programmes long before similar courses were available in mainstream schools. Similarly, the current move towards criterion-referenced assessment has long been advocated by certain special schools.

However, it is not the purpose of this paper to list the advantages of such schools. It is neither a useful nor original exercise (see Ainscow, Fish, etc.). It is the purpose to provide a system for individual schools to identify what they need or have to offer, how best they can achieve collaboration and what objectives need to be met in order for that to be successful. Without such a system teachers will continue to be provided with the solution but no evidence of how to manage that solution *in* the classroom. It is relevant to consider why the transferability of skills from the special to the ordinary school has not been more successful.

TRANSFER FAILURE

The most significant reason for the lack of real developments has been the absence of clear statements from local authorities with regard to the future role of special schools. Where skill-sharing has occurred the *ad hoc* system of development has typified progress (for which the special school is renowned). Lack of policy has determined that certain schools — very often through a falling roll situation and response on a defence mechanism — have instigated their own systems. These initiatives were doomed to failure because the response was not considered in relation to the whole continuum of provision available to an Authority. There are many examples where schools have outreached their facilities which were laudable in the 1970s but have now given ordinary schools false expectations by providing 'extra' resources in the form of curriculum materials or bodies. This results in a collapse when such support is withdrawn. The danger is that no change occurs in the ability of the ordinary school teacher to maintain the educational provision for special educational needs within their own resources.

Transferability of skills must be based on a redundancy model. Experiences of special school teachers must be passed onto ordinary school teachers within a model that releases the special school teacher, after a period of time, to move on.

There are clear implications for local authorities to decide on the future role of their special schools and agree a policy for dissemination of the skills they own.

Recent involvement with teachers from both sectors of the service who are endeavouring to develop links have determined other issues which have caused difficulties.

Paramount for the ordinary school teacher is the absence of practical guidance and support with classroom management. Attitude is a common reason given by special educators for their colleagues' inability to provide appropriately for children with special educational needs. Yet mainstream teachers very often do have a positive attitude and desire to include such children but no one is advising on classroom management.

The suggestions for facilitating special educational needs in the ordinary classroom have, more often than not, been based on a child-centred, individual approach. The cry from mainstream colleagues of 'what about the other thirty?' is very real. We have, perhaps, been attempting to transfer skills that were never likely to succeed in the mainstream classroom.

Unfortunately, methods of accessing the mainstream curriculum in special schools are out of step with many initiatives in the mainstream.

This problem emphasizes the need for special school teachers to be fully aware of current developments in ordinary schools before embarking on sharing skills.

This greater understanding would answer the rhetorical questions posed by secondary colleagues, and in the light of GERBIL concerns from primary colleagues, with regard to demands made upon them by examination, assessment and parents. The flexibility afforded the special school by the lack of constraints has given rise to some excellent curriculum initiatives that cannot be transferred *carte blanche*.

There needs to be a system for identifying such curriculum and teaching initiatives and, within the context of other pressures that mainstream teachers face, to formulate a structure to ensure they are shared.

Class/subject teachers in ordinary schools are now, if not yet accepting, at least aware of their responsibilities for teaching children with special educational needs. Until recently teachers were able to ignore crucial issues of how to teach children with difficulties. There was no call made upon them to monitor progress, record performance or organise their classes to accommodate all pupils. Answers were, and still are, found by removing the problem to a 'specialist'.

The integration concept removes this off-loading phenomenon. This leaves the ordinary teacher feeling de-skilled, vulnerable and believing that they have nothing to offer children with special educational needs. The failure to date in transferring 'specialist skills' has been compounded by the specialists supposedly providing the magic cure.

There is a need to build up the confidence and competence of the mainstream teacher and to challenge the notion of the specialist teacher before transference of skill can be successful.

There are four key areas which must be fully comprehended before skill-sharing between the special and ordinary school can be successful:

- Local authorities must give clear policy guidelines as to the future role of special schools within the overall continuum of provision for children with special educational needs;
- Special school teachers must be aware of current developments in mainstream schools;
- Procedures must be designed for identifying what curriculum and teaching methodologies can successfully be transferred within the constraints in ordinary schools;
- The confidence and competence of mainstream teachers must be enhanced in order that they might recognise the qualities they have in teaching children with special educational needs.

IDENTIFICATION AND TRANSFER MODEL

The prime reason for the transfer of skills between teachers is to improve the learning experiences of the children in their classes. In order to teach children with special educational needs, appropriately, within the overall classroom framework there is a need for a thorough understanding of class organisation, management, openness and child-centred learning. This very often calls for great changes in teacher attitude and style. It also calls for a great change in whole school philosophy. This change manifests itself both in the role of the ordinary school and of the special school. Without thorough knowledge of the effects, such change within an organisation will cause failure in educational innovation. Therefore prior to considering the transfer of skills it is advisable to ensure change is managed in a foolproof way.

Step One: Managing change (based on Bennis et al., 1975)

(i)   Identify strengths: look to the people in both schools and work with those who support the suggested way forward
(ii)   Identify clear goals: ensure that all parties involved have a thorough understanding of the purpose and plan for change
(iii) Identify process: not only what is wanted to happen but how the happening will occur
(iv)   Identify involvement: allow all the persons involved in the change to take a total part — develop the concept of ownership
(v)   Identify a timescale: careful planning and well-thought-out discussion ensure change will not occur too quickly (causing stress) or too slowly (causing frustration)

To reiterate an earlier statement, underpinning all the points above must lie the overall philosophy that special educational needs in the ordinary and special school must be seen within the context of an Authority's total provision. Change will then be recognized as having a focus.

When schools have clearly identified the implications that change will make in their respective schools, the next step is to analyse those skills that can be transferred effectively.

Step Two: Identification of appropriate skills for transfer

Each school involved in skill-sharing will determine its own strengths and weaknesses and identify for itself, within its own context, what it has to offer. The choice will usually be between such issues as: effective class organisation, grouping children, use of extra adult support, team teaching, curriculum designs, curriculum materials, evaluation of curriculum resources, behaviour management techniques, involvement of parents in their child's learning, techniques of assessment, recording progress, identification of special educational needs — the list is endless (Solity and Bull, 1987; Cohen and Cohen, 1986). Hence the problem to date in initially assessing which skills can be taken out of one context and used in another.

Whatever teaching practices, organisational strategies, curriculum materials or learning theories are identified as having value, they will not be shared effectively unless the attitude is positive towards such a process (see Figure 3.1).

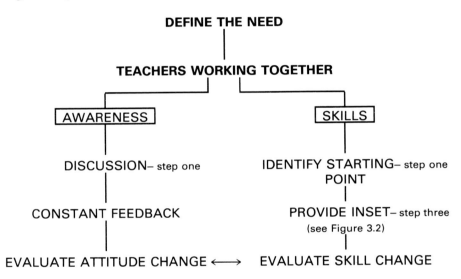

Figure 3.1: Collaboration for Change

If the process of skill change is seen within a collaborative framework there will follow a recognition of the value and purpose of those skills that can be appropriately transferred.

Step Three: Implementation of Transfer

Currently, the majority of staff in mainstream schools have received little or no initial or in-service training for teaching pupils with special educational needs. There is much research highlighting the fact that a team-based, problem-solving approach to curriculum innovation has greater and far-reaching effects than traditional in-service courses (DES, 1974; Hopkins, 1985). The argument is that unless such active problem-solving approaches are used the change in teacher practice will not be so successful.

This format of in-service training requires considerable commitment, time and effort but evidence from teachers themselves suggests that this investment is worthwhile when direct and practical relevances to classroom work can be observed.

Most changes in classroom practice are based on guesswork, experience or intuition. Often such changes are reverted when immediate or short-term improvements are not readily seen. Change must be based on what is actually happening in the classroom and with joint input.

Figure 3.2 illustrates a model, based on action research, that can help teachers ensure a successful skill-sharing exercise. The two main aims which govern the initial idea should be:

- to better match the learning to the child, and
- to relieve the pressures and maximise time use for the teacher meeting special educational needs in his/her class.

Start

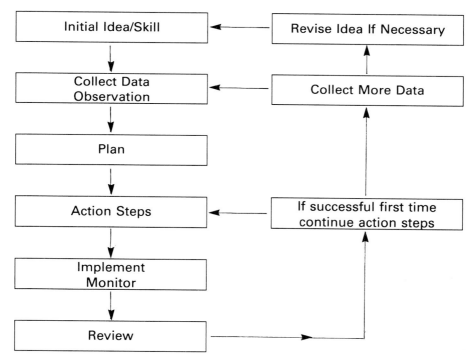

Figure 3.2: A model to implement skill transfer and change in classroom practice to meet the needs of pupils with Special Educational Needs

Collecting data through observation within the classroom ensures a clear analysis of practice (Stubbs and Delamont, 1976). This necessitates looking closely at:

- what pupils are actually doing;
- the measure and variety of learning;
- ways in which pupils respond to the teacher.

This detail of observation is too difficult to undertake single-handed within the busy classroom, hence the pre-requisite that the identified teacher from the special school will undertake to assist in this role — ideally allowing the classteacher to be the observer. This time scale of observation will vary and may require more data once the plan is underway. (Figure 3.2).

The collection of the data will provide the information for the plan. This can then be related in terms of realistic objectives. The plan might include.

- identification of teacher:pupil role;
- objectives of change (curriculum, resources, organisation — whatever);
- time-scale;
- evaluation principles.

Action steps to implement the plan can then be designed. These will be identified by the teachers involved and be formulated in terms of easily achievable stages. Each stage should demonstrate a movement towards the improvement of the initial idea and be managed within the constraints acknowledged to be in existence.

Implementation and monitoring will then follow. Considered judgments of the value of what is subsequently taking place in the classroom must be recorded. Recording techniques will vary from teacher to teacher with their individual preferences but suggestions for such formats can be found in Hopkins (1985), Stubbs and Delamont (1976) and Flanders (1970). The **actual experience of learning** is the reality. If evaluation is to lead towards worthwhile developments then judgment must be made of the learning which pupils actually achieve rather than what is hoped for.

The review after each classroom session must form an integral part of the transfer plan. Question whether the original aims of the plan have been met; identify which parts may need readjusting; move onto whichever stage of the model is failing.

This cycle can be maintained until the review is clearly indicating a successful transfer of change in practice. Ultimately it will have been achieved by:

- collaboration between the special and mainstream teacher;
- timing to suit the individual needs of teachers involved;
- consideration within an overall strategy for meeting special educational needs;
- concentration on within-classroom practice;

- thorough understanding by schools and teachers as to the purpose and value of change;
- permanent assimilation in classroom behaviour.

The skills required to ensure appropriate learning for pupils with special educational needs can only be learnt through working with these pupils. Whilst new ideas in education can come from many sources they will only be manifestly useful if selected and modified carefully to serve particular purposes revealed by specific evaluation in the classroom.

Transference of skills between teachers in special and mainstream schools will be successful if status is given to their work; the management of the school is supportive to their work; a thorough understanding of the management of change is realised; and that school-based, active research in-service is the tool used to assimilate an improvement in classroom practice to meet the needs of all pupils — not only those with special educational needs.

Chapter 4

Special Schools and Ordinary Schools: It's not what you do, it's the way that you do it
Maggie Balshaw

SPECIAL SCHOOLS UNDERGOING A PERIOD OF CHANGE

At a recent in-service course with which I was involved the participants were all from special schools — senior management who were prepared to spend four days of their Easter break examining what they and their schools might do in these uncomfortable times. They were asked to describe their schools in pictorial form and to be honest about what they drew. After they had overcome their misgivings at this exercise which the majority thought was in a curricular area that was not their greatest strength, they got down to work!

The resulting works of art ranged from the primitive to the diagrammatic but were very revealing — much more so than I would have predicted. Maybe the glass of wine they had had with their dinner had loosened their pens! The drawings showed the feelings of a number of individuals that ranged from despair to elation, and seemed to be a real reflection of them, their schools and their colleagues.

Without the original pictures it is difficult to convey to the reader the essential messages in the portrayal of these schools. One was of an enormous white elephant trundling along it knew not where, with its passengers lost, bewildered and insecure. Another was of a battleship waging war over external forces for change, hatches battened down. It was not ready to trade with the outside alien world, only to resist approaches, whether hostile or friendly, by attacking indiscriminately. Another picture showed groups of teachers busily discussing in corners of classrooms and staffrooms the whys and wherefores of the special school curriculum. This appeared to consist of devising numerous checklists of objectives without any thought for the big wide world outside, but the participants were patently very pleased with the levels of communication they had achieved.

In view of these varied pictures of special schools in the post-Warnock era it seems to me that there are some issues to be investigated. In particular we need to consider what staff in special schools might do to avoid these uncomfortable situations. Consequently in this chapter I propose to look at the process of change and how it might effect special schools. In so doing I will be sharing my own experiences and personal interests with the reader. I shall look at how one group of schools responded to the challenge for change, through my role as a participant observer and official evaluator. The description will be by nature brief and less about what the group of schools did than how it went about it. A detailed ethnographic study resulted from the work I undertook as participant observer (Balshaw, 1988).

From that study I shall draw some themes about why the scheme appeared to be successful. The major part of the chapter will deal with some wider issues to do with the future of any scheme of this nature.

The theme of the chapter, therefore, will be to do with the processes of change in education itself, illustrated by the study I carried out and an appraisal of the wider literature relevant to themes and issues drawn out, and is a personal account of my thoughts on the subject.

ONE AREA OF DEVELOPMENT

So, to go back to Warnock, what suggestions lay therein about the future of special schools? An area of development suggested was:

> There should be much closer co-operation between ordinary schools and special schools including, wherever possible, the sharing of resources by pupils in both types of schools, and we recommend that firm links should be established between special and ordinary schools in the same vicinity. (DES, 1978, Ch.8, 8.10).

In one division of a local authority just such an initiative from a special school began to take shape as long ago as 1981, but did not really come to fruition until September 1983. It was formulated along the lines of groups of staff from ten schools working cooperatively to meet a need. The scheme in which they became involved was of their own making, and was grounded in a history of working cooperatively, if less formally in the past. The project became known as the 'consortium'.

The area of need identified by those teachers was that of the special educational needs of the children within their schools. Their response resulted in a consideration of the in-service needs of the teachers in these schools. There were seven primary schools, one secondary school and two special schools in the consortium. The schools served an area which is geographically distinct. There was evidence of a high level of need, both social and educational, in the area and a homogeneity between the schools and community existed.

There was a well-established pattern of meetings by the heads of all the schools, with a history of cooperative ventures in such things as sporting and cultural activities. It was out of this that the consortium grew. From the tradition of working together in the past and the joint appreciation of the difficulties the area encountered, it was recognized that some sort of collaborative approach to meeting special needs in the schools should be initiated.

There had already been a small collaborative venture which started in 1981 involving two of the schools, one special school and the primary school 'just through the fence'. The evaluation of this was the focus of the discussion from which the plan to work as a consortium was formed.

The outcomes of this collaborative venture had been that:

– it had made curriculum compatability between the two schools a real possibility
– it provided a realistic alternative to the withdrawal of children with special needs
– there had been various spin-off effects amongst the staffs of both schools, e.g. shared INSET, shared classrooms
– it provided INSET for both mainstream and special school teachers firmly rooted in the realities of their own classrooms
– it had met the special needs of more children than had previously been possible.

Consideration of these outcomes, alongside the perceived needs of the area, resulted in the drawing up of a proposal to the Chief Education Officer, Divisional Education Officer, Advisers (primary, secondary and special), governors of all the schools and various other officers and members. This proposal was for the formation of the consortium.

It was envisaged that it would work initially in four main phases:

– an identification of the structure required to meet the needs of children in the area
– a detailed appraisal of needs
– planning at both management (heads') level and teacher level to set objectives for the short, medium and long term, for both working groups, the heads' and the teachers'

– an evaluation process by the heads' (steering) group both formatively and informally at regular meetings. A more formalised evaluation was to take place at the end of the first year by the steering group noting evidence and evaluative comments from the working group of teachers.

An evaluation based on a detailed ethnographic study

Although there were built-in forms of both formative and summative evaluation there was a recognition of the need for some more formalised structure of evaluation for the benefit of both the participants and the authority, and possibly a wider audience such as the readers of this book.

The evaluation which ensued involved me, as a participant observer, in gathering data which was hopefully to allow me to share the perceptions of those people involved in the scheme. I sought to furnish myself with information about how people were feeling about the ways in which they were working. The data was gathered in three major forms:

– observation and recordings of the groups at work
– questionnaires filled in by all the participants
– focused interviews with some of the participants.

As a result of the analysis of these data, alongside evidence in the wider literature, some major themes emerged. Firstly, with regard to the scheme itself, an examination of what was making the participants feel positive and optimistic resulted. Some comments about the underlying causes of this followed. Secondly, an examination of some issues in a wider context with possible relevance for groups of teachers or schools who may be considering a cooperative venture and the changes that this involves.

What were the causes of the positive attitudes shown?

In the participants' comments and analyses of what they felt about being involved in the scheme there were feelings of loyalty and motivation which resulted in a sense of optimism about it. These were evident at all levels within the scheme, and came through incidentally when participants were making comments about various facets of the work. There was also evidence in a more practical sense, in terms of calculating the number of 'person-hours' worked. This seemed to be a staggering total, and whether it would be matched in these post-Baker days of 1265 per year working hours is an interesting question in itself!

So what caused this positive attitude? It seems to me that a large part of this was due to the organic nature of the scheme. It was generated from within and not imposed. Within this were several crucial issues.

Because it was in a small locality it was made up of a group of people who already had some knowledge of each other. Therefore, whatever plans were made were small–scale enough to take account of the personalities for whom they had to work. Rather than these people having to fit into a 'grand plan' of some outsider's design, the plans were intended to be tailor–made to fit them. They were therefore able to take account of what each brought into the situation to a much larger extent than if it had been completely imposed from outside.

Taking account of the participants' own style and pace of learning was possible in this situation. The influence of their previous experiences, whether helpful or not, were taken into consideration. This allowed for different schools within the scheme as a whole to develop at different rates but the underpinning of the group structure was a security and a support. It also kept them mindful of what they were about, and what the group aims were. Therefore, in order to take account of individual teachers, and also individual schools, there was a flexibility in the speed and direction of the work. The dynamic nature of the work allowed for pauses, reconsideration, regrouping, evaluation and re-attempting to overcome difficulties. An ability to leave something alone if it wasn't working but not to consider this to be a total failure also seemed to exist. The channelling of efforts into a more productive direction was a decision the groups could make for themselves. They were not compelled to keep re-attempting something because it was in a grand plan, in which they were accountable to outside influences.

This ability to set their own realistic goals was an important factor. Their timescales for achieving targets were flexible, but not avoided. In other words, a target and a date were set but things were not always completed by that date. But this was felt to be acceptable in ongoing evaluation. Their ability to be reflective and accepting did not appear to amount to complacency, because there was usually an intention to try again or do something in a different way.

There seemed also to have been some level of understanding about the aims of the scheme because it had been organically generated. This was particularly evident in the managers' group. There was ongoing debate on the philosophy of what they were about and why, interspersed with the more practical aspects of managing the scheme, such as acquiring more support or resources. Their understanding of what it might realistically achieve within a small locality was also evident.

This brings me into the issue of the in-service needs of the locality. There were four broad areas for consideration within this. There was a 'match' perceived to exist between theory and reality (classroom practice). The teachers seemed to be confident that the theory could actually be transferred to their own practice. One of the difficulties about in-service based outside schools is that very often it does not have any effect on the schools and only a shortlived effect on the teacher who attended the course. Here there were constant references to the feeling that some practical application was available and workable, but alongside this there was a gradual understanding of the theory behind the practice.

Secondly there were also signs that because the groups of teachers had devised much of what they were doing themselves, with reference to their own needs for their own classrooms and schools that it had real relevance. They were reflecting on their own practice and using field-testing and workshop techniques in tandem with discussion at a theoretical level, in the groups.

A third area was that the group discussions involved personnel from other schools, leading to a mutual appreciation of the difficulties others faced and a sharing of difficulties. It also led to sharing of ideas and approaches that worked for colleagues. In all this there was not a great deal of evidence of an 'expert' telling them what to do. They were working it out for themselves.

The fourth area was that this led to an acceptance and understanding, and, crucially, confidence. They felt they were able to be more effective in their own teaching methods and techniques. This confidence generated action in classrooms. Action in the classroom resulted in changes — both in attitudes and teaching practice. This caused a sense of satisfaction and achievement. This sense of achievement, along with plans for future achievement, led to a sense of optimism about the work.

THE MAJOR AREAS FOR CONSIDERATION

With respect to the processes of change in education six key themes emerged from the evaluation undertaken. The collaborative nature of the scheme was such that these may have particular relevance in the light of some of the litreature, e.g. Fish (1985) who refers specifically to the necessity to maximise collaborative responses to provision for children with special educational needs. The new initiatives by the Government for school 'clusters' taking responsibility for the in-service needs and professional development in groups of schools and establishments through the GRIST system (Grant Related In-service Training) which came into being in 1987, have also a relevance for the following ideas. There is no doubt that these clusters might appreciate some guidance about how to identify the needs of the teachers in their schools and, having identified these, in planning and implementing effective in-service training programmes to meet them. The place of special schools within these clusters might also be clarified by an examination of the role played by the special school in the consortium cluster — it was very much just one of the ten schools in the group.

The six key themes

The six key themes are supported to some extent by the wider literature on educational change and staff development. They are as follows:

Change in education is more likely to be effective if:

- it meets the perceived need of those who will have to implement the change
- there is support from senior personnel
- it is based on realistic goals which have been set by the participants
- there are effective procedures for evaluating the development of the project
- in-service training opportunities are provided which relate to the concerns of the participants
- opportunities are provided for participants to support one another.

The perceived need

Meeting the perceived needs of those who have to implement the change is likely to have a positive influence. A change which is organic and happens from within is usually the result of a need which a small group of people, or staff in a group of schools, have identified. It is, therefore, common to them all. This common need provides the focus for the work they might choose to do.

There is more likelihood of a planned change being understood if the people who are to implement it are involved in the planning. Fullan (1982) and Bennis *et al.*(1975) each endorse this view.

However, the whole issue of what I shall refer to as 'multiple realities' needs to be taken into consideration. There is no doubt that even after an involvement in the planning stages of a change people have their own personal understanding of what that change will mean. Within the scheme described the issue of multiple realities was brought sharply into focus by confusion about the concept of special needs in general and the aims of the scheme in particular. It seemed to me that it might be useful for the participants to 'revisit' the concept of special needs. Perhaps they should consider what they feel are the important facts in what creates special needs and how one makes provision for them. Throughout the evidence examined there was a confusion about where the special needs provision lay. In common with findings at a national level (Croll and Moses (1985); Gipps, Gross and Goldstein (1987)), the perceptions of even the most informed of the participants tended towards what is sometimes referred to as the deficit model: in-child factors and a treatment of these by appropriate methods, materials and resources. This was one facet of the way in which the scheme was set up, intending to enable teachers to be more confident about the use of suitable methods, materials and resources. The workshop sessions did much to help in this.

However, in looking further at what might be causing a child to have special needs, the interaction between what the child was being asked to do and his or her ability to do it, alongside the whole context of his learning environment, was often forgotten. The children's experiences in terms of the curriculum on offer, the classroom organisation in which they were expected to learn, and the teaching styles with which they were presented seemed to be getting 'lost' somewhere. This was mirrored in the attitudes shown at management level, with no great changes in curriculum or organisation having taken place or being envisaged. Despite efforts to observe *how* children were going about the tasks demanded of them there still seemed to be a reluctance to consider the total learning enviroment.

Constant debate and discussion are crucial to the process of the multiple realities becoming an understood and shared working reality for the people involved. As Fullan (1982) says, it is the dual understanding of both the content and the process of the change planned that is so important:

> Any change requires knowledge of both the content of a given curriculum or policy and of the planning and process skills needed. It is possible to have expertise in only one of these fields. We must learn to develop expertise in both aspects.

With a small cooperative scheme there is *more* likelihood of this happening than in a large scheme imposed from outside. However, it cannot be assumed that it *has* happened, as the evidence from the investigation I have made has shown. There is no guarantee that it will, there can only be an awareness that the participants should understand that they might strive to achieve it, through constant discussion and reflection.

Support from senior personnel

A localised need having been identified, it is crucial to the success of this need being met that the support of the immediate senior personnel is present. This view is endorsed by Fullan (1982) and Clark, Lotto and Astuto (1984) and borne out by further personal experience in another setting, involving in-service training of support staff.

Although in the case-study schools support may have been assumed to be there, in a closer examination of what happened, it became evident that there was a great variety in the levels of support. This in turn resulted in a difference in the degree to which change had actually happened in individual schools. An understanding by the teachers at group level that they had support from the heads as a group seemed not to be in question. The knowledge the teachers had that their heads were prepared to spend time in meeting to consider and evaluate the progress of the scheme was a positive factor. However, they appeared to be experiencing vastly different levels of support within their schools. Given that the support from outside was seen to be somewhat tenuous it seemed even more crucial that the heads gave both moral and organisational support to the people at the 'chalk-face'.

These were the two main areas of support that were of importance. The first was 'moral' support. This could take the form of privately offered verbal encouragement, time given for personal discussion with the head, and support of an obviously verbal nature in front of other staff. At a personal and professional level this appeared to be more universally present than the second type of support. This was practical and organisational support. It might consist of taking the teacher's class, allocation of resources, organising whole school staff discussion and staff meetings, and timetable or curricular reorganisation of a more radical nature. What undermined teachers' confidence and ability to effect a change in their schools was a lack of this type of support.

There are wider implications about support. Although support within the case-study establishments themselves was important, it was evident that further support was needed. This took the form of support from the LEA in some way, whether at local, divisional or whole authority level. This was clearly seen to be somewhat tenuous in the case study group of schools and was doing much to undermine positive attitudes about what the group of schools might achieve. How can the heads and managers really be expected to stay positive and optimistic when living in a hand-to-mouth way? It seems to me to be an unenviable situation in which it is hardly surprising that the level of support they felt able to give their teachers varied so much. The mixed messages received along the lines of appreciation for all the hard work being done, and forward thinking initiative promises about continued staffing levels, do have the potential to undermine the determination to succeed.

However, the other side to this is that the closeness the groups experienced in the face of these uncertainties did a great deal to cement the working relationships within them. This is reflected in the loyalty, motivation and optimism underpinning it. So perhaps some adversity is a good thing. The question is, how much is reasonable?

An authority which is prepared to show that teachers' time is valued, and that the timing of in-service training should not always be at the end of a teaching day is likely to produce more willing participants than one which does not. This is borne out, particularly in the field of in-service for special educational needs, by Ainscow and Muncey (1983), Browder (1983), and from my further personal experience. This has been through working in an authority initiative which has recognised the need to allow teachers time to reflect on their practice. This has been done through school-based assignments linked to their in-service training course. There is no doubt that developments have ensued in their schools as a result of working in this way.

Realistic goals

Change is also more likely to occur if it is based on realistic goals set by the participants. This is endorsed by Powers (1983), who states that:

> In-service is most effective when teachers are allowed to choose their own goals, rather than when they are presented with pre-established goals. Teacher involvement in the design of specific programme objectives results in objectives that are more appropriately aligned with each teacher's interests and needs.

A flexibility in what might be envisaged, based on the contextual realities of a situation is more likely in a small localised setting. The goals which the participants set may be far more tangible than any imposed from outside. From their identified (common) need a plan for what might be achieved, and in what timescale, can take into account the personnel and organisations involved. A localised knowledge of these is essential if flexibility and reality is to be maintained.

The scheme studied did appear to be sensitive, to some degree, to the realities of the personnel who were involved. It was able to examine in some detail, through the planning meetings, what it was realistic to attempt in certain timescales. Through the discussion there was an acceptance that change does take time and should not be hurried. This created breathing space for busy teachers, and took account of the workload they already had. It may also allow some flexibility with regard to other initiatives with which schools are being faced, such as GCSE. It might even allow for some working alongside these other developments, particularly if they have consequences for the children who are targeted by the chosen initiative. This is borne out by some further personal experience in working with groups of staff at secondary level, whose special needs departments are dealing with the implications of GCSE for their children previously determined 'non-examinable'.

Evaluation

Within the development of an initiative for change there needs to be effective procedures for evaluation. There should be two major strands to this. Both of these are forms of formative evaluation. One involves the progress of the working groups as a whole, the other the individual teachers who form the working groups.

Built-in strategies for formative evaluation linked to the three key areas in the last section: realistic goals, a sensible and flexible timescale, and knowledge of the personnel and their organisations is essential in this.

A system which is not imposed, and is linked through reflection, debate and discussion, into the planning of changes envisaged, will be more effective. This system of evaluation may then allow for alterations in the direction, the pace and the processes of the work. A flexibility of this nature was found to be invaluable in the case-study scheme. The personnel felt they had control over what they might undertake, not that they were subject to an imposition which they might have felt very unrealistic.

This also allowed, in the case-study schools, for dealing with difficulties which were not of their own making. Such outside negative influences had a less damaging impact than they might, because of the flexibility that was already built into the evaluation and planning. It did not, however, totally negate those influences.

This process of flexibility through evaluation is what Fullan (1982) refers to as 'the science of muddling through' — in other words change can occur despite all the possible reasons which might inhibit it, provided people don't assume everything *will* go according to plan!

Evaluation of the changes envisaged in the planning of the programme of work must essentially be in the observation of classroom practice. As Powers (1983) states:

> Evaluation models should be developed which examine the extent to which whatever is learnt during in-service is incorporated into classroom practice by teachers.

The 'proof of the pudding', therefore, lies with teachers reflecting on their classroom practice and evaluating whether change has taken place. This is the second major element of the overall evaluation which should be taking place.

In-service training opportunities

In-service training opportunities should be provided which relate to the concerns of the participants. Teachers have traditionally had very little *real* influence on the in-service opportunities with which they have been provided. A chance to plan the form of in-service and share this planning with colleagues was seen to be of great importance by the teachers in the case-study. A practical relevance to their classroom situations was built into the planning.

The format which the in-service experiences took was varied, but included ways which helped to relate theory to practice. The use of workshops and discussions, devising some practical materials of common use, and field testing them in classrooms were all part of the plan. The evaluation of this through further discussion, together with a feeling that they had been working within their own guidelines meant they were meeting their in-service needs. This view is endorsed by Powers (1983).

The vehicle of special needs may be immaterial in helping a group of people to work in this way. The important issue appears to be that the factors which encouraged cooperative working could provide a platform from which to work on different issues. The groups had already expressed an interest in considering secondary transfer in a much wider sense than just with special needs in mind. They were considering the curricular compatibility which *could* exist if some joint work was done. This could be done by groups of teachers interested in curriculum/subject areas in the top junior age range and the lower secondary years. The cooperative or collegiate approach to this one identified area of interest would be well worth exploring, as it appeared to be a perceived need. The pattern of working established with special needs as a focus could very well be replicated to do this, considering the very positive factors existing which I outlined previously.

A school (or in this case a group of schools) should be a place which has teachers who are learners with the children. A collaborative approach to this learning will allow a more serious approach to school development, and encourage changes in practice, as described by Reed (1986).

Support for one another

The support which teachers are able to give one another through the processes outlined in the last three sections must not be undervalued. In a scheme of the sort documented the mutual support the participants gave each other was crucial to their feeling of optimism about the work in which they were involved. This was particularly in focus because of the perceived lack of constant support from the LEA.

Using all of the existing skills which they possessed rather than relying on outside 'experts' to give 'answers' gave an opportunity for this mutual support. It is reinforcing for teachers to examine the skills they have and share with others, rather than making the assumption that someone else has all the skills. Sharing common problems, with colleagues who are supportive, must be more effective and reinforcing than seeking an answer from outside. Dessent (1984) suggests that this is the case, when examining the role of teachers as in-service trainers rather than using 'expert-consultants', whose classroom credibility may be suspect in the eyes of the recipients. It is also endorsed by Balshaw (1987), in examining the role of the teacher working in support roles.

Not being given 'answers' but learning together to find some possible strategies must be more effective for teachers as learners. In any case, it is highly unlikely that someone else's answers will do in their entirety in each of the participants' classrooms and schools, because they are not context specific.

An answer, or strategy, or teaching method which has been worked out collaboratively with supportive colleagues, will not be seen as definitive. In other words, it is up for trial, personal reflection, further discussion and group evaluation, thus more likely to provide a real change in teaching practice. The professional support of colleagues in a learning situation of this nature is more likely to produce personal and professional development, and therefore classroom and school development, i.e. result in change.

The key issue

The key issue underpinning the six previously outlined themes seems to me to be that change in education is likely to be more effective if the participants feel they have an influence over the change in which they are taking part. There are a number of ways in which this may happen, but an examination of why this is so fundamental is called for here.

'Influence' may take a number of forms: having an effect on something or somebody, often with connotations of power, according to the dictionary. Power is not something which teachers have traditionally held over how their professional development might be shaped. Indeed, professional development in the form of in-service training has offered little opportunity for teachers to make their own decisions. Neither have teachers wielded much power in making decisions about the kinds of changes they might have envisaged their schools making. Change has tended to be imposed from outside or above. The result has been a lack of understanding, resistance, little enthusiasm and a very 'watered-down' version of what was envisaged in the first place. This is usually planned by the government or LEA and as Fullan (1982) states:

> The crux of change involves the development of meaning in relation to a new idea, program or set of activities. But it is *individuals* who have to develop new meaning and these individuals are insignificant parts of a gigantic, loosely organised, complex, messy social system which contains myriad different subjective worlds.

A structure which allows teachers real influence and therefore understanding of the changes in which they will be involved, particularly with reference to professional development and in-service training, must have a better chance of success. It should both effect professional development and increase the chance for change in schools. As Powers (1983) states:

> It is the practice of in-service and not the principle that has generated resistance.

He goes on to describe the importance of teachers being involved in the principles and planning of their own in-service, saying that thus the incentive to achieve is greatly strengthened.

So, where might special schools lie within all of this?

If special schools are to become 'ordinary', perhaps take on the skills, experience and attitudes of mainstream schools, whilst retaining relevant skills of their own, could this be then one way to do it? Should it involve collaborative ventures using the combined knowledge and experience of all participants? Should it involve giving the participants understanding through in-service training which they have planned themselves, with their own needs in focus? This may well result in a feeling of influence over the inevitable changes that are involved. It may also reinforce feelings of optimism about the future, which have tended to be sadly lacking in special schools in recent years.

CONCLUSION

Somebody once said:

> Some people make things happen, some people watch things happen, and some people wonder what the hell *did* happen.

If schools wish to be in the first category of this statement and *make* things happen then perhaps they should be mindful of the following thought:

Change is more likely to happen successfully if the people experiencing the period of change are involved, understand and plan the period of change themselves.

It may be that in this process they still get into 'the science of muddling through', and that they understand that not all they envisage for themselves will go to plan. However, if they feel they have influence over the processes through which they are going this is more likely to be acceptable to them. If they feel better about it because of this level of understanding, and subsequently influence, they will still feel they can 'make things happen'.

Perhaps at future in-service courses dealing with the nature of special schools the pictures or allegories produced by the staff of those schools will be different from the ones described at the beginning of this chapter. Maybe the white elephants, battleships and a narrowly developed curriculum will no longer be depicted? Maybe the drawings will show a more positive attitude and an understanding of what can be done? Hopefully there will be a sense of optimism within special schools about their ability to 'make things happen'. It could be that the process of making the special school more ordinary will be facilitated by collaborative ways of working to produce change.

Chapter 5

Reaching Out: The Background to Outreach
Allan Day

THE BACKGROUND TO OUTREACH

Links between special and mainstream schools have taken on increasing importance in recent years, as attempts are made to move towards a unification of the two sectors. While there is also a need to plan for the linking of children, curricula and resources, this chapter will focus on linking teachers across the boundary between special schools for children with moderate learning difficulties and ordinary schools. This activity in some of its aspects is often called 'outreach'.

An enquiry by the author into links in fifty LEAs led to follow-up visits to twenty recommended special schools where innovative work was taking place. Where teachers based in the special schools were reaching out to the mainstream, their reasons for doing so and the local patterns of provisions and administration within which they worked were very different. These factors produced a variety of constraints and opportunities. Special schools inhabit a particular ecological niche in their own area which confers upon teachers moving off-base a range of powers and limitations. Despite the variety which exists nationally in both the special schools and local mainstream learning support structures, there was nevertheless a likelihood that the special school teachers in reaching out to the mainstream would favour one of four outreach models, which are explored later in this chapter.

Before we examine specific models, however, what do we already know about links between special and mainstream schools? The perceived need for

Allan Day is Head of Southall School in Telford, Shropshire. This chapter is based on a report which was made by the author following a one-term secondment by Shropshire Education Authority to a Schoolteacher Associateship at Crewe and Alsager College of Higher Education.

such links certainly goes back at least as far as the Warnock Report (DES, 1978), in which it was seen that increasing integration would tend to leave surviving special schools a narrower range of children and force them to become more specialised. According to Warnock, links would bring benefits both to the mainstream, in a spreading of expertise, and to the special school children and staff, in a reduction in their isolation:

> 8.12 The expertise in special schools is likely to be of considerable benefit to teachers in ordinary schools in a range of areas...Moreover, by collaborating with staff in ordinary schools teachers in special schools will avoid the professional isolation which many of them feel at present and which would otherwise tend to increase if, as we envisage, special schools become more specialised institutions than they are now...(DES, 1978).

The recommendations made by the Warnock Committee very clearly widened the concept of special educational needs and emphasised integration, and yet these recommendations were seen as entirely compatible with placing a high value on the remaining special schools and their teacher expertise.

Many of Warnock's procedural recommendations have been incorporated into the 1981 Education Act, which deals almost entirely with procedures, duties and rights, and does not attempt to take Warnock's ideas any further. Although Section 2 specifies that it shall be the LEA's duty to educate the 'statemented' child in an ordinary school, this must be compatible with

(a)   his receiving the special educational provision that he requires;
(b)   the provision of efficient education for the children with whom he will be educated; and
(c)   the efficient use of resources.

It is therefore left to individual LEAs, under varying pressures from local and national ideological, economic, pressure-group, and litigious processes, to move towards integration in different ways, and choose their own interpretations of the future roles of special schools in their own area. This has resulted in extremes of local variation, from almost total run-down of MLD special schools to 'business as usual'. Furthermore, different LEAs have moved towards establishing county special needs policies at different rates. In some areas this has meant that special schools have had some years' grace in which to take their own initiatives in establishing outreach work or other links and have managed to pre-empt county policy decisions, and in some cases strongly influence them. This may be particularly true in areas without well-established remedial or psychological support to the mainstream, where special schools have stepped into a vacant niche.

It is no coincidence that links between special and mainstream schools are being established as some special school rolls are falling, as foreseen by the Warnock Report, where the major effect should logically be on special schools for children with moderate learning difficulties, and those for children with physical handicaps. However, the special school falling rolls situation is not yet clear, and seem to be very patchy nationally (Swann, 1985).

Numbers on roll in a given special school may depend on how several factors balance out. On the one hand, there may have been an increase in referrals since the 1981 Act, or the school may be in an area of population growth, linked to high levels of poverty which generate problems at a rate with which an under-resourced mainstream is unable to cope. On the other hand, the LEA may have recently invested heavily in mainstream units or support services, and the special school may be located in an area of stable or shrinking population. It is therefore likely that any national statistics will conceal an enormous variety of situations affecting MLD special school rolls. In the schools which I visited, however, mainstream links, and teacher outreach in particular, were often given impetus by a falling-rolls situation, and this is borne out by the findings of a large-scale NFER survey (Jowett, Hegarty and Moses, 1988).

Nevertheless, although some heads of special schools have developed outreach work in response to what was perceived as a threatening situation, the NFER study also observed other situations where changes in special school rolls and roles were seen by heads as a valuable opportunity to display expertise and show the rest of the educational world what was possible. Outreach work might therefore be viewed by individual schools in a negative sense to maintain staff and credibility in a threatening situation, or as expansionist, providing opportunities for growth, diversification, and community with mainstream education.

It is only relatively recently that a few reports of special school outreach work have been available. Pioneering work at Heltwate School was described by Hallmark and Dessent (1982) and Hallmark (1983) and outreach from Castle School was described by Bond and Sharrock (1984). These schools developed very different models, which are explored later in this chapter.

Mullins (1982) analysed the roles of special school-based primary phase support teachers in Sheffield, following an LEA policy reorganisation in 1976. This valuable study explored the perceptions of the outreach support staff and the mainstream teachers, as well as the expansion of the service within an LEA policy framework. Galloway and Goodwin (1987) have used Mullins' survey to suggest that the net effects of such an outreach support service were mainly to 'de-skill' mainstream teachers further, and provide an avenue for increased special education placement. The Mullins research and the subsequent commentary by Galloway and Goodwin raise important issues about the function of any learning support service. There is obviously room for conflicting interpretation of support service functions, since the setting up of any service will result in that service justifying its existence. Special schools will tend to reveal children in need of special schooling, support services will identify children who need support, statements will lead to children being 'statemented', and so on. On the other hand, special educators will argue that the children are all 'there' waiting to be discovered and that their service meets the needs of children which would otherwise go un-met.

Further exploration of the perceptions of the different parties involved was pursued by Armstrong (1986), who undertook useful research in six LEAs in the London area (five metropolitan and one county), in which he interviewed many of the agents involved in MLD school outreach projects to illuminate not only the different models, but also the perceptions and attitudes of those involved in different roles. In each authority he interviewed the following, or their equivalents:

AEO (Special)
Adviser (SEN)
Principal Educational Psychologist
Head (MLD special school)
Outreach Support Teachers (MLD special school)
Head (mainstream primary school)
Teachers (mainstream special needs coordinator or class teacher).

Armstrong found on-going outreach support from MLD special schools to mainstream schools in five out of the six LEAs. In four of these areas the instigators were the special school heads, in three cases with strong SPS support, following a history of psychologist involvement in the development of special school programmes, and in two cases falling rolls were a major factor. Although Armstrong explored important issues of the policies and perceptions of LEA officers and advisers, perhaps the most relevant observations to the practice of outreach concern the views of the outreach support teachers and the mainstream teachers.

Most of the special school outreach teachers were in minor promoted posts and had been actively recruited by their special school head. The sources of greatest dissatisfaction to the outreach teachers were:

(i) (where applicable) Having a teaching commitment and responsibility in the special school, alongside their outreach work, which was highly demanding.

(ii) Not having in some cases a clearly-defined brief to work from, and not having clear role definitions. Some of the outreach projects were pilot schemes, so support teachers bore a heavy responsibility for making a go of it, and therefore felt under extra pressure.

All special school outreach teachers were keen to differentiate their role from that of the remedial advisory teachers. Those who had both primary and secondary learning support experience found the primary sphere easier to work in, largely because their skills analysis approach was more appropriate there. All worked on a task analysis and objectives model. In two cases, there had been conflict between the outreach teachers and area special needs advisory staff, but outreach staff invariably deferred if there was a territorial problem. (Only in one area was there centrally coordinated differential allocation of the two services to different schools or children).

Mainstream heads agreed that previous and current remedial advisory teacher support was too infrequent and spread too thinly to be of much help, and felt that special school outreach was more helpful in terms of level of involvement.

All mainstream class teachers, of whom several were their school's named SEN coordinator, were very positive towards the special school support, mainly because of:

(i)   the specificity of the programmes for individual children
(ii)   materials provided by the special school
(iii)   training given by the outreach teacher to pass on skills to the mainstream teacher
(iv)   the evidence of progress, in relation to a sequence of objectives
(v)   support given in the classroom demystifying expertise
(vi)   regularity of contact for fine-tuning and moral support
(vii)   in some cases, the attraction of other support by the outreach teacher.

Like their headteachers, mainstream class teachers were most annoyed when children with special educational needs were placed in their class without consultation or support.

Armstrong's research is useful in highlighting the perceptions of the different parties involved in such support networks spanning the special and mainstream sectors, and the importance of coordination and role-clarification.

It is important that he should also have established the popularity of special school outreach support independently of the viewpoints of special school staff, since there is in some quarters a great deal of suspicion about the outreach role. Galloway and Goodwin (1987), for instance, assert:

> To be accepted as resource centres, then, special school staff will need to demonstrate that they can offer something of practical value within an ordinary school. Demonstrations of success in a different

context will be of little value. This also has implications for their possible training role. Teachers in the mainstream will not want in-service courses that urge them to adopt the classroom organisation, curriculum and teaching methods of a special school. Quite rightly, they will demand something which helps them adapt their existing methods to become more responsive to individual needs.

All this is asking a great deal of special school staff. It requires not only the ability to work with children in the necessarily sheltered setting of the special school or unit. In addition it requires the ability to carry out in-service education with colleagues in a quite different context. While there are some notable exceptions, there is little evidence that special school staff are equipped to fill both of these roles.

Galloway and Goodwin underestimate the popularity of outreach support among mainstream teachers, although they do raise a valid issue of exactly what skills and approaches are to be transferred, and what interface can be found between special school and mainstream approaches. As will become clear in the link models described, the interfaces will be quite different at primary and secondary levels. Most special school outreach takes place at the primary level, where a task analysis of basic skills is more readily transferable, whereas the secondary phase is more conductive to subject-based curriculum analysis, which could only be approached as a partnership between the special and ordinary schools.

It is also evident that there is a trade-off between intensive involvement with a small number of children in a few mainstream schools, and casting a wider net, but losing the impact of closer involvement within a given school. As any outreach service grows, and more demands are made of it, it is more likely to run into the problems of the thinly spread remedial support service. It is not clear how much of the widely agreed benefit of special school outreach work is due to the objectives model and the special-school-based skills, and how much is simply due to the high levels of involvement with individual children and teachers, which is a luxury not enjoyed by the remedial advisory teachers who have a wider responsibility.

Armstrong also makes the point that outreach could not prevent some children being referred to special schools. It cannot modify or replace whole mainstream curricula, nor can it replace all of the functions and benefits of the special school.

In quantitative terms, our knowledge of special school-mainstream links has been brought up to date by a recent nation-wide survey undertaking by the NFER (Jowett, Hegarty and Mosses, 1988), who sent a questionnaire to a random quarter of LEAs in England and Wales. This evoked responses from

268 special schools, of which 91 catered for children with moderate learning difficulties. The percentages of the different types of special schools declaring some involvement in links with mainstream schools was as follows:

moderate learning difficulties	70%
severe learning difficulties	80%
physical handicaps	67%
emotional and behavioural difficulties	69%

The NFER study looked at the movement of staff, pupils and resources between the special and mainstream sectors. This concept of movement or mobility of special school and mainstream elements can usefully be incorporated into models for teacher-links.

In the first instance, movement of teachers could be analysed as follows:

(i) Movement of special school teachers to mainstream schools: this could involve the special school staff moving out to pick up mainstream skills and knowledge to bring back to the special school, but is more likely to involve the special school staff in 'outreach' support work, since what essentially is being moved is the special school's expertise, particularly in the primary phase. When special school staff do outreach support work, it may be focused on individual children, groups of children or teachers. It may emphasise teaching (of children), or guidance and consultancy (with mainstream teachers). It may be linked strongly to provision of material resources, or aim primarily to teach techniques.

The teaching model applied could range from a behavioural-objectives model to a diagnostic-remedial one.

In the NFER survey, in 35% of special schools, staff were on regular weekly outreach work, in 32% less regular, and in 33% no staff were involved. On average in those special schools undertaking mainstream staff links one teacher in five was involved.

Nearly a quarter of MLD schools had regular weekly outreach work going on. Half of the teachers involved were out for less than three hours per week, nearly half of them for between half a day and two days, and one teacher full-time. Table 5.1, a re-working of some of the NFER data, shows interesting differences between the activities undertaken by special school teachers on outreach work according to type of special school.

The table suggests that the outreach rationale for teachers from schools for children with moderate learning difficulties involved far more of a consultancy role. Their main activity was providing support for their colleagues, although teaching accounted for a third of their outreach work. On the other hand, for the teachers from schools for physically handicapped children and children with severe learning difficulties, the main activity was

Table 5.1   Percentage of total number of activities undertaken on outreach in mainstream schools

	TEACHING			ADVISING/LIAISING	
	Teaching pupils from the special school	Teaching pupils from the main-stream school	Teaching combined groups	Advising Colleagues	Liaising
Teachers from schools for children with moderate learning difficulties	17	10	6	65	2
Teachers from schools for children with physical handicap	31	0	38	6	25
Teachers from schools for children with severe learning difficulties	17	0	71	10	3

teaching, mainly accompanying special school children in integrated lessons, and mainly for short periods of time.

(ii) Movement of mainstream teachers to special schools: this could simply involve the collection of materials from a special school resource-centre, or could involve a commitment to regular meetings, or a period of part-time or full-time INSET or teaching based in the special school. It could also involve a transfer of mainstream expertise to the special school, perhaps to extend the curriculum for more able children.

In 38% of the NFER sample, some movement of staff to the special school was reported — much less than in the reverse direction. Over half of these contacts were to enable teachers in mainstream schools to make use of resources based in the special school or draw on the experience of special school staff. The rest of the contacts involved either regular direct work with pupils, often in teams, and usually timetabled, or more occasional meetings and workshops. The figures are not broken down by type of special school.

(iii) In a more evolved situation, the movement of staff could be less polarised than in (i) and (ii) above, and a network of special school and mainstream support staff established. In such a situation, there is more likely to be a need for centralised planning and role-definition.

OUTREACH MODELS

In the schools involved in outreach work visited by the author, it was possible to identify four main conceptual models for teacher links, which could be described as:

(1)   Exporting the behavioural objectives approach
(2)   Resource-delivery
(3)   Consultancy
(4)   Partnership

It was possible for a special school to be involved in more than one of the above, but in practice most had put most of their energy and allegiance into one model. One could envisage a progression from (1) to (4) in terms of reducing the egocentricity of the special school, and yet the situation is not as simple as it seems. In any outreach work, there has to be some rationale for the activity, and this usually centres around the concept of expertise. If special school staff are to reach out to the mainstream, the rationale is usually one of exporting for the benefit of others expertise which has been concentrated in a special school. However, closer examination will show that while this stance is usually defensible in the primary phase, it breaks down very quickly in the secondary phase. Secondary schools, unlike most primary schools, all have learning support departments of their own, with staff experienced in remedial methods. The basis of mainstream secondary education is clearly the school subject, and special needs support has to work within subject boundaries, as well as within the school's pastoral system. Given both of these factors, there is a less clear picture of where expertise lies: subject teachers have subject expertise, mainstream learning support teachers have expertise in remediation and in-class support for children with mild learning difficulties, and special school teachers have expertise in child-centred curriculum adaptation with a narrower range of very low-ability children. Given also the lack of subject breadth and expertise in many special schools, there may even be a perceived lack of competence in special schools at secondary level, requiring input from mainstream expertise. At this level it would be naive to see the special school teachers as the experts and a partnership is the only basis on which links could work.

It is worth exploring concrete examples of how the four proposed models work in practice.

Model 1. Exporting the behavioural objectives approach

This model is the most common, but is perhaps the most contentious. Its basic premise is that what special schools have perfected is a method of linear task analysis linked to the setting of behavioural objectives, and that this can be applied to children with learning difficulties in mainstream situations. At its most simplistic, it involves the direct application of the special school's own basic skills curriculum and materials to the child in the ordinary school. In a more evolved form, such as ELSA or SNAP, it is a method which is being exported, and therefore can exist without the involvement of the special school's own curriculum.

The prime exponent of this model has been Castle School, which is an all-age (4–16) day special school for children with moderate learning difficulties, in an urban setting. It has gained a national reputation as a pioneer of the behavioural objectives curriculum run according to the open/closed model described by Ainscow and Tweddle (1979), and it is this behavioural objectives model which has been used in outreach support work.

The development of the pilot outreach support project from 1980 to 1984 has been described by the subsequent Head and Deputy (Bond and Sharrock, 1984): in the autumn of 1980, forty-eight local primary school heads were invited in to Castle School to see their approach to implementing individual programmes for children with learning difficulties, at which point the possibility of applying similar methods to children in the primary schools was discussed. Staff discussions in the spring of 1981 led to the agreement among the Castle School staff that support should primarily be through cooperative working with class teachers rather than working directly with the children. The emphasis was therefore to be on transferring skills from the special school staff to the mainstream staff.

The project was planned from the beginning in liaison with the educational psychologist attached to the primary schools, although referral was by the primary schools themselves, and the psychologist was simply to be kept informed.

Two Castle School staff were chosen and each was given a half day per week on the project, involving eight children from two primary schools (the first two schools to ask to be involved). The model followed this pattern:

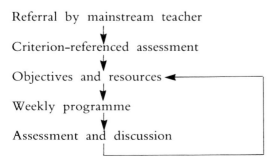

Referral by mainstream teacher

Criterion-referenced assessment

Objectives and resources

Weekly programme

Assessment and discussion

The key features of the model were the criterion–referenced assessment and targeting of behavioural objectives. The assessment would take place in the primary classroom, but using the curriculum of the special school, each area of which is specified in terms of behavioural objectives. This assessment would determine the point at which the child entered the special school programme, and focus on setting individual objectives, specifying:

(a) the required pupil behaviour
(b) the conditions under which that behaviour was to occur
(c) the performance criteria which the child must meet in order to pass the item.

The special school support teacher would leave the mainstream teacher a 'package' of objectives and resources to match, taken from Castle School's own Language/Reading and Math resource areas in which banks of materials are coded to match each objective in their programmes. Each week the special school teacher would assess and chart the child's progress, so that each week would bring:

(a) progress for the pupil in the specified curriculum area
(b) collated accurate data on each child's progress, with regard to accuracy, rate and maintenance, which were made available to all external agencies such as parents and educational psychologists
(c) familiarity by the mainstream teacher with techniques of identifying specific areas of weakness, teaching programmes, strategies and resources, and techniques for recording data.

By 1985, the programme had expanded to include five members of staff supporting five primary schools, and three in secondary schools. Clearly, both consultancy and resource delivery are involved in this approach, but the emphasis is arguably on the exporting of the behavioural objectives approach. In this author's survey, a similar model was used by several special schools, usually where special school outreach had been encouraged by behavioural psychologists who had been involved in the development of the special school programmes. (This, too, was noted by Armstrong, 1986).

Model 2. Resource-delivery

This model is less tied to the vision of the special school as a behavioural-objectives hothouse. It is more pragmatic about what resources it will deliver to mainstream schools, and is therefore more able to work within the mainstream school's own materials and perceptions. To a large extent, this means that the special school involved partakes of the traditional roles of the peripatetic remedial teaching service, and the rationale for basing the outreach in the special school becomes less obvious, since it is less tied to esoteric special curricula. Nevertheless, schools operating within this model report that the special school's involvement is highly valued by the mainstream schools, even where other remedial and support services exist.

The prototype and paradigm for the resource-delivery model is Heltwate School, whose outreach support service has been described by Hallmark and Dessent (1982) and Hallmark (1983). The emphasis was to be on the prevention of transfer of children to special school, and the focus would be on the infant school. In devising a support model, various alternatives were rejected:

> ...we soon realised that strategies such as workshop courses, short in-service courses and opening up the special school to other teachers, were by themselves quite inadequate, for there was no guarantee that they would be followed up by changes in actual classroom practices. Also, the temporary placement of a pupil in a special school or class meant that possible opportunities for helping other pupils and actively involving the class teacher were missed. (Hallmark, 1983).

The essential features of the support given were to be a weekly visit by a special school outreach teacher, the delivery of a constant supply of material resources, and on-going weekly written work objectives for the pupil concerned. Although the operation has considerably expanded over the years, this remains the basic framework. The development in relation to a particular infant school is described in Hallmark (1983) as follows:

1. Initial approach to referred pupil in the ordinary school. Head teachers meet and agree on weekly session by a visiting teacher.
2. Visiting teacher discusses procedure with head and class teacher. Discussion with class teacher on needs of pupil, work to be left, written down when agreed. Work done by pupil helped by class teacher.
3. Curriculum needs of child assessed. Practical considerations of how these could be met in a particular classroom. First week's work written down. Resources left.
4. Learning resources introduced gradually in response to the developing needs of the child. Any specific classroom problems noted.
5. Regular weekly visits maintained to monitor child's progress and write new work programmes. Class teacher thus encouraged to carry out work plans.
6. Visiting teacher devises record-keeping system, which is open for scrutiny and which details what has taken place on each visit.

7. Materials and teaching support clearly suitable for other pupils, who are therefore included in the scheme as far as possible.
8. Other mainstream teachers 'volunteer' to be helped, this willingness being the best way of guaranteeing success.

Among the many excellent features of the scheme is the way a definite commitment is demanded of the mainstream school, which is then drawn into a learning-support network. In the first instance, the primary school has to ask for help (having heard of the support service through 'the grapevine' or through educational psychologists). The primary school has to make a commitment to at least ten minutes' teacher-time per day for each child's programme, and a payment to the special school for resources used. The primary school staff must agree to go to the special school for an induction meeting, and their 'named teacher' must be released for the last quarter of one day per week to attend a weekly meeting at the special school with the support service staff and other primary school teachers in the same role as themselves. The same teacher must attend a review meeting twice a year with the educational psychologist and give a progress report on work in her own school. In return, the commitment of the special school outreach staff is constant. (They will even undertake parents' workshops and attend the primary school parents evenings, if requested).

There are five staff involved in outreach work, with from approximately 30 per cent of their teaching loads devoted to the support service. The head of the support unit visits between five and eight schools per week. The outreach goes in to about twenty primary schools, and up to 250 children are being given support of some sort, as many as 30 in one large primary school. The teachers involved are quite certain that among these children are a significant number who would previously have been referred to special schools, and that they are in fact supporting some pupils in the ordinary schools who have more difficulties than some of the pupils who come to the special school from mainstream schools which are not supported by the scheme.

All of the four staff are also involved in the creation and development of the impressive resources bank based at the school. Given the scale of the operation, this has to be highly organised, and now involves the full-time work of two ancillary helpers who duplicate and pack individual kits, based on the teachers' weekly request-forms. All materials are printed outside the school at some expense with high quality print, paper and card.

It is interesting to note how the outreach support service has developed in relation to the other support services. One feature of the scheme is that infant teachers are encouraged to identify their own problem children annually by listing them in order of priority. These children are then assessed by the outreach staff, using a very simple set of tests. In all of this process, there is no recourse to either an LEA screening or normative tests, and it is thought to be an important feature of the scheme that screening and assessment should be devolved from the LEA to the infant classroom in this way, and linked directly to teaching strategies and materials.

It should also be noted that more recently, special education resource centres have been established in some primary schools. Staff are aware that, because of a lowering of the average ability of the special school's intake, it is arguable that future resource-based learning support might be better located in primary schools. However, it is reported that the credibility and popularity of the special school outreach staff remains consistently high. This would perhaps suggest that special schools could still play a key role in support networks, because of their proven expertise and credibility, even when other mainstream support services are available. It would also suggest a need for the outreach staff to maintain at least some teaching commitment within the special school, in order to retain both their teaching involvement and their credibility, although this dual role is consistently found to be a burden to outreach staff.

Model 3. Consultancy

While consultancy is definitely involved in models 1 and 2, it is not the central process. Some schools were found, however, where consultancy was seen as the main outreach role and where the activity was staffed and resourced accordingly. One school, which I will call City School, was exemplary.

City School has a large Outreach Unit of seven teachers working in the moderate learning difficulties field. The school has strong links with area psychologists, but there is no peripatetic remedial advisory teaching service. The development of outreach work has therefore been a joint SPS-special school venture, which began as a joint pilot project. From the outset, the allocation of time to mainstream schools was generous, allowing two half-days' support per week for each mainstream class teacher. This would allow in-depth assessment, use of observation techniques to allow mainstream and outreach teachers to collaborate, and further training of the mainstream teachers through workshops back at the special school.

Of special interest is the strategy of the support teacher teaching the mainstream teacher's class for some of the time to allow that teacher the freedom to concentrate on the individual child's programme. This emphasises cooperation and reduces the possible 'deskilling' effect on a mainstream teacher caused by bringing in an expert to deal with her child.

In devising the above model, the teaching staff spent a great deal of time looking at existing practice and preparing themselves for their outreach role. The 'resource-delivery' model described in the previous section was among those considered, but it was decided that a resource-based provision could give support without bringing about long-term change. The emphasis was to be on training teachers, rather than providing resources, so it was decided that the outreach staff would above all need consultancy skills. Experts were brought in to give the staff an intensive course in consultancy skills and cooperative teaching, and the outreach staff were then given a month's straightforward primary school practice, both as a simple refresher and as a way of focusing their perceptions on the predicament of the mainstream primary teacher faced with children with learning difficulties. The staff regard both of these initial orientation procedures as valuable.

Staff describe the present running of the scheme much as in the pilot project. These are seven teachers, each out for four and a half days per week, offering an input of about half a day per child per school per week. This means a total of more than fifty children being supported in the mainstream. None of these children are statemented, since no change of placement is involved, but the outreach staff are quite sure that their outreach work is preventing some of the children being referred to special school.

The outreach unit's staff have taught within the special school, but not since moving into the unit, which has, consequently, relatively detached status. The staff have therefore become operationally separated from their special school building. This would seem to detract somewhat from the logic of basing the unit in the special school.

The sheer amount of weekly time which each outreach teacher spends with each supported pupil seems relatively generous, and is considerably more than most peripatetic support teachers could hope for, and many times more than in most special school outreach services. Simply looked at in terms of cost-effectiveness, there are clear relationships between the number of staff made available by the LEA and the sort of support model which it becomes realistic to apply.

A comparision of five outreach link models for which I have managed to obtain data allows the calculation of approximate time available for each child being supported in the mainstream is shown in Table 5.2.

The right-hand column clearly indicates the different levels of staff resourcing in relation to the numbers of children receiving support, and must impose severe restraints on what is possible. Time allocation is an obvious gross variable, although it is not yet clear how it interacts with type of model to limit the optimum conditions for change.

Table 5.2   Time available for each child being supported in mainstream

Number of outreach teachers	Total outreach hours per week	Total number of children supported by outreach	Average weekly time available per child*
4	74½	250	18 minutes
7	175	50	3½ hours
1	12	22	33 minutes
1½	32	30	1 hour 4 minutes
9	60½	56	1 hour 5 minutes

* takes no account of group work, travelling time, or discussion-time with mainstream teacher.

Model 4.   Partnership

While Models 1 to 3 are of particular relevance in the primary phase, the different conditions prevailing in the secondary phase require a different approach, as one head who has previous experience of primary outreach has realised in setting up teacher links from his large urban secondary MLD school, which I will call Urban School.

In setting up his secondary phase outreach, the head found it necessary to firstly look at the mainstream learning support background. Most of the local comprehensive schools are working on or moving towards a mainstream learning support model based on extra teachers in class and little or no withdrawal. Secondary schools already have learning support staff who have trained in the remediation of learning difficulties, many of whom need little guidance on basic skills intervention. Some of the secondary schools are developing extensive departmental learning-analysis structures. Given this background, and the sheer number of secondary-aged children in the city, it is thought to be pointless for this special school's outreach staff to involve themselves with individual children. They are therefore involved primarily in working alongside mainstream learning support teachers, or subject teachers, and the focus of their work is on curricular modification within subjects. They have therefore moved away from the linear, sequential, skills-based model of primary remedial work to a depth-analysis of subject areas at secondary level. The secondary schools are largely working on modular work, with some non-negotiable core elements and some negotiable open-ended choices for the senior pupils, linked to programmes running in three local comprehensive schools. The intention is therefore to run the special school curriculum in several structural ways parallel to the mainstream secondary curriculum. The basis of their support to mainstream schools is therefore their experience of modifying the secondary curriculum for slow learners in the special school, although at this level expertise has clearly a two-way flow, and outreach becomes partnership.

In several other special schools, mainstream links were made with a view to gaining input from mainstream teachers into the special school curriculum, often in the mainstream base, with special school and mainstream colleagues team-teaching. This was seen as a process of normalising and extending the special school curriculum, and support was therefore unavoidably acknowledged and welcomed as a two-way process.

THE FUTURE

The future of special school outreach will depend largely on LEA attitudes to special schools, following the progressive formulation of local integration policies. Such policies will affect both special school rolls and the value placed on special school expertise. The period of freedom for individual special schools to independently establish their own ecological niche in mainstream support must be drawing to a close, and future links will require greater LEA coordination. Both planners and practitioners will still have to address the same issues as those who have pioneered outreach work, among which will be the following:

In the primary phase:
(1)   The role of the special school teachers within the LEA learning support network. (Isolated or integrated).
(2)   The nature of expertise, its location, its relevance, and its transferability. (Based on behavioural objectives curriculum, or standard remedial model).
(3)   Target group for outreach support. (Individual children, with mild, specific or moderate learning difficulties. Statemented children. Class teachers).
(4)   Objectives for outreach. (Prevention of special school placement. Mainstream support for statemented children. Generalised mainstream support. Transfer of skills and attitudes to mainstream staff).
(5)   Strategies and outreach models relevant to objectives and target group. (Teaching or consultancy).
(6)   Scale and intensity of outreach work. (Number of special school staff involved, for how much time, working with how many children, teachers or schools. Role of outreach staff in the special school base).
(7)   Level of back-up resources. (Problems of funding, time, production. Can they be delivered by the teacher, special school, LEA?).

In the secondary phase, in addition to all the above:

(1) The interface between the special school and mainstream curricula at subject level. (Problems of achieving an interface, if the average ability of children left in special schools drops. Narrower range of subjects and subject-teachers in the special school).

(2) Change of emphasis from outreach department to a more generalised interchange of subject staff. (How many staff to involve? Staffing implications, if this is ever to progress beyond token links).

Few professionals now doubt the need for more links between special school and mainstream teachers, for the mutual benefit of schools in both sectors, and for the career mobility of the staff involved. There is evidence that many special schools are already reaching out across the great divide, but there is still a yawning gap between minor local experiment and full LEA resourcing. The models for special school outreach and teacher links which have been tried should now be drawn upon to bring special school and mainstream staff into a truly integrated service.

Section 3
Special Schools:
A Positive Response

Chapter 6

The Special School: A Part of, not Apart from the Education System
Keith Bovair

THE PERCEIVED CLIMATE

Special schools in Great Britain have been waiting for a change to occur in special education provision since the inception of the Warnock Report on Special Educational Needs. It was a national report which has been implemented in an *ad hoc* manner; much depended on the responsiveness of the local authority where one worked. If you were in Sheffield in 1978 you would have found yourself in meetings about steps to implement the suggestions of the report and would have a *Readers Digest* condensed version of it to assimilate. If you were with another authority, you might have found yourself trying to find out if anyone besides yourself had read it.

The report broke ground in initiating our rethinking of the way we were meeting the individual needs of children. It tackled the issues of labelling, early childhood education to post–16 provision, initial teacher training, identification, assessment and recording, special education in ordinary and special schools, parental involvement, curriculum matters, teacher education and training, advice and support networks and relationships with other services concerned with children with special needs.

The Warnock Report was the 'Way Ahead' for an education system, which did not perceive the selfish society we were heading for; that which ignores our human and social inter-dependence. After all, humanistic approaches to children and young people have often been perceived as an unfortunate residue of the late sixties and early seventies. Because the financial cost of the idealism of that time has been perceived by some as a financial burden that should not occur again, we find ourselves depending on the creative financial manoeuvrings of those 'caring authorities' who are trying to maintain a humanistic approach within the restraints of the current financial climate.

One of the key points to have come out of the Warnock Report was the concept of integration. It was also to be included in the 1981 Education Act, which supported many of the issues identified in the report. As an educational philosophy it can mean that children and young people who are considered to have special educational needs are educated in the ordinary educational settings of their local community. Unfortunately, it has been overshadowed by the financial opportunities it offers certain authorities to rationalize existing services as cost-cutting exercises under the pretence of protecting the rights of the individual who may be unfortunate enough to have a handicapping condition.

The lack of capital investment in these new initiatives was blatantly obvious when the 1981 Act came into existence. Lady Young was quoted in the *Guardian* at that time as stating that she welcomed the Act but pointing out that there would be no additional resources to implement it, thus leaving overstretched local authorities to meet the cost. Rather than incurring more financial burdens and under the guise of best intentions, a cheap form of integration has occured avoiding the cost of special school placement, yet without the necessary resource input in the ordinary setting, all too often at the expense of the population that truly has the right to benefit from the concept.

The loss to children and young people with individual needs is the provision of proper resources for the ordinary school to meet their requirements. The resource that is truly required is time. Time to make oneself aware of the needs of those with learning and physical handicaps, the time to see to their pastoral needs, the time to create appropriate and adequate materials that would allow access to many of the curriculum areas. Time is money.

Unfortunately, the money that has been created for the ordinary school setting has gone on Assistants to support a child in a classroom, not on additional teaching staff. Additional teaching staff would allow a teacher to be released at key times to focus on an individual's need and create the educational materials that would individualize a child's programme in a large class setting. This is not to negate the value, at times, of the Assistant. It is to recognise that such appointments can water down the problem, but not alleviate the educational need of the child.

Another creation in the ordinary school setting is that of teachers responsible for special needs. They have two dilemmas. The first is that they often have not experienced the intense subjectivity of dealing with children in a specialised setting because they are recruited from the mainstream. So, when they are setting up their departments, the model is often shaped not by their knowledge but by the demands of the school, which can often lead to a glorified remedial department. The second is that they may not be seen as being on the same level as heads of other departments, thus having an in-built difficulty in acting as an advocate for the principle of integration. This dynamic occurs often because although the senior management may be in tune with and agree with the ethos of integration, unfortunately, no groundwork has been done to work with and influence the attitudes of the staff. The teacher responsible for special needs is then stretched by having a population of pupils with diverse needs, colleagues expecting some form of assistance, or colleagues not wanting any assistance at all, just removal of the pupil from their classes.

Classroom teachers, until now, have had no training to help them deal with these youngsters suddenly present in their classroom, and often no idea of where to begin to help them cope with the complexities of their special subject area. The aim of classroom teachers has been, and for many still is, to impart their knowledge and skills to their pupils, teaching them to retain this knowledge and these skills. Because some pupils with learning difficulties may not be able to master those skills or retain that knowledge for more than a very short time, the teacher considers that they have failed with these children, and that perhaps they should therefore not be placed in their class. Since they can see no possible success with these children on these terms, they consider that a more suitable placement would be in a special class where such pupils could be offered something more appropriate to their abilities. If enough teachers took this approach there would soon be no subject areas deemed appropriate for children with learning difficulties.

It could be argued, and, for the sake of the children concerned, should be argued, that what is important is not necessarily absorbing or learning all that a teacher has to offer, but being given the opportunity to experience a subject in the same way as other pupils without an arbitrary judgement as to whether this is worthwhile. The teacher of a foreign language, for example, expects his pupils to learn some French or some German, and may consider that a very poor long-term or short-term memory would preclude any success in this subject. Indeed many children have been excluded from foreign language classes on this basis. But is it true to say, because some children will never become fluent in a second language, that they gain nothing from exposure to another language? It is the expectation of the teacher which must change, not the ability of the children.

AFFILIATION: A SHORT-TERM RESPONSE FOR SPECIAL SCHOOLS

There has been, for a long time, an either/or approach to the problem of children with special needs. Either you segregate children in special schools or units or you integrate them into the ordinary setting. The terminology, segregation and integration, is divisive and lends itself to a dual system of education. This has created two separate bodies of professional — special and ordinary — which has not allowed for an overlap in practice and has not encouraged collaboration to resolve the educational needs of individuals. We have the situation that either ordinary educators manage the problem, or it escalates to a point where it is seen as necessary for a special educator to take over responsibility.

Segregation is the more honest of the terms and the clearest to see in action. When initiatives are described as integration, the majority of programmes are only partial; there is some form of removal at some point in a day or week in the ordinary setting. Often this arrangement is not one desire by the professional involved, but one dictated by financial limitations, and thus there is containment by default.

The problems we encountered in meeting the changing pattern in special education have encouraged our present *modus operandi*, which is described in the next section. It was developed from the observation that the commitment to the practice of integration was more of an illusion than a fact; and because of that we turned to the children in our care and created a model which allows them access to curriculum areas and experiences which we are unable to provide in our own setting. In fact, all of our initiatives have been dictated by finding opportunities to show the strengths of the children and raising expectations of their abilities. Our intent is to encourage our officials to believe that the effort and expense is worthy of their consideration for future planning.

We use the term affiliation to describe our work. The intent is that, in our developing relationship with our colleagues, we are to be seen as an integral part of education. We are a resource that is created not by our own perceptions of what is required in our education community, but by being responsive in a collaborative relationship.

In 1958, Haring, Stern, and Cruickshank identified four areas important to intregation:

(a) The classroom provides for all the needs of the child.
(b) The child can become a contributing member of the group.
(c) The physical facilities of the school are amenable to the child's needs.
(d) The teacher with whom the child is placed understands and accepts him or her.

It is now the 1980s and some thirty years have elapsed since this was written. Items (b) and (d) are feasible in attainment, but, because of limited capital investment, (a) and especially, (c) are less likely to occur in the current educational and political climate.

Our approach of affiliation is being developed with an eye on this and a hope that in the future it will be assimilated into the ordinary school setting.

ONE APPROACH

The approach we have initiated at a school for children with moderate learning difficulties is based on the previous observations. It is one that is dealing with the day-to-day realities of the education system at this time but is readily capable of being assimilated into the ordinary setting, if and when the latest educational initiatives such as the introduction of a National Curriculum, In-Service, Assessment and Testing, Technical and Vocational Initiatives, etc., begin to settle down to ordinary day-to-day practice.

To initiate the assimilation of special education into ordinary practice properly, there needs to be a clear policy and plan. It needs to start at the beginning with initial teacher training, staff awareness, adequate support and a flexibility within ordinary school settings to meet the individual needs of children. Until that time, our proposed model (Figure 6.1) attempts to address this need practically.

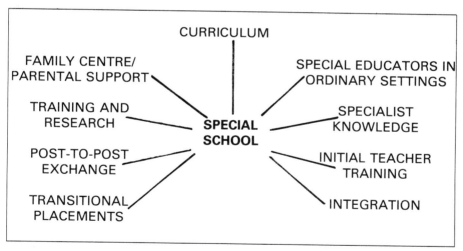

Figure 6.1: Affiliation model

Curriculum

The special schools, particularly the schools for moderate learning diffi-culties, have developed a deficiency-based curriculum. Its content has focused on English and Maths, with Art, Physical Education and more Art under the guise of Project Work and topics which interest the teacher.

In order to meet the needs of individual children who may have a future opportunity within the ordinary school setting, a special school needs to develop a curriculum that runs as parallel as feasible to that of the ordinary school setting. It creates the structure which will be met by the pupils if they are integrated. It also allows special educators to meet the problems encountered by colleagues in their ordinary settings in trying to make a certain curriculum area accessible to those with limited abilities. A close relationship with the schools in the local community is necessary, so that an enhanced curriculum can be provided by partial integration not only of children but of staff. (See Chapter 7).

Special educators in ordinary settings

If it is expected that colleagues are to take on the responsibility of children identified as having special needs, special educators must be able to work in ordinary settings. The benefits to be gained are the understanding of the pressure colleagues are under in both settings, the raising of expectations of standards for the special pupil, the opportunity of collaborative approaches to the curriculum and the respect gained by being seen as an educator, not someone who has opted out from the rigours of the ordinary setting.

As our experience has proved, when initiating involvement with a local ordinary school, there was an imbalance that needed to be addressed. Special educators were getting paid more than their mainstream colleagues for teaching children with special needs. How can one approach colleagues to accept children with greater needs, without the financial resources to redress the problem?

Our answer was to encourage staff in the special school to teach in the ordinary school; not necessarily to be only involved with the children with special needs but with those 'ordinary' children of the local school population in a specific subject area such as Personal and Social Development or English. By doing so, some pressure is taken off our colleagues' timetable and a quiet transposition takes place without forcing the issue. Special educators will be seen as educators.

As this relationship was growing with other comprehensives and primary schools the Technical and Vocational Education Initiative arrived with its Related In-Service Training. TRIST brought together diverse institutions including Further Education, to work collaboratively in 'clusters', the famous English buzz word of the 1980s.

This encouraged cooperation and respect for each other's professional skills. It allowed release time for teachers to either attend courses or visit other institutions that would assist them in being more flexible in the changing pattern of education. Although this was obviously not its intent, it allowed for special schools to break out of their moulds gradually.

Unfortunately, the momentum under the TRIST exercise was short lived and we are now waiting for it to be resurrected under the Grant Related In-Service Training as soon as or if the finances will meet the expectation levels raised by TRIST.

Specialist knowledge

It is necessary to have a strong base of specialist knowledge in the area of language and speech, behaviour and physical needs to meet the complex problems children and young people can present to any school. Working from a base where there is a population of children with a variety of needs, special educators could establish locums for ordinary educators to participate in in-service under the direction of these professionals. These same professionals can assist those with designated responsibility for special needs in the ordinary school to run their own internal in-service training.

Many of the materials being developed in schools by those tackling the latest initiatives in exams and curriculum development can be enhanced by the collaborative relationship between the special and ordinary school to make the materials more accessible for pupils, particularily those in the low ability range. The specialists' skill in breaking down tasks into attainable steps has much to offer all children, not just those fortunate to have been identified as having special educational needs. But this relationship is one of collaboration and it must be acknowledged that the special educator in this context has as much to gain as the ordinary educator.

This collaboration of professionals is very important if we are to move from what is termed in this chapter 'affiliation' to assimilation. Attitudes and values need to be addressed constantly; the majority of teachers did not enter the educational field to work with children at the lower end of the spectrum of individual needs and the issue cannot be forced. Whilst the special school exists as a base and there is a close professional interaction with the schools with which it is affiliated, encouragement and skills can be developed, children themselves can be better prepared and materials and resources can be created which would encourage rather than discourage the majority of educators towards integration. A direct onslaught with little or no resources will only harden negative attitudes and the pendulum will swing in a retrograde direction.

Initial teacher training

If integration is to occur in the future, educators being trained today need a wider range of expertise than their predecessors. They will no longer only need the knowledge and teaching skills related to their subject area. They will need skills that will prepare them for the variety of individual children who will be in their classroom.

These professionals will need the skills of identifying those children who have individual needs which may limit their ability to tackle the set tasks and comprehend them. They will be required to be cognizant of techniques and materials that can alleviate these children's difficulties and enhance their learning potential. This is why a placement at a special school should be an integral part of their training. (See Chapter 13).

Special school placement offers an intensive opportunity for contact with children who are having difficulty; it heightens the awareness of the professional. The real speciality of the special school becomes apparent. Time is allowed for concentrating on an individual and individuals dictate what they need rather than the system doing so.

While working alongside seasoned teachers in a special school setting, a student can pick up the subtleties in working daily with pupils; the unwritten technique of helping a child calm down when frustrated by a task, or how to break a task down into basic steps for learning. These and others are things that cannot be learned or emotionally dealt with solely in lecture format or by a short visit, but only by day-to-day interaction in an educational setting.

Special school placement for teachers in initial teacher training offers the opportunity for a student to perceive the ramifications of handicapping conditions and to see beyond the often visible disability and find the strength within the person, developing an individual approach. It also, as we have found, alleviates anxiety for a young teacher, during the first years of practice, when informed that at least three of their pupils in any class are likely to have special needs.

This interaction in initial teacher training should be extended to those who lecture in colleges and universities. They will be responsible in guiding these young professionals into a world often different from their own experiences. They will need to be able to encourage young teachers how to identify and meet the needs of a school population which in the first instance could be more daunting than Form 3D. Because of this, lecturers will need similar experiences to help shift established perceptions of special schools and their children and to realign a few values related to those with physical or learning disabilities.

A benefit for the children in the long term is the possibility of limiting special school placement by improved ability to deal in the ordinary school with a child who has difficulty with a learning task, and, if still having difficulty, being aware that the special school can be approached for support and direction, rather than seen as the end of the line.

Post-to-post exchange

In our setting, we began to work from the premise that if we are moving toward the eradication of a dual system of education and encouraging the integration of not only children but staff from special school settings, then those who have worked in day-to-day isolation must find avenues to exchange knowledge and expertise and familiarize themselves with other educational settings. If the ordinary school is to take on a large population of children with special educational needs then the same is true for them.

This is true in-service training. Educators either in ordinary or special school settings need to be aware of the complexities facing the whole education system. When working in isolation from each other, myths develop. Special educators are either seen as 'Florence Nightingales' or, as stated previously, as educators incapable of meeting the rigours of the ordinary setting. The ordinary educator can be seen as an indifferent species to the child with special needs. These myths need to be eradicated if we are to move ahead constructively as educators.

The ordinary educator may feel that the cart has been thrown in front of the horse in relationship to the education of children with special needs. They may feel as though they are treading water in their day-to-day interactions with a population with whom they have been presented, without proper support. This view is reinforced by a wealth of current information emerging from the United States pointing to the lack of understanding by the ordinary educator of the educational characteristics of children with special needs.

For the sake of all educators and children, this needs to be rectified by in-service related to actual involvement. What better way to learn about special needs than to be placed for a day, a week, a half term or a full term, in a setting where the population dictates specialist skills being applied to a large group in all curriculum areas? It is also one where the system of educational process is broken down into accesible steps for pupils and where an educator could feel secure in knowing that the school structure lends itself to the support of the child and the staff members themselves.

The special educator, in this climate of change, may have felt the cart has been removed from the horse. The uncertainty of working in an ordinary setting is very daunting for someone who may have worked in specialist settings for a majority of their career. The post-to-post exchange lends itself to the opportunity to work in the ordinary setting, yet return to the specialist base at the end. This has led, in our experience, to a staff member persuing a career in a comprehensive school, after their exchange had been completed.

Training and research

The special school is an excellent setting to encourage training of other professionals. Many colleges and universities have students who are pursuing research that has effect or impact on the population of children with disabilities and learning difficulties; psychologists investigating cognitive development, physiotherapists exploring means of alleviating motor development problems, social workers developing family work techniques, etc. Such initiatives may be on one's doorstep. One just needs to be more multidisciplinary in one's outlook, and to encourage one's own staff to be analytical of the work they do and to address it to a wider audience, if appropriate by lecturing or publication.

Family Centre/Parental Support

The most neglected individuals involved with children with special needs can be those within the family. The child is identified as having a learning problem often after a year or two of formal education. The family is informed that the statementing process is beginning to ensure their child will receive the most appropriate education. Alternatively it may be that the child has difficulty at birth, with either a physical or mental impairment. The parents may have difficulty in coming to terms with their feelings or there may be difficulty in obtaining information on their child's condition. They may simply feel the need to meet and talk to others in a similar situation.

If the special school is being encouraged to be a resource, it has an exciting opportunity to develop a network for parents of children with special needs. It can build up a library of practical information. It can establish an additional base for all the voluntary agencies who work for the individual child to meet with the parents. It can act as an advocate for parents, to ensure they are receiving appropriate services for their child. It can provide the context in which parents can meet to support each other or organise speakers who can give parents the feeling of a better status than victims of circumstance manipulated by professionals. (The example of a Family Centre that we are planning to use is based on one that exists in Sheffield, South Yorkshire).

Transitional placements

Often the prospect of attending a special school is seen as a one-way ticket to educational oblivion. The trepidation with which parents have often initially approached a special school was with this in mind, but they rarely voiced it because in doing so it would deny the child the opportunity to have their personal needs met and it would be challenging the professionals who made the recommendation. Finally, in Britain, parents are finding their voice at the same time that special schools are readdressing their relationship within the education system.

We have actively encouraged short-term placements in our setting, having these objectives written into the statement. Also, we have been building up such relationships with our colleagues that a child or young person can come to our setting for short periods to receive specific assistance. This is in much the same way that approximately forty of our pupils a week attend other schools for varying amounts of time to meet their curriculum needs.

In addition we are involved with several schools for children with Severe Learning Difficulties. The children from these schools spend time in our setting with the assistance of pupils from our local comprehensive and our own pupils. This is a step towards integration for these young children with severe learning difficulties. It is also an active means in making children who themselves have not been limited by disability, well aware of the personalities and strengths of these young people. It helps minimise the negative labelling of children within their local schools.

Integration

At all times our model seeks to encourage and enable young people to return to the ordinary setting. It is not designed to replicate ordinary schools for the sake of keeping a school population existing within a special school. The difficulty in which we find ourselves is that many of the ordinary schools in which we desire to integrate children are still limited by lack of physical access, appropriate additional staffing and a true desire to assist these children.

Chapter 7

Curriculum Development in one Special School
Andrew Hinchcliff and Carmen Renwick

The Warnock Report and the Act that followed it sought to bring about a situation when the great majority of children with special needs would be able to continue to attend ordinary schools in the future, in preference to special schools.

Whilst attempts to translate the report's recommendations into practice have been many and varied, the future role of the special school has been a key issue common to most. In some cases it has brought about closures, in others the challenge of a new and developing role.

We are fortunate enough to be involved with a school which has been evolving in response to the needs that the Warnock Report has created. In particular, we have sought to work towards a common provision for all children; a principle that the report wholeheartedly supported and which can embrace diversity in the size, organization and purpose of schools but not in the quality of the provision within them.

The need for special schools to broaden their curriculum has become generally accepted. In a note by the DES it was acknowledged that the children with moderate learning difficulties cannot be expected to cover the full extent of the secondary curriculum. Nonetheless, it goes on to stress that 'the range of curricular elements to which they should be introduced is similar'. Similarly in the DES publication *Better Schools* it is clearly stated that the curriculum offered to every pupil, 'whether at an ordinary school or a special school' should be broad, balanced, relevant and differentiated (DES, 1985a).

Cooperation with nearby ordinary schools has afforded our school the opportunity to dramatically extend and enrich the curriculum we offer (Table 7.1).

Table 7.1: *Curriculum*

SUBJECTS	INFANT	JUNIOR	YEAR I	YEAR II	YEAR III	YEAR IV	YEAR V
Project Work	·········▶						
Clumsy Group	·········▶						
Maths at Arb.	·········▶						
CDT at Arb	·········▶						
Science at Arb.	·········▶						
Language at Arb.	·········▶						
Cooking at Arb.	·········▶						
Music at Arb.	·········▶						
PE at Arb.	·········▶						
Language	···▶						
Handwriting	···▶						
Maths	···▶						
Computer	···▶						
Art/Craft	····························· Incl. GCSE Art at M. ··▶						
Drama	···▶						
Music	··························· .Performing Arts ········▶						
Dance	···········▶ · · · · · .Performing Arts ········▶						
PE	···▶						
History	···▶						
Geography	···▶						
Health Ed.	···▶						
Science	···▶						
Social Skills	···▶						
Printing at Ch.	·················▶						
Textiles at Ch.	·················▶						
Pottery at Ch.	·················▶						
French with Ch.	·················▶						
Technical St. at Ch.	······························▶						
Typing	······························▶						
Sherbourne Grp. St L., RS	···▶						
Typing at M.	···▶						
Music at M.	············ Performing Arts ··········▶						
Env. Studies	···▶						
Childcare	···▶						
Performing Arts with M. GCSE Pilot	···▶						
Camb. Maths with Ch.	···▶						
Newspapers in Education NIE Pilot	···▶						
Community Inv.	···▶						
P.S.D. at Ch.	···▶						
GCSE Eng. at Ch.	···▶						
RSA Eng.	···▶						
Careers Prog.	···▶						
Work Exp.	···▶						
Engineering at C.C.F.E.	···▶						

KEY:
Arb.	Arbury Junior School	
Ch.	Chesterton Community School	
M.	Manor Community School	
C.C.F.E.	Cambridge College of Further Education	
St L	St Lukes Junior School	
RS	Rees Thomas School (SLD)	

Yet as anyone who has been involved in such a process knows, the impact goes beyond extending the opportunities of the children within the school. Such cooperation between teachers, together with the chances for observing other situations and practice, can broaden thinking about the curriculum. Brennan suggests that special schools may come to the realization that their 'pupils should not be denied the experience of as much of the common curriculum as possible... [and that they] should take account of mainstream curriculum and seek ways of replicating it in a manner appropriate for their pupils' (Brennan, 1985). Similarly it is suggested that ordinary schools may be prompted to go beyond thinking about 'how pupils with special needs might participate in mainstream curriculum... [to think-ing] positively about how the curriculum may be modified to allow more pupils with special needs to participate' (Brennan, 1985).

Our school's experience tends to bear out such a description, so far as it goes. During the development of our curriculum framework, a conscious effort was made to relate to mainstream courses and wherever possible to involve colleagues from ordinary schools. This resulted in the establishment of a core of subjects which are similar to those in ordinary schools.

In this way it was envisaged that through developing such areas of the curriculum for our children, ultimately our work could have a direct bearing upon aspects of mainstream practice. Similarly, an awareness of areas of common experience and a desire to promote further such areas can only enhance the prospects of cooperation between schools at the level of curriculum development.

Cooperation at this level, however, is more difficult to achieve and does not necessarily follow from the kind which simply generates new oppor-tunities for extending the curriculum. An extensive network of links with other schools requires that there be opportunities for joint planning and evaluation.

Our school's early involvement with another school at the level of curriculum development was a credit to the dedication and conviction of the staff involved. Acknowledging the worth of such cooperation, the LEA later funded further work in order to explore and promote the kind of opportunities that may be developed for children with special needs within the GCSE framework.

The fact that GCSE seeks to place a new emphasis on understanding, the application of knowledge and oral and practical skills, represents a significant development which could make it more accessible to special needs pupils.

Weller, writing from the Secondary Examinations Council, states: 'We believe that by widening the range of abilities which properly qualify as creditworthy, by teaching these in contexts which relate to pupils' everyday lives and by improving assessment techniques such as 100 per cent coursework and accessible papers, significantly more pupils will gain access and reward from public examinations' (Weller, 1985).

The SEC also believes that differentiation in GCSE will give opportunities for pupils to show positive achievement across the grade range from G to A. Furthermore, if G and F are to be seen as 'foundation' grades which should be accessible to the large majority of pupils, it should also include many from special schools.

To explore fully the possibilities that GCSE offers requires the involvement of those concerned with special needs both in mainstream and special schools. In our case, this has involved piloting courses within our own school and working with colleagues in mainstream schools during the development of courses in which our pupils were involved. (See Note 1.)

Our involvement has been in those areas of the curriculum that are most readily accessible to our children. This may be due to the nature of the subject, the organisation of the course or the willingness of the staff involved to seek ways to accommodate our pupils.

Not surprisingly the Arts have provided much scope for development. The practical nature of the subjects favours our pupils and underlines the importance of continuing to develop a more experiential approach in other areas of the curriculum.

Such a shift in emphasis should serve to redress the balance. For whilst an undue emphasis is put upon the ability to read and write during the education process, those whose difficulties show themselves in these areas are at a major disadvantage. This situation not only reinforces their weaknesses but tends to detract from their areas of competence.

The fact that many courses are being organised in modules provides much scope for the involvement of those concerned with special needs. A module is a more manageable unit which may readily be developed within a special school setting with a view to it being included in a course being run in a mainstream school. The modular organisation makes it possible for a variety of modules to be offered which provide different routes to the final qualification. This situation may operate within a single school or be created through cooperation between schools.

Such organisation can make parts of a course accessible despite, in some cases, the final qualification being unobtainable. To be able to be involved in this way not only creates further opportunities for our pupils but their presence can make those involved in the design of the course ever mindful of their particular needs.

During our involvement the concern has been mainly for the quality of the experiences being made available and less for the qualification at the end of a course. Nonetheless the fact remains that, despite our pupils taking part in a wide range of courses and exhibiting a variety of abilities, little of this may be formally acknowledged.

For this reason, and in order to complement our work with GCSE, we have been prompted to consider the City and Guilds/B Tec Foundation Programme of Pre-Vocational Studies. Not only does it emphasise activity-based learning and the development of a profile of skills across the curriculum and cross-curricular themes but it also requires tutorials and some negotiation of learning objectives. It is our belief that it will provide a framework within which much of our best practice may comfortably fit and be further enhanced.

There are fears that by being associated with special needs and non-examination pupils the course may be seen as an alternative to GCSE and as such of lower status. Such fears detract from the possibilities that it offers for pupils of mixed abilities to work together at activities whilst pursuing different ends and being assessed upon different criteria. Within our context, it would allow our pupils some recognition for the work done within areas where presently the likelihood of an exam result is remote. By allowing pupils with special needs to work within such areas arguably the hopes for GCSE may ultimately be realized.

Nonetheless, cooperation at this level still requires a commitment on behalf of the LEA and the establishments involved to provide opportunities for planning and evaluation. Whilst the competing demands on teachers' time have made such a commitment difficult, opportunities have arisen through involvement with TVEI.

The current GRIST arrangements owe much to the transformation brought about by the TRIST organization. By requiring schools to work together in consortia, these in-service arrangements have provided the kind of forum for discussion and a focus upon curriculum development between schools which previously could not have been envisaged.

That the submission for the TVEI Extension required a commitment to making the full range of benefits available to all students across the full ability range has made the involvement of special schools a desirable, if not essential, part of the process. At the same time the planning of the submission has afforded an opportunity for special schools and ordinary schools to discuss common needs and interests.

The establishment of such a need for cooperation, together with the enabling organisational structures, has provided considerable scope for developing the role of the special school. The extent to which such opportunities are made available to special schools will depend on the LEA and the visionary zeal of the head.

The development of the special school curriculum has served to highlight some of the limitations of the systems of recording and assessment that operate and has prompted a re-appraisal of existing practice. Interestingly enough, such limitations within a mainstream setting have formed part of the argument for developing the Records of Achievements; 'the final global grades available...conceal more than they reveal about the student'; 'There is a second, equally important weakness in existing methods of assessment — the tendency to assess (and therefore value mainly those kinds of skills and behaviour that can be most easily tested)...We have given less attention to many personal and cooperative skills and attributes which we all know students must possess in order to learn effectively as individuals and as a group' (CPRA).

It may be argued that the traditional emphasis upon the areas of reading and number is a natural consequence of the fact that much work has been done in these areas. The content is well-defined and there is a good understanding of the heirarchy of skills to be developed. As a result they can be most easily tested.

The fact that there has been a concern in special education for the development of skills within these areas and that this has tended to operate at the expense of the wider curriculum reflects not only their importance but also the difficulties that arise when attempting to consider their development through other areas of the curriculum.

We feel that both the Foundation Programme and the Records of Achievements involve approaches which could help to overcome such difficulties. By seeking to profile the development of particular skills and behaviour within a variety of educational contexts, they bring us nearer to the point when meeting a child's special needs will involve all aspects of the curriculum.

The practical difficulties associated with broadening the curriculum cannot be overlooked since a failure to overcome them could seriously impede the process. In our school's experience they have required a series of organisational responses which in themselves have been very positive.

The development of links with other educational establishments puts the school and those involved under considerable pressure. Whilst more generous staffing levels may go some way towards helping the situation, arguably the major source of pressure is what could be called the process of re-orientation which can arise when staff and children are experiencing an increasing amount of movement between different educational settings and adjusting to the variety of expectations and experiences that come with this.

At the same time, the kind of flexibility that is required to take advantage of opportunities as and when they arise may result in a period during which there may appear to be little coherence in curricular terms. Interestingly enough, such a situation may be necessary since the need to maintain balance, continuity and progression throughout the curriculum could frustrate the spontaneity and imagination which often lies behind such developments. Nonetheless, it is also the case that as a school develops in this way the sense of security felt by the staff and the children will be under siege.

It is interesting to reflect that staff in special schools commonly derived security from teaching a class for the majority of the timetable and that this permits a high level of tolerance to the vagaries of the timetable or curriculum that can exist.

In our experience, the movement away from this situation following the development of wider opportunities reaffirmed the need for a coherent curriculum structure which in turn prompted a review of the organisation that underpins it. (See Note 2).

Our involvement with the wider educational community has helped us to raise the quality of the education we provide and increasingly involved us in issues and areas of work which have a direct bearing upon the response to special needs in mainstream schools. Whilst there continues to be much that can be done at an inter-school level to promote such interaction, we have been heartened by some of the recent developments and welcome the opportunities they offer.

NOTE 1 — GCSE INVOLVEMENT

Expressive Arts

The fundamental importance of the recording of positive achievement and the assessment of coursework of a practical nature was possible in the expressive arts. The Mode 3 CSE Art allowed students to explore a wide variety of media — drawing, painting, printmaking, photography and three-dimensional studies and to draw upon themes from the existing curriculum or the environment. Coursework could be negotiated with each individual student and their classroom work formed the basis of their final, externally moderated exhibition.

Our links with mainstream schools meant that many of our students could participate with mainstream students for most of their coursework, supported by extra specialist equipment and the high quality of teaching. Our Welfare Assistant was also an art graduate and so was able to be absorbed into the general teaching of the fourth and fifth year art class in the local school — helping not only our students but the mainstream students also. Our students were able to be stimulated by the work of the others, whilst often having to work at a faster speed than they might be used to and having the demands of regular homework.

The exhibition of work at the end of the two years was integrated with the mainstream students and may as a result, have changed some teachers' and pupils' attitudes about the capabilities of students from special schools, particularly as the standards were compatible with average and occasionally above average CSE grades.

The new GCSE Art exam is soon to be taken by ten of our students. Coursework is to be assessed by a ten-hour paper on a set theme. Our students will work on the paper over several days but it is difficult to predict how they will manage to sustain both their interest and attention to the task in hand.

Performing Arts

The Performing Arts — dance, drama and music, have always featured strongly in our school. Students have opportunities to dance in school and at a local dance studio where a teacher and, on occasions, performing arts students work with our students.

Drama has, until recently, always been taught by a drama specialist, whilst the Head of Music at a neighbouring school has been able to offer us one morning a week to work with the fourth and fifth years. More recently, a 'dance animateur' appointed by the City Council has been working with us for one morning a week.

A Performing Arts GCSE was sought which would most suit our students' needs. Our experience pointed to the need for a modular structure involving group and individual work which would be experiential in approach and planned on the basis of objectives or learning outcomes which were expressive in nature and able to be continuously assessed without a final written exam.

A pilot year is in progress and students appear to enjoy the flexibility of the modular organisation which is designed to suit their interest and capabilities. This together with the use of collaborative learning and teaching methods seems to sustain high motivation and can be evaluated by all concerned, pupils and staff alike, as the course is still in progress.

The emphasis is on the process rather than the performance although small performances of the students' work do take place within our own school and other special schools, as well as a planned joint project with a local old people's home, based on the theme of 'Music Hall' song and dance.

The Mode 3 GCSE, which was designed by staff from an out-of-county comprehensive, has adapted beautifully to our particular students' needs and indeed is now offered to students from a local SLD school. Our drama inspector has agreed to oversee our progress as he also moderates the school from which the course originated.

English

English specialists from the mainstream school welcomed the challenge of our students joining the course and from the outset a teacher from our school was included in the planning and teaching.

Our students found the first year of GCSE English extremely taxing, despite the fact they were a selected group with what was considered to be adequate reading and writing skills. The amount of writing required was challenging enough but work also had to be typed, taped or transcribed at our school to support their coursework and this slow process meant that the modules were often too short for the completion of their work. In order to allay the sense of panic that grew as several of our students 'got behind' in the subsequent modules, 'base groups' were established to enable some catching up to be done. This did not, however, leave our students feeling confident about their capabilities compared with their mainstream classmates.

Nonetheless, their enjoyment of good literature, poetry and drama was immediately apparent. Orally the students blossomed and their assessments proved to be well on target.

Such a situation seems to underline the need for the oral component of the coursework to be given higher status and even to be validated separately. Certainly a pass on oral work and an overall fail mark does not give our students, who can have quite remarkable oral skills, the credit they deserve. There must be many students with similarly uneven levels of communication skills in the mainstream schools.

It also fuelled our concern about the accessibility of certain texts for our students who, despite low reading ages, can cope with higher interest level and literary content. Where possible video was used to supplement the novel but this is unlikely to be the answer in the long run.

Assessment during the course also presented problems for teachers who were meeting our students for the first time and who were unsure about how much help to give and how to mark fairly.

Such experiences underlined the need for further GCSE training in order to promote the use of a variety of learning routes and methods and the adaptation of work for special needs students.

The fact that our school day is shorter than that of the local comprehensive made it impossible for the present fifth year to attend some lessons. Thus whilst they were unable to continue to follow the course in total, appropriate modules could be offered to them and be developed at our school. Fortunately a new, smaller group of fourth years have started on the second wave of GCSE English and it is hoped that they will be able to continue to a final assessment.

The RSA Practical Skills Profile is now being used for the fifth years in order to provide some recognition for the work they have been engaged in and their achievements. Through the use of such profiles, students who are unlikely to gain a pass at GCSE are still able to take advantage of the experience, and receive recognition for what they have done. In this way the use of profiling can compliment rather than detract from the use of GCSE with special needs students.

NOTE 2 — CURRICULUM STRUCTURE AND TIMETABLE

The curriculum provides for the children to enjoy a core of activities throughout their schooling. It also provides for a wider range of activities to be available as the child progresses through the school. The establishment of a core has provided a backbone throughout the secondary years. Alongside this other opportunities exist or may be developed which enhance and complement this and which provide experiences that would not otherwise be possible.

The establishment of a core curriculum which is organized sequentially provides a desirable structure which can ensure continuity and progression and facilitate aspects of the mainstream organisation. However it has had implications for the nature of the class groupings and movement within the school as a whole.

Consideration of this was aided by viewing the school population in terms of their year bands. As a result of this process the class groups have been organised in order to permit more intensive work to take place in the significantly smaller Infant/Junior classes. The Middle School classes cater for first and second year Secondary and some fourth year Junior. They, like the Infant/Junior classes, are vertically grouped in order to encourage the fostering of relationships through more stable groups. At the same time, such groupings afford sufficient flexibility to allow for the varying numbers and ages of the children referred each year. By contrast, the Senior School classes are grouped horizontally and cater for the third, fourth and fifth year Secondary.

Such a structure has provided a clear and predictable guide to movement throughout the school. Nonetheless it is always stressed that it should never be envisaged as being so rigid as to go against the individual needs of the children. Important also are the insights that can be gained from viewing the individual needs of the children in the context of the mainstream organisation.

Another aspect of the structure which becomes highlighted through the process of development is that should a child progress through the school then they will experience ever increasing changes in teachers, groupings and the range of courses. Nonetheless, the extent to which this is the case will be determined by the staff according to the needs of the children.

The timetable is intended to provide flexibility and scope for further development and experimentation. It provides opportunities for teaching within class groups by the class teacher, another teacher or by team teaching. At the same time, opportunities are provided for groups of varying sizes to be formed according to the children's needs and interests.

Courses may form part of the core which runs throughout the school or may be part of an optional element which may be organised in half-termly, termly, half-yearly or yearly modules.

Chapter 8

Searching for Solutions: Approaches to Planning the Curriculum for Integration of SLD and PMLD Children

Barry Carpenter and Ann Lewis

Education for children with either severe learning difficulties (SLD) or profound and multiple learning difficulties (PMLD) has undergone major changes in recent years. April 1971 marked the implementation of the Education (Handicapped Children) Act (1970) which transferred responsibility for providing education for mentally handicapped children from health to local education authorities. Establishments catering for mentally handicapped children had both a change of title (from Junior Training Centres to Special Schools (ESN-S)) and a change of role. For the first time in Britain, children who had previously been deemed ineducable had a legalised right to education.

Staff in the (new) special schools looked to both existing special education and ordinary schools for models of successful classroom practice which could be translated into work with children with SLD. At this time, the early 1970s, many curriculum innovations and experiments were being carried out. Piagetian approaches, ability-training and developmental curriculum models all had their adherents. Superficially, curricula based on developmental checklists appeared very tempting. However, their inappropriateness both in step size and for some pupil age groups meant that more detailed and pupil-specific learning programmes had to be developed for children with SLD. What emerged, and to some extent still exist in various SLD schools, were eclectic approaches to curriculum development which combined significant features from many of the approaches mentioned earlier.

The range of experiences, initially presented in a trial and error manner to children with SLD, has generated a number of dominant strands of curriculum practice (Coupe and Porter, 1986). Several authors refer to SLD curricula that utilise the identification of skills written, for teaching purposes, in terms of observable pupil behaviours (Gardner, Murphy and Crawford, 1983). However a strict behaviourist approach is now less popular than previously as practice has shown that structured teaching programmes can be effectively implemented within highly stimulating class, school and community environments. Some educationalists have developed successfully a variety of programmes using cognitive approaches to learning (Rectory Paddock, 1983). These emphasise the active role of the child in exploring learning situations. Recently both behaviourist and cognitive approaches have been challenged in the light of the development of principles of normalization. However no viable alternative SLD curricula have been recommended (Shears and Wood, 1987).

What has emerged clearly through this evolution of SLD curricula is the necessity of designing curricula for individual children (Carpenter, 1984; Blythe School, 1986). This individualized approach to curriculum planning is consistent with that advocated for children with moderate or mild learning difficulties in ordinary and special schools/units (Haring *et al.*, 1978; Ainscow and Tweddle, 1979; Brennan, 1985; Gulliford, 1985).

INFLUENCES ON SLD CURRICULA

Traditionally, a school's curriculum policy has been regarded as the autonomous responsibility of the head (Day, Johnston and Whitaker, 1985). However the present educational and political climate has led to a change in this. Agencies external to the school are endeavouring to influence, and in some cases determine, the nature of the school curriculum. These agencies include the DES, through for example the proposed National Curriculum (DES, 1987a); HMI through their survey and discussion documents (for example the Curriculum Matters series, e.g. DES, 1985b) and local education authorities (LEAs) who have, over the past five years, increasingly produced documents (for example, Croydon Education Authority, 1985) which identify objectives to be attained by all children of specified ages in the LEA. A number of themes recur in these documents. These themes have been promoted as characteristics of good curriculum practice. They include consistency, continuity, balance, breadth and differentiation. These themes have been intrinsic to many of the developments in special education. The notion of differentiation or match, for example, underlies the individualized approach to curriculum planning for children with SLD which has been described above. Other groups external to the school have also influenced curricula. These groups include parents and representatives from industry. In sum, a wide variety of groups ranging from the DES to local parent bodies have, rightly or wrongly, eroded the traditional autonomy of a head to determine the curriculum in the school of which he/she is the titular 'leader'.

In addition there have been changes within schools which have altered this traditional position. A major factor has been a revision of staff roles within the school. In particular the image of the class teacher operating within her four walls with little reference to other staff in the school has been replaced by an emphasis on collegiality and staff working as members of the school team. A model of curriculum development has evolved, in both special and ordinary schools, in which this activity is shared by all staff (Campbell, 1985; Day, Johnston and Whitaker, 1985; ILEA, 1985a). The curriculum development team may be led by the head or a member of staff with a relevant responsibility. In ordinary schools this may be a responsibility for children with special needs and in special schools the post may be for curriculum development. In either case curriculum development is led and coordinated by one teacher but the decision-making process rests with the whole staff.

We have been involved in trying to put into practice an individualized approach to education for children with SLD in mainstream settings. The special school involved is located in a semi-rural area of North Warwickshire and caters for seventy children (ages 2 to 19) with SLD. The staff of the school are strongly committed to the development of integration programmes.

The first integration project from the school began in September 1983. Ten SLD children, age 5 to 8 years, joined a mainstream class of 6 to 7 year olds once a fortnight for a fifty minute session including PE and story time. The session was taught jointly by the first school class teacher and the deputy head from the school for children with SLD. Negotiations concerning resources, timing, staff and curriculum content were initially carried out by the heads of the two schools. However, once links had been established, the teaching staff carried out detailed planning and development of the work. The aims of the integration experiences encompassed the personal, social, and educational development of special and mainstream children.

This first project was regarded by parents, children and teachers, as very successful; consequently links were made with other schools and the local FE college. These links extended beyond the immediate locality to more isolated rural areas in which some of the children with SLD lived. Projects were usually part-time and involved class groups from the SLD school.

Staffing for integration projects has usually consisted of one teacher and one classroom assistant from the SLD school plus one teacher from the mainstream school. In projects involving children of nursery/infant age an additional classroom assistant has sometimes been involved. Recently this has been supplemented by an integration support teacher (see below).

Most projects have taken place in mainstream schools but occasionally integration has been located in the SLD school because of specialist facilities there (for example, specialized home ecomomics area, soft play area). The integration experiences based in the SLD school are summarized in Table 8.1.

Table 8.1   *Age phases and curricular areas of integration projects located in the SLD school*

| | Age phase of mainstream pupils | | |
INFANT/FIRST	JUNIOR/MIDDLE	COMPREHENSIVE	FURTHER EDUCATION
One-off visits:	cookery,		cookery,
– art,	environmental studies, including computer-based learning.		
– music,			
– activities in the soft play area,			
– joining in major school events			
		personal and social development.	personal and social development.

Children from mainstream schools often ask questions about the children with SLD, for example 'My friend Edward is brain–damaged; what does that mean?' or 'The girl I'm working with, Janet, has Down's Syndrome; what's that?'. One interesting aspect of these questions is that the child, and not the handicap, is seen first.

In preparation for any integration project preliminary discussions have been held with the pupils involved using, with the younger mainstream pupils, videos and stories about children with SLD. Initially these discussions were led by one of the special school staff; more recently this has been carried out by the integration support teacher (see below). Messages about SLD embodied in the materials for discussion have been reinforced during the project; for example the inappropriateness of treating children with SLD as helpless babies was emphasised. The mainstream children learned basic Makaton signs (Walker, 1978) in the preliminary and early integration sessions, and used them with their SLD peers. The reflections written by mainstream children about their integration experiences illustrate the development of positive attitudes. Some extracts from these accounts are illustrated in Figure 8.1.

Handicap awareness courses have been developed for middle and comprehensive school children. The courses have been devised and carried out jointly by staff from the ordinary and SLD schools. Particular materials that have been found to be useful in this context include The Community Attitudes to Retarded Adults (CARA) project (McConkey, McCormack and Naughton, 1983; McConkey and McCormack, 1983) and Mental Handicap: Patterns for Living (Department of Health and Social Welfare, 1987). In

On the fourth week we had drama and then we came back into the classroom and started on our masks again all the masks were very good and I think that it would of been into impossible to choose a best one. But if I had to choose one I would probbly choose s omeones mask from Blythe school because the people from B ly the s chool must of tried the most

Ruth liked to tip the powder into · her palet unl then mix the Nowder She started to put lovely colur coleur on to the paper then

The next week they realey Settled in. kieran was trying to tie me up he was getting behind Me and getting my arms and pulling them behind me. I was stuck. But it was all right I did not mind. I think they are really nice.

The next week he had carried down But he dropted water all over the floor. Kieran Said his birthday was In January and he had a whach. it was a red one.

This picture is of keieran.   then for the first time with blythe we went into the hall to act out the first part of the story the crift. We took are shoes and socks off and I had to take Richard sock of and as I found out he had trwo pairs of Socks on.

Figure 8.1: Observations by Children

some instances the handicap awareness courses have led to placements of older children in the SLD school as part of their personal and social development courses. Anxiety and apprehensions expressed in initial discussions have been resolved through the positive relationships which emerged between pairs of mainstream and SLD pupils.

Integration with younger children may be regarded as relatively easy; at the primary school stage children are usually with one class teacher throughout the day, the discrepancy between attainments of mainstream and SLD children of the same chronological age is smaller, prejudices about 'handicapped' people have not been established and, generally, young children are thought of as more tolerant than adolescents. Research evidence concerning this last point is ambivalent. However, Towfiquey-Hooshyar and Zingle (1984) investigating the attitudes of American second, third and fourth graders towards multiply-handicapped peers found that an integration programme had more influence on developing positive attitudes (towards the handicapped pupils) of the younger than the older age groups.

The developments towards greater integration of children with SLD have not been entirely without difficulty; however, the challenges have been met and resolved successfully. As confidence has increased challenges are seen as sources of growth rather than obstacles to progress.

One of the most pleasing results of the integration projects has been the development of friendships between pupils from the comprehensive and SLD schools. For example, at the beginning of one academic year fifth formers in the comprehensive school, who had worked at Blythe during the previous year, took the initiative of inviting their friends from the SLD school to share in their 'elective studies' which included keep fit and badminton. A further extension of these friendships has been the joint planning of a canal holiday for SLD and comprehensive school pupils.

The process of implementing an integration project is summarized in Table 8.2.

RECENT DEVELOPMENTS — THE INTEGRATION SUPPORT TEACHER

Recently in Warwickshire the integration of children with SLD and pupils in ordinary schools has been expanded and consolidated through the introduction of integration support teachers (IST). These are permanent posts, appointed by the county, and are not included in the staffing establishments of special schools. The IST is a full-time post specifically oriented to work with staff and children on integration programmes. The work of the IST has enabled links to be developed beyond the local area and twelve educational

Table 8.2 Processes in implementing individual integration projects.

1. Staff of the SLD school identify type of integration needed (pupil(s) and/or curricular areas)
2. Initial discussions between heads of SLD and mainstream schools
3. Mainstream head and staff debate the idea of an integration project
4. Curricular area(s) for the focus of integration sessions are clarified
5. Preparation (led by special school staff) of mainstream pupils:
   – preliminary input using books, videos, etc.
   – sharing of apprehensions, preconceived ideas, etc.
6. Staff from both schools jointly plan first phase (i.e. sessions for the first half-term) including dates for commencement and evaluation
7. Evaluation of first phase including:
   (i)   curriculum content
   (ii) teaching techniques
   (iii) programme modifications
8. Planning of future shared learning experiences within a specified time framework
9. Appraisal of scheme:
   (i)   quality of pupils' learning
   (ii) pupil interaction
   (iii) resource implications
   (iv) staffing needs
10. Decisions about 'Shall we carry on?' – if so, are amendments necessary?

establishments are now involved in integration programmes with children from Blythe School. Existing projects have continued, and are planned and implemented by the staff involved. Developments carried out under the auspices of the IST include:

(i) an increase in integration of individuals and small groups of children with SLD with the IST acting as a support teacher alongside mainstream colleagues. This has permitted more children to be integrated for part of the school week in their neighbourhood ordinary schools. This has fostered friendships between children with SLD and classmates. All the neighbourhood ordinary schools have been prepared to go ahead with partial integration of a child with SLD and there has been no selection of specific schools.

(ii) greater liaison between class teachers from the ordinary and SLD schools. The IST is able to cover a class for one teacher while she/he visits the other teacher(s) working with her/his pupils. This is particularly useful for mainstream teachers who are, through this scheme, able to observe the 'integrated' child/children in the SLD school. It has also meant that time can be given to matching particular children with SLD to specific mainstream contexts.

(iii) more joint planning has been possible. The vital importance of this was noted in evaluations of one of the early integration projects developed by the school (Carpenter, Lewis and Moore, 1986; Moore, Carpenter and Lewis, 1987). The IST has been able to lead joint planning sessions with staff for several schools and to raise pertinent issues, concerning, for example, discipline, appropriate curriculum areas and levels of skill of children being integrated.

(iv) the use of some of the link schools as work experience placements for further education students from the SLD school (i.e. in a local nursery and an infant school reception class). These may be seen as the obverse of the work mentioned above in which pupils from a comprehensive school had placements in the SLD school.

(v) the monitoring and evaluation of integration. The IST has been able to monitor practice and to meet challenges as they have arisen. Gradually a bank of knowledge and experience about successful practice is being built up. This includes information about which of the curriculum areas provide particularly effective means for integration. To date, as discussed earlier, the non-core/open curriculum areas (Ainscow and Tweddle, 1979; Gardner, Murphy and Crawford, 1983), such as Art, Music and PE, have often been the focus of joint activities.

(vi) coordination of related INSET needs. The IST is in a good position to identify the INSET needs of teachers, in both special and mainstream fields, in relation to integration. Similarly she is able to keep teachers informed of relevant publications, courses and meetings about which they might otherwise not have heard. For example, teachers in ordinary schools will often not be aware of developments reported in the special education press. Conversely staff in the SLD school may, through the IST, receive information about specific curriculum initiatives being undertaken in mainstream schools.

(vii) organising workshops for parents, teachers, administrators, advisers and councillors. These have provided a vehicle for overview, planning and evaluation at a wider level than the individual school.

(viii) liaison with parents of children with SLD. The reactions of parents of children with SLD have differed widely. Initially some parents were apprehensive about 'mainstreaming' even on a partial basis, as they feared that their child would be bullied or 'called names'. Certain parents were concerned that partial integration of their child would be a precursor to full-time transfer from the special school, with the possible loss of support on which the parents had come to rely and trust. The IST post has enabled a teacher to spend time arranging, and in some cases accompanying, parents on a visit to the mainstream school attended part-time by their child. The IST has also developed a diary system in which she records for the parents what their child has done during the integration sessions and particular gains made, for example joining in a particular activity for the first time. This is an extension of the 'chatterbox books' (school-home diaries) used by the SLD school. The diary system means that although questions to the child directly may receive little response, parents do know something of what the child has done in school.

The parents of the children with SLD have been overwhelmingly supportive of partial integration. One parent's comment that 'James is being integrated not to be educated well but because he's well-educated he can be integrated' crystalises the centrality which many parents still give to the work of the special school. An unexpected spin-off of partial integration has been the extent to which it has helped certain parents come to terms with their child's severe learning difficulties. One parent said that seeing her daughter, Rebecca, in a mainstream class of children of her own chronological age had helped the mother to appreciate why Rebecca had seemed so slow to learn to walk. Previously Rebecca's mother had convinced herself that Rebecca, who has an unknown cause of SLD, was really 'normal' and one day everything would 'click right'. Partial integration helped Rebecca's mother to accept the differences between her daughter and mainstream peers.

The parents of children with SLD have also cited awareness of handicap by mainstream pupils as an important (for some parents the crucial) aspect of integration. One parent recounted an incident which occurred when she was out shopping and passers-by became angry with her when she strongly reprimanded her son who has SLD. She had found this public condemnation embarrassing and hoped that integration would eventually lead to more understanding about people with SLD, thereby preventing other parents of children with SLD from having such experiences.

(ix) liaison with parents of mainstream children. The IST has also had the opportunity to talk with parents of mainstream children and to learn of their enthusiasm for integration projects. The only complaint received from a mainstream parent has arisen because a child was *not* in the group of mainstream children working with children with SLD! Parents of mainstream children often voice their nervousness about the 'handicapped' and do not want their children to be embarrassed when meeting handicapped people in their communities. Partial integration is seen as one means of reducing, and perhaps preventing, this embarrassment.

The integration projects, described above, which are located in mainstream schools, are summarized in Table 8.3.

The pattern of integration activities outlined above reflects a development, from tentative beginnings towards a commitment to maximizing

Table 8.3   Age phases and curricular areas of integration projects located in mainstream schools

Age phase of mainstream school:	NURSERY	INFANT/ FIRST	JUNIOR/ MIDDLE	COMPRE-HENSIVE	FURTHER EDUCATION
	Art	Art	Art	Art	Art
	–	–	–	Badminton	Badminton
	–	–	–	CDT	CDT
	–	Cookery	Cookery	–	–
	–	–	–	–	Dance
	–	–	Drama	–	–
	–	–	–	–	'Elective' studies (including haircare, pottery)
	–	–	–	–	Home management
CURRICULAR AREAS:	–	–	–	–	Industrial skills. (e.g. horti-culture)
	–	–	–	–	Leisure education (e.g. use of Sports Centre)
	–	Music	Music	–	Music
	–	Number	–	–	–
	–	PE	PE/ movement	–	PE
	'Pre-reading'	–	–	–	–
	Structured and unstructured play	Structured and unstructured play	–	–	–
	Swimming	–	–	Swimming	–

educational opportunities for individual children, in whatever school these may best be developed. The types of integration described provide flexibility, so that ordinary schools provide children with SLD with what segregated special schooling often cannot — contact with mainstream children in the immediate neighbourhood of home; and the SLD school provides what, at present, ordinary schools usually cannot supply — expertise and resources oriented specifically to children with SLD. From the point of view of ordinary schools these integration projects enhance the development of their children, as is illustrated in the findings and quotations concerning attitudes and discourse cited earlier.

A significant aspect of the developments outlined has been the introduction of the IST post. Perhaps the most valuable aspect of this role has been the maintenance of communication between all parties involved. The vital importance of this has been noted in many of the case studies on integration (Shearer, 1983; Orton, 1986). If, as a first step, LEAs and/or central government support integration by making IST posts an integral and central part of SEN provision then the goodwill of practising teachers may make effective integration a reality. Research by Croll and Moses (1985) concluded that:

> For any particular type of handicap, having had experience of a child with that disability in the classroom was associated with an increased willingness to have a child of that sort in the future (p. 152).

The expressions of support for integration, in spite of the acknowledged difficulties, by the mainstream teachers involved in these projects support Croll and Moses' optimistic finding. We have also found that the willingness to integrate has spread to those mainstream colleagues who were initially sceptical about the feasibility of integrating children with SLD. Mainstream teachers have also said that integration has sharpened their awareness of other children with special educational needs in the class.

NATURE AND QUALITY OF THE INTERACTION

One of the integration projects which involved lower school children (age 4 to 8) from the SLD school working with mainstream 6 and 7 year olds has been monitored in detail. This project was studied over two school years during which the integrated sessions took place approximately fortnightly. In each session ten children with SLD were paired with ten mainstream children. Children chose their own partners and so pairs varied from week to week. Ten mainstream children were involved throughout the first year and a second set of ten mainstream children involved in the second year. Most of the children with SLD were involved in both years of the study.

(i) Observational data

A structured observation schedule, using observations every thirty seconds, was administered during the fortnightly afternoon integration sessions. Focus was on each of the mainstream children in turn. This data showed four stages of interaction between the SLD and mainstream children.

The first stage was characterized by mainstream children's high levels of interaction with adults, particularly those from the special school. The novelty of having a number of adults in the room was so stimulating that the mainstream children initially overlooked the children with SLD. The second stage involved high to moderate levels of solitary activity, often including mainstream children staring at the children from the special school. The third stage began around the beginning of the second term. At this time most of the mainstream children tried to communicate with the children with SLD using gestures, including, in some cases, Makaton signs. The final stage emerged during the third term when both groups of children tried to communicate verbally with one another. Many occasions were noted when the attempts by children with SLD to speak to mainstream children were understood and acted upon.

(ii) Attitudes

The mainstream children involved in the second year of the project were interviewed near the beginning and end of the second year. These semi-structured interviews explored attitudes after brief (two sessions) and more substantial (sessions over one school year) involvement with children with SLD. These interviews suggested that in the short term many of the mainstream 6 and 7 year olds were confused about the behaviour of children with SLD. Some children were upset at the apparent double standards operating in the classroom. Children with SLD appeared to 'get away with' behaviour for which mainstream classmates would have been severely reprimanded. A minority of the mainstream children had evolved coherent explanations of SLD based on concepts of the SLD group as normal children, younger than their actual years (Lewis and Lewis, 1987). In the longer term, after involvement with children with SLD over one school year, these explanations had been eroded. They were replaced by concepts of SLD as a sensory disability. The explanation then given for misbehaviour of children with SLD was not that they were very young, but that they had not heard the instruction or could not see the materials properly (Lewis and Lewis, in preparation).

(iii) Discourse strategies

The conversation between children involved in the attitude interviews and partners with SLD was monitored over fortnightly integration sessions during one school year (Lewis, 1987). This data has shown the skilfulness of the mainstream children in adjusting their language to the perceived linguistic needs of the children with SLD. The mainstream children appeared to be struggling quite hard to communicate with their SLD partners, sometimes repeating a phrase and sometimes guessing at the part of the phrase which has not been understood and modifying it. The following extracts illustrate these.

(During an art activity involving painting over candle wax):
Marie: (1) Debbie, do you want to do another colour?
               (2) Want to do another colour?

(3) Right we'll do this colour.

(4) Shall we do this?

(5) Shall we?

In each of these successive utterances Marie is re-phrasing the instruction slightly, dropping words which seem to be redundant (e.g. 'Debbie, do you' from line 1) and switching from a question (line 2) to a declarative statement. The child with SLD may or may not comply but a behavioural rather than a verbal response (line 3) is anticipated. By line 5 Marie has reduced the eight-word utterance (line 1) to two words, giving Debbie a much shorter and simpler utterance to which to respond.

Similar characteristics are evident in this extract from Eddie's speech to Andrew (a child with SLD) during a treasure hunt game in which they searched for pieces of their purple jigsaw:

Eddie:
(1) Come on Andrew.

(2) Are we going to find our other one?

(3) Come on then.

(4) No we're not looking for them sort now.

(5) Come on.

(6) Andrew come here.

(7) Andrew.

(8) Andrew.

(9) Going to find purple?

(10) Going to find purple?

(11) Come on.

(12) I've got purple.

[Finding missing peice]

(13) Is this ours?

(14) Andrew is this ours?

(15) Is that purple?

(16) Is this purple?

(17) Yes, we've found ours.

(18) We've found ours already.

Eddie uses questions quite frequently to prompt Andrew into a response (e.g. lines 2, 9 and 10) in the same way as teachers and parents often do. He uses Andrew's name at the beginning of an utterance (lines 6 and 14), possibly to make sure that he is listening to him. It is also interesting to examine the ways in which Eddies uses 'I/you' and 'we/ours'. He is clearly conscious that the activity is intended as a joint enterprise and although he found the missing jigsaw piece (line 12) he shares the credit with Andrew (lines 17 and 18).

These examples may give the impression that the mainstream children always dominated interaction. However, the following extract illustrates how one of the children with SLD (Jane) tried to stand up for herself in conversation with her mainstream partner (Rachel) (during a dressing up game):

Rachel: (1) D'you want a dress on?
                     (2) Want this on?
                     (3) Wait there.
                     (4) D'you want to be a nurse?

Jane: (5) Yes.

Rachel: (6) Right let me do it then.

Jane: (7) (?? — not interpretable)

Rachel: (8) What?

Jane: (9) Want to be a doctor.

Rachel: (10) No.

Jane: (11) Yes.

Rachel: (12) Might.

Jane: (13) Might.

This dialogue was recorded from before the beginning of the dressing–up game and there had been no talk of a doctor until Jane mentioned it (line 9). This shows that she was able to draw on knowledge from outside the immediate situation and apply it appropriately in the game. Four minutes after the end of the above extract Rachel again raised the suggestion that Jane dress up as a nurse. Jane still maintained, '[I] don't want to be a nurse' and only agreed to do this when Rachel said 'That's for nurse', producing a very colourful, glittery piece of fabric for the nurse's dress. It is debatable whether it was Rachel or Jane who 'won' this exchange!

Comparisons have also been made with discourse between the same mainstream children and (a) classmates and (b) younger mainstream children. It is evident that speech to children with SLD is characterized by a relatively high proportion of commands and few questions, suggestions or monitoring of the joint activity. The integration setting has provided both sets of children with a highly demanding situation linguistically. The discourse data, of which only part has been discussed here, suggest that both mainstream and SLD children are developing linguistic skills that would probably not be generated in segregated settings.

CURRICULUM DEVELOPMENT IN RELATION TO CHILDREN WITH PROFOUND AND MULTIPLE LEARNING DIFFICULTIES

Children with profound and multiple learning difficulties (PMLD) have not generally been separately identified when considering the curriculum for children with SLD (Johnson and Werner, 1980). Until recently there has been little discussion about the highly specific curricular needs of children with PMLD. However, in the last two years publications about this issue have begun to appear and specific approaches to be devised (Brudenell, 1986; Hogg and Sebba, 1986; Evans and Ware, 1987; Ouvry, 1987). An increase in expertise concerning teaching techniques and curriculum content for children with SLD has enabled special educators to examine the challenges offered by children with PMLD.

The learning patterns presented by these children are often complex owing to the profundity of their intellectual disabilities which may also be accompanied by physical and/or sensory impairments. The presence of such impairments suggests the need for an inter-disciplinary approach to the education of these children (Carpenter, 1987). Education is an inter-active process between teachers(s) and child and the intricate design of the PMLD child's individual programme demands considerable cooperation amongst all those involved with the child. The interdisciplinary approach to assessments and programme implementation involving specialists such as physiothera-pists, speech therapists, occupational therapists and audiologists can be linked with assessments of the child's needs made by those people most closely involved daily with the child — parents, teachers, nurses and/or residential staff. The aspirations for the child of all these agencies can be met through a corporately-planned individual programme. This programme needs to define skills and activities realistically and to maintain existing skills as well as developing new ones.

The implementation of the PMLD curriculum raises issues about the optimum learning environment. Will this necessarily be the Special Care class? If the curriculum in the SLD school rests on individualized pro-grammes then each child's needs should be able to be met within any classroom, regardless of the degree of a child's learning difficulties. It is likely that the levels of activity in an integrated SLD/PMLD class will be higher than in a unit catering only for children with PMLD. Consequently the integrated classroom environment, with its talk and activity, is likely to be a source of stimulus to the child with PMLD. This is not to suggest that there is no longer a need for a resource base offering facilities specific to the additional learning difficulties displayed by children with PMLD. The aids and apparatus for physiotherapy require adequate storage space as well as a suitable room in which they can be used unhindered. Similarly children with visual difficulties may require the use of a specialist dark room containing visual stimulation materials.

The expertise of staff in handling and educating children with PMLD must also be considered. There is certainly a role for a coordinator for children with PMLD on an SLD staff team. This coordinator could offer advice on physical management, support children with PMLD in each SLD class and organize sessions which bring together PMLD children for highly specific learning activities (for example sensory awareness). Most importantly, this coordinator could lead curriculum planning for children with PMLD. This planning would involve specifying in minute detail skills in curricular areas that may not be priorities for SLD children.

In advocating the integration of children with PMLD into SLD classes (Ouvry, 1986) the need to maintain a curriculum relevant to PMLD children cannot be over-stated. This will require that the teacher manages two curricula in tandem. Areas of overlap, as well as areas that differ considerably from the normal SLD curriculum, will quickly become apparent. To endeavour to fit the educational needs of children with PMLD into an existing SLD curriculum may generate so many targets that the school's curriculum becomes unwieldy. Conversely to use only existing SLD curriculum targets may pose problems for the child with PMLD as the hierarchy of learning steps may be inappropriate and the steps between targets too vast. This would only reiterate the criticisms of many teachers of SLD children that very little commercially-available material provides the intricate detail needed by the child with PMLD.

A MODEL FOR INTERACTION

The integration needs of children with either PMLD or SLD can be seen to encompass common goals. One of these is for increased contact in a shared learning environment with slightly more competent peers. The uniqueness of the curricula for PMLD and SLD children has been emphasized, but some curricular areas are common to both groups. Can the curriculum provide a strategy for identifying starting points which may lead to constructive shared learning experiences in integration settings?

The structure of an individualized programme for a child with SLD might look something like Figure 8.2. This profile identifies the component (subject) headings given to each target in the curriculum for a child with SLD. Certain areas of learning have been designated as core or closed areas of the curriculum because they are to be attained at mastery level. They are learning/teaching priorities for that child and his teachers. Other targets are

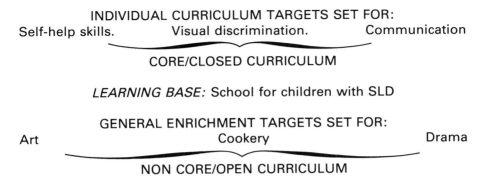

PROGRAMME PROFILE   PUPIL: Jenny (SLD)

INDIVIDUAL CURRICULUM TARGETS SET FOR:

Self-help skills.   Visual discrimination.   Communication

CORE/CLOSED CURRICULUM

LEARNING BASE: School for children with SLD

GENERAL ENRICHMENT TARGETS SET FOR:

Art   Cookery   Drama

NON CORE/OPEN CURRICULUM

LEARNING BASE: Mainstream setting, appropriate age phase

Figure 8.2: An individual programme profile for a child with severe learning difficulties

defined as non-core or open because they enrich the curriculum offered to the child and provide opportunities for the generalization and adaptation of skills (Haring *et al.*, 1978).

It is in the sphere of this enrichment learning that the spectrum of learning experiences may be sufficiently broad to encompass both PMLD with SLD and SLD with mainstream children. Here the breadth of curricular activity can be such that all children can participate at a level appropriate to them and gain from the experience. This situation is similar to that faced by a mainstream teacher of a class of 9 year olds who has to plan, for example, art activities, which will develop aesthetically both a 'gifted' child and a child with mild learning difficulties.

This analysis of the curriculum enables teachers to identify an avenue into the mainstream setting for the child with SLD. Similarly a route can be found into the SLD curriculum for the child with PMLD. An individualized programme for a child with PMLD might look like Figure 8.3.

In both Figures 8.2 and 8.3 the key to planning for the child with SLD or PMLD is the curriculum for the individual child. An analysis of that child's needs illustrates the potential areas for shared learning experiences. Other curricular needs such as personal and social development are also promoted when children engage in shared learning.

To summarize, a curriculum is required for children with PMLD which can meet their highly specific learning needs. This curriculum should be tailored by an inter-disciplinary team to meet the individualized needs of each child. This team should include parents and caregivers. New and imaginative

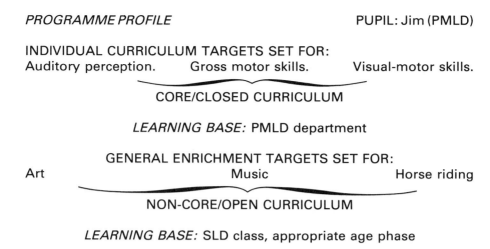

PROGRAMME PROFILE   PUPIL: Jim (PMLD)

INDIVIDUAL CURRICULUM TARGETS SET FOR:
Auditory perception.   Gross motor skills.   Visual-motor skills.

CORE/CLOSED CURRICULUM

LEARNING BASE: PMLD department

GENERAL ENRICHMENT TARGETS SET FOR:
Art   Music   Horse riding

NON-CORE/OPEN CURRICULUM

LEARNING BASE: SLD class, appropriate age phase

Figure 8.3: An individual programme profile for a child with profound and multiple learning difficulties

patterns for the placement of children with PMLD should be explored to ensure maximum effectiveness for the delivery of their curriculum. Placing children with PMLD in classes with pupils with SLD requires that both the needs of staff for support from a teacher with expertise relating to the PMLD curriculum and children's needs for a specialized resource base are acknowledged.

NEW CHALLENGES

The integration debate has been fuelled by sociological, political and philosophical issues (Tomlinson, 1982; Children's Legal Centre, 1985; Dessent, 1987). These issues include examination of concepts of equality and discrimination and have parallels with deviance and labelling theorists (for example, Kitsuse, 1962) who have held that those who are regarded as odd or undesirable by influential members of society are progressively marginalized and lowered in status. In the process negative attitudes towards these groups harden. Those who take this line have argued that to remove children for any reason from the 'normal' provision is discriminatory and undesirable.

The term integration encompasses a spectrum of provision from highly segregated, as in the traditional special-mainstream system in the 1950s and 1960s, and the target of much criticism in the late 1970s, to provision which enables strong links to be made across the two sectors. The Warnock Report (DES, 1978) classified integrated provision as locational, social or functional.

One challenge for teachers of children with SLD or PMLD is to identify the form of integrated provision which will optimize progress for those children while retaining an individualized approach to their educational programme. Teachers of children with special needs are not in favour of integration at any price and wish to be assured that integration will not, in any way, disadvantage the child with special needs. For this reason schemes which have involved a full-time re-integration of children with special needs into ordinary schools have, like the initiatives described here, gone about this process cautiously and systematically (Bond and Lewis, 1982; Adams, 1986).

It is our belief that integration experiences presented to children with SLD or PMLD should be based on curricular decisions. It should be possible to identify, among the range of educational experiences presented to the child, those which overlap in content with those offered in appropriate ordinary schools. Initially a simple matching of timetables should achieve this. However, if integration initiatives are to be successful then teachers in both ordinary and special schools must be committed to the development. This commitment rests on their understanding of why they are making these changes.

Normalization is the goal now advocated for people with a mental handicap (Wolfensberger, 1972; Independent Development Council, 1985). This concept revolves around the notion of people with moderate or severe handicaps living, working and spending leisure time in their own communities alongside people without those handicaps. The educational counterpart of normalization is integration. Both share a common aim: to achieve societal integration for all handicapped people. The class integration projects described, particularly those located in schools near the SLD school, are generating continuity of experience between the mainstream children and pupils with SLD. Mainstream children who worked with pupils from Blythe three years ago in the first school now work with them in the middle school; at 15 or older the friendships begun at age 6 may be sustained and in due course the mainstream children involved in these projects will, we hope, welcome, for example, the building of local hostels for the 'mentally handicapped'. At that time we may say that some of our aims for citizenship have been achieved.

Normalization implies raising levels of awareness about the needs of handicapped people in society as a whole. Society must accept responsibility for its disabled members and explore with them new and imaginative styles of living together. The education service has to reappraise its service delivery just as the health and social services need to evaluate theirs in the light of desired changes. It is inevitable that there will be reorganization as well as a continuing need for close collaboration among agencies.

Over two hundred years ago Samuel Johnson wrote that 'A decent provision for the poor is the true test of civilisation'. This statement is still valid if the word 'poor' is replaced by 'handicapped'. Does Britain today pass this test of civilization? Those working in the education system have a responsibility to nudge society towards being more 'civilized' and, in so doing, broaden all children's horizons.

Section 4
The Wider Context

Chapter 9

A New Curriculum for the Later Years
Ian Galletley

Special schools have always prided themselves on their 'leavers' classes. Why they should have done so entirely defeats me, since their curricula and their intentions were almost always normative, conservative and based on a deficiency model of underachieving students. This was hardly surprising, in view of the all-consuming nature of most special schools, particularly where these were all-age, and most particularly where they were designed for moderate learning difficulties or physical disability.

Brennan (1979) reported that half of his surveyed special schools had 'successful' leavers' courses. Quite what 'successful' meant is not clarified; one should acknowledge, however, that the prospects for employment at the time of his work had not taken the nose-dive of the early 1980s. Of all socio-economic groups in Britain, none was hit harder than the one which we in special education seek to serve. Now, at last, there seems to be some faint revival for our students: the upper years of special education, however, have been chronically slow to react, even to the original decline, let alone the subsequent signs of recovery. In fairness one must also say that the curriculum for less able children over the age of fourteen in many comprehensive schools is as bad, if not worse, but does have the single advantage of taking place in an unsegregated setting.

Either we help our students to compete in an unequal world, do not help them to compete, or by default let others determine what our function is to be. The author maintains that it is not elitist to encourage our children to try to take the world on: a stance which would have been mocked ten or fifteen years ago, and probably by people just like ourselves. The recommendations in this chapter to revitalise the upper years of secondary special education curriculum have their origins in two areas of experience: in advising a Local Education Authority at a time of reorganisation, and in the findings of a small-scale piece of research which involved listening to students talking about the curriculum they would like to receive.

LOCAL EDUCATION AUTHORITIES

LEAs sometimes have a comprehensive policy for Special Needs education, but more often this policy is no more than the total of all the activities which it undertakes. This usually adds up, in the late 1980s, to a declining number of MLD schools, static SLD provision, secure and enlarging provision for children with emotional and behavioural difficulties, and varying degrees of school and unit facility for sensorily and physically disabled children. Squadrons of peripatetic teachers also proliferate. In other words, provision is still based around types of disability rather than types of curriculum. Children are still grouped according to what others perceive their short-comings to be rather than around the sorts of learning experience which will be of value to them.

Many LEAs have responded to the pressure of changing circumstances rather than actively proposing a new kind of future based on entitlement to curriculum. However, development has become polarized. Some LEAs have pursued a policy of closing down schools on ideological grounds, making decisions on the issue of human rights. Such a process is valid, if contentious and can be sustained through philosophical, if not always psychological logic.

The other polarity exists where schools are permitted to become the prey of market forces, with officers and psychologists ruling school roles (and rolls) by the operation of the 1981 Act procedures according to personal definitions of 'need'. This leads to the arbitrary run-down and closure of certain MLD schools with the flimsiest of rationale. Such schools have had the hardest time of all in recent years, and one has to say that in many cases they deserved it. It is not so easy conversely to say, however, that what the students who would have attended the special schools did receive in mainstream schools was of much greater value. In the absence of clear curriculum direction from either local or national government, many special school heads felt cut off and unsupported. Chapter Eleven of the Warnock Report (DES, 1978) was the greatest disappointment of all: heads who were genuinely looking for a lead were left holding the piety of aims being the same for all, and uplifting words about the quality of the curriculum. Not for special education the driving forces of new examinations, or, except in a few cases, inclusion in the early stages of TVEI. It is hardly surprising, therefore, that special schools often felt that LEAs were both judge and jury, failing to define what was expected, judging what was delivered and controlling the source of supply of students.

It was too easy to see the crisis over admission to special schools as generated entirely by an ideological process about where children should be educated. Rarely did the debate transcend to a discussion of 'what?' and 'why?'. Williams (1980) described the curriculum for slow learning children in both special and mainstream schools as the 'wilderness' of education; his point was largely ignored in work with older children, and now we find a curriculum crisis in our own backyard.

COLLEGES OF FURTHER EDUCATION

A proliferation of courses, both full-time and linked to special education in schools has occurred over the past decade. Further Education was both well-intentioned and opportunist in the wake of the Warnock Report. Suddenly, an interest was evinced! This was where teenagers should be, learning about real life! Teachers in special schools winced and passed students on. Liaison between past and present curricula was often poor and curriculum repetitious. Functional integration within Further Education is, even now, virtually unheard of. No one questions the competitive and hierarchical structure of courses in FE departments, since they are based around graded qualifications with strict bands of admission criteria.

Good courses for special needs students do, of course, exist, and these are much valued by students and parents alike. However, they are not, nor can they be, part of an integrated structure. The qualifications to which they lead are cosmetic in comparison with those of other departments and the attachment of special education to Departments of General Studies increases the chances of their being marginalized. All too frequently the 'special' course takes place in reclaimed derelict buildings, or off-site on the wrong side of the curricular tracks. Admittedly, the students can say that they are 'going to College' in an attempt to render themselves anonymous, but this can too often lead to an ultimate loss of oversight, and diminution in the quality of care.

The DES-sponsored *From Coping to Confidence* (DES, 1984) demonstrated sound teaching strategies at work with young students. The title of the project was fine, but begged the question of what the confidence should be ultimately directed towards. There was insufficient emphasis on the direct ways, in addition to general confidence, in which young people can be assisted in the search for work. Confidence can with equal validity be acquired by learning to do something which others will value sufficiently to pay for.

THE BASIS FOR A NEW CURRICULUM CONTENT

It is the intention of this chapter to propose a curriculum for the later years of special education, be they in segregated or mainstream settings. The curriculum will be based on six premises:

(i) a vocational curriculum has equal validity to a traditional liberal approach provided that it has depth and width;

(ii) young people should be encouraged to do new things and to see the fruits of their labours quickly and in a way they will value;

(iii) students must have as wide a choice as possible, and must be involved in the negotiations of the learning process;

(iv) students with learning difficulty feel an affinity for, and a greater understanding of living things and natural phenomena than of abstractions;

(v) schools regularly underestimate the capacity for enterprise and inventiveness of children with learning difficulties;

(vi) scientific, mathematical and literacy principles are more easily learned by students with learning difficulties through the medium of varied interest courses.

The sample curricular outline shown in Figure 9.1 is an organizational, content-based description currently in use. Within such a framework, teaching methods can vary, but certain attitudes will be necessary. The most significant is the need to move away from thinking about levels of intelligence at the expense of levels of interest. Motivation should be sought by thinking about what students will do, and how they will be rewarded for what they have done.

The courses offered require a modular approach. Students taste several different areas before deciding the area in which they wish to undertake an Enterprise. The final proportion in tenths is that which the student will have undertaken by the end of a year, rather than what every week of life contains. In the example shown, science is within environmental studies and PE within leisure. Religious education is an essential element of PSE, which is undertaken within Enterprise. Students eventually concentrate on fewer areas as their courses develop, but Enterprise is compulsory and permanent.

The aims of such a new curriculum are to make children more employable (or make them more productively unemployed) and to demonstrate to them the significant connection between what we are like and what we achieve. This can be properly achieved by a new approach based around interesting activities and working together to attain predefined goals which are valued by students and staff alike.

Sample model curriculum

Status	Curriculum activities	Time in tenths
Inner Core	Enterprise groups/pastoral care/religious studies.	1.5
	Basic skills in Numeracy Literacy embedded in work on options and outer core.	1.5
Outer Core	Integrated arts course (run in conjuction with other Schools)	1
	Environmental Science (including residential experience)	1
	Technology (in conjunction with College of FE)	1
	Leisure pursuits (especially sailing)	1
	Agriculture and horticulture	1
Options	Agriculture/horticulture Textiles Understanding machines Child and Family Care/Home Economics Work experience Community service Business Studies/Typing	2

Figure 9.1 TVEI SUBMISSION

The fruits of a student's labour may be demonstrated through profit, the creation of a service to others, or both. The evaluation of such an approach is found by listening to the consumers, who are the students, their parents, the people they service through their work, and the staff of the schools from which the students come.

The head of a small or medium-sized special school could be excused for thinking that the range of courses required to offer a broad and interesting approach of this kind was beyond the school's means. Of course it is. And therein lies the key to the matter; it should not be offered alone. It has no point unless it is offered collaboratively with mainstream schools or colleges. The course is the product of a pooling of abilities. The skill of the special school in fostering sound relationships, and in some cases, of breaking down curricula into teachable and learnable chunks, is complemented by the skills in mainstream education which focus on interesting activities and subject-based motivation.

A major problem of special school children and the Warnock 18 per cent in ordinary schools is not so much that they cannot learn, but that they do not know enough to be useful to others, and thereby, be of value to themselves. The interest- and motivation-based curriculum can render them in a new light to others, and if pursued with appropriate conviction, can make them more likely to be employed. It is not a crime to be useful, but utilitarian knowledge was mocked in the heyday of the 1970s. An entire generation of teachers was convinced by the prevailing orthodoxy that it was selling a child short to concentrate at 14+ on what was to happen next.

In special schools, the 'leavers' class' has largely been based on a passive view of adjustment to the real work waiting outside. It has not grasped the opportunities which really exist for generating self-sufficiency and wealth, either financial or spiritual.

Resources beyond the expectations of the special school lie within the mainstream. It is not necessary to replicate them inside the special environment. The special head should sign over 14+ staffing, equivalent to a bold approach arrived at by collaboration with other schools and the LEA. If a special school waits for it to happen spontaneously, however, it will wait forever. The education of children with special needs is only one of many concerns of the mainstream head, whereas it is everything to the special education counterpart. It is the special head's fundamental responsibility, therefore, to propose change which is at the same time:

a) supportive of mainstream schools,
b) likely to enhance the opportunites of children with special needs in either setting, and
c) an exciting and interesting thing to do.

The schools which thrive and survive are those which do exciting things. They are the schools which take bold steps, move on and develop. Too many special schools have sat through a decade of decline, passively assuming that all the powerful cards were held by outside agencies such as the LEA. Times are changing, and from a national level, schools are being encouraged to broaden their scope by taking far more of the future into their own hands.

With all its other faults, the legislation of the late 1980s does provide an impetus for special schools, many of which are under consideration for reorganization, to adopt a bolder profile. The issue of where children are taught has for too long masked the even greater issue of whether what has been done in special schools over the last twenty years is of any real interest or value to the students. In that sense, therefore, we are in a post-integration stage; integration is now only one of several issues affecting special education.

The significance of *Enterprise Education* cannot be over estimated in the new curriculum for young adults with special needs. A knee-jerk reaction is sometimes encountered to such a proposition. A powerful opinion has evolved over a generation; that children with special needs cannot create profitable activities and sustain them unaided. Thus, a dependency curriculum has become normal, which, because it does not challenge, because it still seeks primarily to care rather than to elicit, is limited to serving rather than liberating students. Stories abound in special schools of students who show remarkable persistence and insight outside school, even though it is sometimes in, let us say, inappropriate channels. People are surprising, and often schools get it wrong.

It is not proposed that the usual bank-sponsored mini-business course is used as the basis of Enterprise. Rather it is a course which seeks to permit students to become enterprising. Their activities may lead to the creation of a profit, or a service to others, or both. The fruits of their work should be theirs to dispose of. The nature, style and disposition of their enterprises should be determined by students advised but not controlled by adult help. As Bruner (1966) discovered, students return, through an organised course of study, to the same piece of understanding at progressively higher levels.

Being enterprising *can* lead to enhanced employment opportunites.

Colleagues in Careers work report that what a student is like and how hard she/he tries in every bit as important as what she/he <u>knows</u>. Thus 'Enterprise' should also encompass Personal, Social and Religious Education. Our students see more sense in moral, ethical and religious values when they are rooted in real choices about what needs to be done to make money or help others. 'Doing' the value leads to a greater chance of either conceptualizing abstraction, or accepting socially approved moves, rather than merely acting them out through compulsion.

Another major strand of the new curriculum is the 'elemental' component. A core aspect of all students' experience should be an awareness of forces, energies and living things. This comes from the study of machines at work for us, of natural forces through such activities as sailing, and of living things through agriculture and horticulture. At the heart of these studies will be the concept of things which *move* for us, which have significance in what they do.

Young adults, with special needs, who have a developmental lag, respond intuitively and sensorily to things which have bearing, or into which they direct bearing. Successful learning environments are alive, and because of the intellectual capacities of the students, the special school must have actual rather than reported life. 'Let us see what it does; let us see how we can use it' should be the way in, rather than 'Let me show you what to do'.

However, the length of time for which interest-based curricula can be taught, or interest sustained, is limited by all the same factors in special schools as anywhere else, unless new dimensions are added. One such dimension is that of financial motivation. Money. Students want to earn money, or get those things which money can buy. They also understand the power, if not the value of money in the lives of others. Cynical staff might say that it is debasing education to learn how to make money, or perhaps mock the likelihood of special needs youngsters ever successfully sustaining any enterprise which involved such a process. Atkinson's (1984) work contradicts this. Special schools have housed thousands of students who have gone on to self-sufficiency despite the courses they undertook at secondary age, not because of them.

Atkinson's findings as a result of a longitudinal survey of special school leavers over many years were, *inter alia*:

(i)   the large majority of ex-pupils had made acceptable personal, social and economic adjustments;

(ii) most of the subjects showed no striking divergences in their personal and family behaviour from the standards prevailing within the locality.

(iii) most former pupils showed considerably less than average social participation, but when they did take part they joined organisations similar to those of other people; and

(iv) almost without exception, former ESN school children did not become 'social menaces'.

He concludes, 'Observation strengthens the need for obtaining greater knowledge of their problems and, of equal importance, taking positive action to improve the quality of their education and...If presented with the opportunity, many less able students can be good, conscientious and reliable workers with a good deal to offer. The greatest need is to be given an initial opportunity!' (p.24).

THE INITIAL OPPORTUNITY

Thus we arrive at the concept of a vocational department in a special school, or, by pooling resources, the creation of a vocational college. The evidence exists that children with special needs learn best through the pursuit of courses which are not only interesting but also in the interests of the students (Evans, 1965). Atkinson (1984) has demonstrated that, given a chance, these same students can make it, and, it would seem, actually hang onto employment longer than many of their more able counterparts.

The collapse of substantive employment possibilities and their replacement in the 1980s by YTS has meant that the real process of selection has been delayed for many students until they are 18 or 19 years old. Most secondary schools are now involved in the Technical and Vocational Education Initiative. TVEI was regarded with suspicion at first, but many secondary school heads are now glad of the precision, point and evaluative processes which a scheme, when well-run, can bring to a school. Special education's involvement in this process has been minimal and slow, reflecting the conscious distancing which many special needs (and some LEAs) regard as natural between the special and mainstream curricula. This, however, underestimates the flexibility of vocational initiatives. Even the traditional leavers' class activities would have been better if some of the expertise in mainstream vocational work had been tapped.

Mainstream teachers often speak of the 'expertise' of the special school. The payment of extra salary to staff in special education also adds to the mystique of a closed process, yet many readers will know that much of this is based on a myth of discrete ability.

Equally, there are many young people in mainstream secondary schools with needs almost as great or as great as many in special schools. A bridging of this gap in provision can be made through a vocational enterprise. The curriculum previously outlined can form the basis of a course which creates a cooperation of separate establishments, or, by being bolder, the creation of a distinct new type of establishment, specializng in small-scale support and intervention in pre-employment and substantive employment.

Although it is beyond the means of most special schools to set up a vocational department unaided, by joining forces with other resources it may become possible. Imaginative joint-staffing strategies between special and secondary schools or Colleges of Further Education liberate the greater facilities of larger establishments to special school students. They also enable underachieving mainstream students to come into contact with special school staff. Outreach schemes from special have long existed, but they have usually revolved around child support and reintegration activities. The author here proposes that the course of study should be the primary focus of staff.

For many students of lower ability, the *Youth Training Scheme* has become the primary means of paid study and employment in the immediate post-school years. Although in many authorities, a Careers Service has had a significant input into the design and balance of training opportunities, special schools for older children have by and large fought shy of attempting to either become involved in the delivery of YTS or seeking to give advice on the nature of its content. Similarly, after the completion of YTS, many students simply 'fall of the edge', with nothing left by way of continuing educational support. This author proposes that special school heads should not eschew the chances of housing YTS, becoming involved in its development or seeking the chance of offering facilities to adults in their post-YTS years.

There is a common misconception, presumably rooted in the originality of sin, that young people are naturally poorly disposed towards education, and that, given half a chance, they would get as far away from it as possible. Every reader will recall students who were loath to leave what the school had to offer, and for whom it formed the major improving influence in their lives. Such children, and those who almost felt that way, need more education, not less. Careers Officers often complain that students with special needs have limited opportunities in young adulthood with neither work nor appropriate continuing education available to them. Many turn to Adult Literacy groups which by definition are somewhat limited in scope. There is a need for extended appropriate educational support for young adults with special needs. How much better for them if this grew out of a process which had overseen the transition from remedial education through vocational education, perhaps through a training scheme and on to work or non-work. The students would perceive the delivering agency as the one which sponsored them into adult life, and to which (if the quality of the courses was sufficiently high) they would continue to relate. Atkinson (1984) found that few special needs students moved far from the area in which they grew up, so the potential clientele is large.

THE LOCATION OF THE NEW CURRICULUM

A redesigned curriculum should be a means of organizing events, people and understanding, not an institution in itself. There is no necessity, therefore, for the curriculum to be delivered in any one place; rather the students might go to wherever the most appropriate courses are being delivered. The quality and reliability of the courses depends on the input of special educationists. This can be achieved either by training or retraining in vocational areas, or by experienced trainers undergoing a reciprocal INSET process. This author holds that it is more likely that more children will be functionally integrated into society if some segregated special education provision is retained. This can be at a much lower quantity than is currently the case in some LEAs, but if special education is to be a process, the possibility of an alternative environment, particularly for fixed periods of time, is of very great therapeutic significance, and essential in the process of rehabilitation and re-education.

Special education can, of course, take place in mainstream schools and colleges. Dessent (1987) argues for a continuum of provision, and that progress will only be achieved towards this by starting within mainstream schools. A fine sentiment, but not one which instils confidence in this author. An alternative approach is one of *sponsored change* through the medium of special education taking place in a variety of settings. A vocational curriculum for special needs must be available in alternative places. Government legislation in the late 1980s seems in many ways to contradict the 1981 Act, or at least to make it more difficult to implement. Those authorities which have initiated large-scale closures of schools in the wake of the earlier Act may well live to regret their lack of provision. The advantage of having a variety of placement possibilities is that the same curriculum can take place in a setting which is right for each child. In the past, a different place has too often meant a different curriculum, when in fact all that needs to be adjusted within a vocational curriculum is pace and depth.

The client group for a new curriculum may be either statemented or non-statemented, from special or mainstream backgrounds. Special school students may join a course in mainstream or vice versa. Either group might undertake part of their modular course in a College of Further Education. The staffing of such a process should be on a 'service' model, tied to the needs of the course rather than a crude pupil-teacher ratio. The greater the learning difficulty of the students, the greater the likelihood of them taking more modules within the special school. Where specialist facilities are only available off-site, however, all students will undertake modules at the site of activity concerned.

Crucial to the success of a continuous view of need across mainstream and special boundaries is the means by which the progress of students is profiled. Special schools have a great deal to learn from mainstream secondary education in this respect. Profiling is a process rather than a summative document. Special education abounds with recording systems but rarely uses them to motivate students or negotiate future directions. Not the least part of securing a special school's future lies in making the relationship between student and teacher a more active one; this can be achieved in a variety of ways. Negotiations over modular choices match exactly the tone of education for Enterprise. Equally, they have the style which frequently characterizes successful businesses. Given the right support, and free from the worst nonsenses of what passes for a liberal education, students from a wide variety of educational backgrounds can benefit enormously from a reinvigorated, modular and vocational curriculum.

The teachers within a new and enterprising curriculum must have open minds, and must learn from mistakes. A new strategy calls for new enthusiasm. It is often said that teachers become demoralized in middle age, and turn to cynicism about change. Often, however, they are either bored or frustrated. Recent experience in Newcastle upon Tyne suggests that if teachers are also given an initial opportunity to work with students on new courses and under new conditions, they will respond extremely favourably. This author has written elsewhere (Galletley, in Bowers [Ed.] 1984) that collective descision-making can be an important part in drawing innovation from a group of teachers. An open management method encourages debate, and industrial experience proves that it increases commitment and efficiency. Therefore dogmatic personalities might find a negotiated curriculum hard to support or enjoy; usually students do not have anywhere near as great learning difficulties as some adults in this respect. A new curricular process needs to be well-led, but it also needs lively senses of humour well and truly embedded within it; the process of change can be a great deal of fun!

SUMMARY AND CONCLUSIONS

If you are working with students with special educational needs and you want to change the means by which a vocational and life-preparation course is delivered, the following recommendations may be of interest:

(i)   Pool all human and material resources in an area and see how much they amount to;

(ii)   Write a new curriculum outline within which you would love to work;

(iii)   Ask students what *they* enjoy;

(iv)   Ask your school or college governors for support in outlining a new curriculum;

(v)   Approach senior LEA officers and ask for their help in doing what you have already decided to do;

(vi)   Involve parents in discussions;

(vii)   Get help from voluntary organisations, but retain school control;

(viii) Find other places where it is already happening;

(ix)   Recruit all new staff from mainstream secondary schools and colleges;

(x)   Retrain all existing staff who are to be involved in the use of Enterprise
in the curriculum and create a link with TVEI;

(xi)   Make the course modular, involve the students and try to make money
which is ploughed back in;

(xii)   Do not duplicate facilities which exist unused nearby;

(xiii) Do not discriminate between statemented and non-statemented students;

(xiv)   Leave all visiting students on the roll of the 'home' establishment;

(xv)   Try to get staffing detached from a ratio. Press for the 'service' concept of staffing;

(xvi)   Try to lengthen school terms into holidays, and give staff time off in lieu. Students can also be offered 'flexi-time';

(xvii) Set up small businesses and encourage young people to try their own process with your support;

(xviii) Talk to MSC and ask their advice (you may be very pleasantly surprised!);

(xix) Always propose changes to the LEA as a matter of joy rather than an endless series of problems;

(xx) Be prepared for an overwhelming demand from secondary schools.

Many are seriously concerned about what to do with less able and disaffected students over the age of 14.

If your particular concern is not in the list, contact the author, who will gladly advise from his own experience of unarmed combat in this developing area of education. And by the way, good luck!

Chapter 10

Making Education Accessible: Parents' Role in Special Needs Provision
Sheila Wolfendale

The purpose of this chapter is to described and demonstrate significant innovations in parental involvement which have been initiated within special education and special needs. Special schools themselves have played less of a poineering role than have many mainstream schools, but work taking place within broader contexts of special needs within the UK has provided inspiration to teachers in special education to adapt and maintain initiatives that are suited to their settings.

So an intentionally holistic perspective will be adopted, in order to demonstrate inter-connnectedness within the education system and between other agencies and personnel, wherein parental and multi-disciplinary cooperation has been shown to be effective. The many ventures of this kind have exposed and dissipated any myths that divisions between sectors in education and with other agencies have to be maintained or are sacrosanct. Children, parents and professionals can be the beneficiaries when the boundaries of demarcated practice are eroded. How this chapter can be compatible with the theme of the book will, it is intended, be via exemplification of parental involvement initiatives that are applicable within special schools and which could fit comfortably into their metamorphosing role.

INVOLVING PARENTS: CHRONOLOGY AND CONTEXTS

Although parent-teacher collaboration is very much a contemporary pheno-menon, it is possible now from the vantage point of the late 1980s to look in retrospect at the take-up and spread of so many projects. A number of texts have chronicled these events from a mainstream and community perspective (Craft *et al.*, 1980); some have sought to incorporate special needs within an encompassing perspective (Wolfendale, 1983; Bowers, 1984; Cullingford, 1985; Bastiani, 1987) whilst others have presented an intact special needs focus (Pugh, 1981; Mittler and McConachie, 1983). In the ever-developing area of parental involvement in reading, the bulk of the work has taken place in mainstream schools, and effectiveness has been demonstrated with children learning to read, with those who are maintaining and extending their reading skills, and others who have reached plateaux in performance (Topping and Wolfendale, 1985). Keith Topping gives a résumé of the involvement of parents as 'reading tutors' (1988) and provides a diagrammatic model of a whole-school policy on parental involvement in reading. This chart sets out the stages of school life, thus demonstrating convincingly its applicability to special as well as mainstream schools, in terms of choice of relevant techniques.

We are moving from earlier models of parents-as-helpers, a rather simplistic notion not unallied to the fund-raising *raison d'etre* of many a parent-teacher association, towards a rather more sophisticated conception. Whilst there remain some fundamental issues to be explored and resolved, such as the desirability of and limits upon power-sharing (Beattie, 1985), nevertheless there is a broader acceptance of parents-as-educators (Topping, 1986) and commensurate acknowledgement of the prime part played by parents in their children's development, socialisation and education.

EXTENDING PARENTAL INVOLVEMENT — A MORAL IMPERATIVE?

Making special schools 'ordinary', for the purposes of this chapter, is making them accessible to very many more people, less closed than hitherto, and less 'special', that is, less remote and only available to a few. Thus the ease of access should extend to parents and the opportunities for parents to contribute to school life as recorded in countless projects available in all schools, irrespective of designation.

This exhortation might at first read rather starkly, were it not for the fact that for many schools and professionals working with or on behalf of children parental participation is nowadays a 'given', routinely part of school and professional practice. Thus, on the premise of equal opportunities, it behoves all educational institutions to reappraise existing practice regarding the place of parents, with a view to articulating policies of the kind of involvement that will best benefit children. On the last point, which for many parents and teachers is the sole enduring criterion which justifies their cooperation, Bloom (1979) goes so far as to posit that a significant degree of home-school collaboration leads to measurably enchanced learning. This can be attributed to the matching of teachers' and parents' skills, 'equivalent expertise' (Wolfendale, 1983) in the promotion of effective learning, whether this takes place at school, at home, or in any other milieu.

A number of parent-professional ventures, within the special needs realm, some of which are described in this chapter, have been predicated on these principles. Successful working relationships have been created which can inspire replication, the impetus for which can come from special or mainstream schools, local groups of parents and professionals or even from the LEA itself.

THE IMPACT OF THE 1981 EDUCATION ACT AND THE PLACE OF PARENTS IN SPECIAL NEEDS

The Act itself seems to have galvanised action locally and nationally, towards the setting up of increasingly effective parents' groups, as well as by the creation of mechanisms designed to effect better working relationships between parents, community and schools (Kramer, 1987).

These effects are not, of course, incidental, since the philosophy of the Act is explicit: 'the involvement of the child's parents is essential', and 'close relations should be established and maintained with parents and can only be helped by frankness and openness on all sides' (DES, 1983 p.2, para. 6). And, after all, the direct influence upon the framing of the Act was the Warnock Report, which, in its chapter on 'Parents as Partners' examined the expressed needs of parents of children with special educational needs, the few examples in existence in the mid 1970s of successful collaboration between parents and professionals, and concluded 'it is... an essential part of our thesis that parents must be advised, encouraged and supported so that they in turn effectively help their children' (DES, 1978, p.150., 9.1).

However, whilst some initiatives in cooperation may seem now to have been logical developments, compatible with such philosophies, others were not necessarily foreseen or anticipated. The rhetoric of grand statements provides no indicators or prescriptions for action. The only area of possible parental involvement in any of the Act's procedures that is mentioned explicitly, and even then quite briefly, is assessment (see below). The intentions and effects of the 1981 Education Act in so far as parents are concerned will be highlighted in this chapter, in connection with specific areas or projects.

However it is worth dwelling a little more at this point on the extent to which the existence and provisions of the Act generally may have altered the attitudes and practice of professionals and parents, for possible changes would have a bearing upon attitude and practice within special schools, since they are so often recipients of children who, with their parents, will have already gone through a number of mandatory as well as optional stages of discussion, assessment, and possibly been assigned to different teaching and intervention programmes. Thus special school teachers, notwithstanding their own view and practice on working with parents, may, at the later stage of a child's admission to their schools, inherit certain 'sets', preconceived expectations by parents as to the perceived advantages or disadvantages of working with teachers, based on their prior experience.

Several local studies, as well as the Select Committee Report into the working of the 1981 Education Act (1987), reveal that we are at present still some way away from agreeing: that partnership with parents is a priority area; the requisites for effective parent-teacher, parent-professional coopera-tion; the mechanics of implementing cooperative ventures.

We are witnessing and are part of a transition from erstwhile educational practice which kept parents at arm's length, towards a participant model that acknowledges and embraces the vital part played by parents in their childrens' development and education. So 'good practice' inspires emergent practice; successful models are replicated and eventually those proven examples of effective practice will be adopted on a wide scale.

The several studies referred to in the preceeding paragraph have explored at local level the interface between parents and professionals in and around the procedures of the 1981 Education Act. These singular micro-cosms graphically illustrate the state of flux and shifting attitudes that characterise the realignment of professional practice that is taking place in respect of the place of parents. Stone (1987) highlights an uneasy relationship between professionals and parents going through the assessment and statementing process, documenting, in so many instances, a sorry tale of misunderstanding and inadequate communication, despite best intentions. Parents in her study confessed to uncertainty about what kind of information professionals (social workers, psychologists, teachers) wanted to elicit from them, and how best to convey it. She is explicit in the observed fact that parents in her study were not partners in the decision-making process, that is, were not consulted and negotiated with on equal terms. These observations are crucial in respect of special school placements, since, as stated above, teachers in special schools inherit sets of parental attitudes. The provisions of the 1981 Education Act were supposed to eradicate the anomalies and unfairness of a system that so patently excluded parents from each stage of a process that led to a major change of education placement. Yet Stone's survey confirms that vestiges of what should by now be ertswhile practice are still in evidence, and so does another study carried out by Cornwell (1987) in a London borough. Again, the mis-match between parental and professional perceptions is arguably serious, given the affirmation of principle contained in the Act and Circular 1/83. It seems that 'parents describe an experience of being heard but not listened to by professionals and administrators' (p.59 'Key Points') and that parents' own 'special needs' in respect of having 'special needs' children are not sufficiently acknowledged and dealt with. These findings are echoed in yet another such exploratory study carried out in another London borough (Sandow, Stafford and Stafford, 1987). It is evident from these studies, as well as from an as yet unpublished survey carried out during 1987 by The Greater London Association for the Disabled (GLAD) in three other London boroughs, that professionals are feeling their way tentatively into a changing relationship with parents. They are unused to power-sharing (Gleidman and Roth, 1981) and open communication and information exchange on an egalitarian basis. As Sandow *et al.* remark, the 1981 Education Act was very forward-looking but 'perhaps the ground had not been adequately prepared for some of its innovations. It is possible to legislate to change practice, but changing attitudes is more difficult' (p.156).

Other, national-level surveys and appraisals of the Act's effectiveness have also confirmed the slow pace of change towards the spirit of partnership envisaged by the Warnock Committee. It has taken many Local Education Authorities several years, since the implementation of the Act on 1 April 1983, to produce written information for parents on special needs provisions of sufficient quality as to be of actual use to them (CSIE, 1986).

A number of factors for this slow transition towards 'constructive engagement' have been considered by J. Evans (1987) in summarising the findings from a DES-funded research project into the implementation of the 1981 Education Act. She reports that, overall, parents expect a certain degree of formality and bureaucracy — they are more concerned 'about the quality of the interactions which they had with the various LEA and DHA personnel with whom they had to deal on behalf of their child' (p. 16).

Finally, and most recently, the evidence given by parents' and professional associations to the Select Committee during 1987 suggested that the same complaints as reported in Warnock are still as pertinent, ten years on — 'inadequate or unclear information... insufficient help... lack of weight given to their (parents') views... a lack of choice from a range of forms of provision' (Select Committee p.XI, para. 16).

As with any complex societal issue, there are a number of 'truths' competing simultaneously, since progress is rarely smoothly linear.

Juxtaposed alongside this rather negative catalogue of evidence that progress towards effective cooperation is sluggish comes equal evidence that joint work, even partnership ventures, are taking root and flourishing.

Attention will now be given to a number of developments which have come about specifically as a consequence of the Act's provisions or which are reflective of the broader context of parental involvement in education. A number of special schools are already associated with these initiatives, of course, but it will be seen that the particular message of this chapter is that, at this juncture in the history of special education, it is timely for all special schools to reconsider the place of parents.

INVOLVING PARENTS IN ASSESSMENT AND PROGRESS REVIEWS

There have been exhortations by a number of educationalists to involve parents routinely in reviews of children's progress as part of generalised accountability procedures (Ainscow and Tweddle, 1979). As part of a report on the outcomes of a national pilot study into the take-up and potential of parental involvement in Section 5 assessment and statementing procedures, this author (Wolfendale, 1986) examined the evidence, mostly American to date, that there is a high degree of agreement between professional and parental perceptions of the rate and type of developmental and educational progress made by children.

A number of measures are potentially suitable. Wolfendale (1988a) reports on the try-out and application of several of these in the UK. They include ratings, parental completion of itemised check lists, the open-ended construction by parents of a parental profile, 'My Child at Home', based on the provision, if needed, of a set of guidelines, an *aide-memoire* to help generate thinking. The effectiveness of this particular approach was demonstrated in the national pilot study referred to above. The revised Guidelines for parents in constructing a child profile are in use in a number of local education authorities, and have been taken up by several voluntary and professional organisations, amongst which are MENCAP and the National Union of Teachers.

The application of these and other measures has tended to be concentrated at initial assessment stages (for example, Section 5 assessment) and yet they are suitable for use at statutory annual review, or routine non-statutory review points. There is little empirical evidence as to how widespread parental input into review procedures is — it seem that practice is haphazard, variable, and unsystematic even within LEAs, let alone between them. At an anecdotal level, teachers in special schools, who will describe other kinds of parental involvement activities, admit that parents are still held at arm's length when it comes to assessment and re-assessment of their children's progress. A circular argument is in danger of prevailing: teachers remain unaware of the significant and valuable contribution parents can make to progress review until they include them in these processes!

Currently much attention is being given to the place of Records of Achievement and Pupil Profiling in school-based assessment (Broadfoot, 1986; Task Group on Assessment and Testing, 1987). The part that parents can play has hardly yet been considered, even though some writers are of the view that there is much to gain from including the parental perspective (see Bray, 1986).

Inclusion of the parental view within progress appraisals of children with special educational needs would be compatible not only with these developments just described but also with the curriculum-based assessment and individualized learning approaches now in use in many special schools.

PARENTS AS EDUCATORS AND 'MANAGERS' AND THEIR INVOLVEMENT IN INTERVENTION PROGRAMMES

There are many examples nowadays of parental participation in educational programmes, wherein parents have amply demonstrated their competence as 'teachers' and 'tutors'. As Adams (1986) states 'parents are, first of all, home teachers, ... Parents teach their children the skills of daily living, they serve as models for appropriate behaviour and by listening to and talking with their children they make the most of the environment around them' (p. 142). The pedigree of parental involvement in intervention programmes within special needs contexts is long and honourable. From the early days of the American Headstart programme, in the 1960s, introduction of Portage in America in the late 1960s, its advent in the UK in 1976, and its widespread application by the end of the 1980s, all attest to the powerful influence parents can exert in their own children's development.

These initiatives have been chronicled, generally, across the special needs and disability ranges by Wolfendale (1983, ch. 7), Cunningham and Davis (1985, ch. 7), Cunningham (1985), McConachie (1986, ch. 10), and Topping (1986). The views of these writers are not always unequivocal about the success of methods employed. As with any human learning experience, there are lessons to be learned from first applications of innovative approaches; these pave the way to modification and improvement, and so we are clearer now about the requisites for effective parent-teacher (and other practitioners) co-working. Skills appraisal exercises (Wolfendale 1987a) can also provide a foundation for a match between what parents and practitioners can bring to joint enterprises.

Some of these facets have been explored with reference to specific special needs and curriculum areas, as, for example, parental involvement in acquisition by children with Down's Syndrome of reading skills (Buckley, 1985; Buckley *el al.*, 1986). Carr (1980) and Newson and Hipgrave (1982) provide blueprints for parents along the lines of 'helping your handicapped child' which include teaching and behaviour management strategies. West-macott and Cameron (1981) and Herbert (1985) in books written specifically for parents deal with 'problem behaviour' and suggest a number of handling and coping strategies.

There is considerable potential for a greater amount of cooperative work between school and home, in devising and carrying out learning and behaviour management programmes. Some of the work referenced above has been project work of hypothesis-testing, exploratory nature, whilst other texts are explicitly and exclusively aimed towards home settings. A case can be made now, on the basis of pioneering work, for marrying these elements into corporate school-home programmes which could form part of routine school provision. A model for introducing a systems approach into schools for involving parents in behaviour management has been proposed (Wolfendale 1987b) which postulates four levels of situational analysis and planning for joint programmes to take place and staff/parent training needs to be catered for. A flow chart demonstrates possible procedures at level 4.

Published 'how to' manuals for teachers and parents (of which there are many hundreds in the USA) may well provide the initial impetus and encouragement to proceed. However, it could be a fruitful exercise for teachers in special schools to get together with groups of parents and representatives from local voluntary and community organisations to devise home-grown materials that are then tailor-made for each uniquely differing individual school and community setting.

PARENTS, COMMUNITY GROUPS AND VOLUNTARY ASSOCIATIONS: TOWARDS PARTNERSHIP WITH SCHOOLS?

We have witnessed in recent years a dramatic and significant growth in parents' and community groups with a focus on special needs.

There is an explicit and undeniable link between the mushrooming of lobbying, pressure and self-help local groups, the advent of an national network and special needs legislation in the form of the 1981 Education Act. Also notable, and associated with this growth of parental power-exercising groups, has been the increasing parent-focused activities of established national organisations for different handicaps and disabilities.

The apparent militancy and high public profile of some groups has been born of concern about the implementation and provisions of the Act. For example, one Midlands-based parents' group came about as a result of frustration on the part of a number of parents who wanted integrated education for their handicapped children, and who believed that collective pressure on the LEA to implement Section 2 of the Act would be more effective than lone campaigns.

Parents in such groupings are becoming seasoned campaigners, developing skills of lobbying, contacting, negotiating with local authority administrators, professionals, and elected council members. Initial confrontation in many instances has led to constructive dialogue, and shared activities, such as day conferences for parent and professionals. One major London-based parents' group now has an impressive track record of such participant events.

During 1986 a national umbrella coordinating group was formed, called '81 ACTION which has an agreed set of aims. It publishes a newsletter and initiates meetings and conferences. Any reader who is interested in finding out about local and regional groups is advised to contact '81 ACTION, 52 Magnaville Rd, Bishop's Stortford, Herts, CM23 4BW.

Some groups have established themselves as the agreed local point of contact for families going through Section 5 Assessment and statementing procedures. For example, in the London Borough of Newham, the routine LEA letter to parents makes mention of the help and support available to them from the Parents' Support Network, which itself is a part of Newham Parents' Centre (the author is associated with this venture). The PSN produces information and guidance leaflets, sponsors meetings, provides individual casework support for families, and liaises with schools and the support services (Smith, 1986).

A number of funded family support groups have demonstrated solid and valuable services in recent years. Examples include: the *Elfrida Rathbone Society* which first produced a parents' guide to the 1981 Education Act towards the end of 1983, runs family projects, such as 'Parents and Co.', and liaises with special schools; *Contact A Family,* which, as a national charity, links families of children with special needs, on a one-to-one basis, to a support or self-help group or to voluntary/statutory organisations (Hatch and Hinton, 1986); *Kids,* which, via its Family Centres, provides general advice, information and counselling to parents of children with special needs (Dale, 1986).

The national, long-established voluntary organisations, each with a remit to a particular disability area, also responded and contributed to the changing special needs climate by developing services for parents and families. Barnardo's, the National Autistic Society and MENCAP have run awareness and training courses for parents — MENCAP, in partnership with several local educational authorities, is involved in a major initiative recruiting and training voluntary parent advisers to work with parents, offering them guidance and support as they go through the assessment process (the author has been involved with these initiatives). Also MENCAP has produced a detailed and comprehensive Directory of services for families and their young children with special needs, in the London area. Recommended as an account for self-help groups and family casework in the Liverpool area is Evans *et al.* (1986).

How important is it for teachers in special schools to know of these developments? Should the activities of local national parents' and voluntary groups impinge upon schools? A charge familiar to this author, over the years, is that teachers are not sufficiently aware of the various statutory, personal and voluntary services. Such knowledge is usually acquired incidentally, often in an *ad hoc* fashion. It is rarely imparted on initial teacher training courses, and even on INSET courses may only figure tangentially, if at all.

This author is of the view that it is a vital concomitant of teachers' responsibilties that they are aware of available and local resources. Basic knowledge of what is available and of local contact persons can provide the foundations for mutually advantageous work on behalf of children in special and mainstream schools. The LEA and community and voluntary groups themselves have an equal responsibility in setting up liaison mechanisms. There are a number of legitimate points of contact between schools and community groups, as far as parents of children with special needs are concerned — guidance and support over statutory procedures of assessment and review, cooperation in running parents' workshops, educational programmes, public debates and attitude — changing exercises — not to mention fund-raising activities and social functions. The accumulated expertise of practitioners, voluntary and parent workers in the special needs sphere is now just waiting to be shared.

FORUMS FOR JOINT PLANNING AND MANAGING OF SPECIAL EDUCATIONAL NEEDS: THE CONTRIBUTION OF PARENTS TO SCHOOLS

The many ways in which home-school links manifest themselves in contemporary Britain have been illustrated diagrammatically in the form of a 'wheel of parental involvement' (Wolfendale 1987c). The activities, radiating like spokes on the 'wheel', denote the range and type of face-to-face involvement, as well as illustrating *in toto* an ideal of practice towards which schools could aspire, if they were committed to an articulated policy on parental participation.

Forums for the exchange of information for communicating concerns figure prominently on the wheel. Due to legislative provisions, one of these forums is made formal and explicit, that is, the composition and duties of schools' governing bodies. Parents and teachers are represented on the governing body, which has several new duties assigned to it, in respect of special educational needs, under the 1981 Education Act. A paper has been produced by the National Association of Governors and Managers (NAGM) which spells out these duties and ways in which they can be carried out.

This is the most formal 'interface' between schools and home, and it can be paralled, at less formal levels, by utilising existing PTA networks to promote frequent, relaxed interactions between staff of special schools and their parents. Of course, this is standard practice in many schools already, but PTAs can have an imprecise function and may not be easily amenable to restructuring and redefining. A model to pursue could be the Home-School Council, proposed in the Hargreaves report on secondary education in the ILEA, and implemented by staff and parents in one ILEA secondary school during 1987 (this initiative, how it was set up, and how it runs will be described in Wolfendale, 1989, currently in preparation). The HSC is a forum for the exchange of views and concerns between parents and teachers; matters of mutual interest can be shared, such as curriculum plans, teacher provision, sex education, to name but a few of the many topics discussed during the first year of operation in the school referred to.

At the direct, face-to-face level of contact between individual teachers and parents, and class teachers with their group of parents, several options are available. These range from standard practice of meetings-by-appointment, e.g. traditional case conferences or open evenings, to what is termed 'parent-teacher conferencing' by some American educators. Two books are commended to readers which comprehensively explore the dimensions of parent-teacher conferences, how to initiate them, skills required for conducting them, and which also suggest materials to facilitate and sustain the dialogue (Lombana, 1983).

CONCLUDING COMMENTARY

The central theme in this chapter has been on empowering parents to increase their participation in the provision of services, and to exercise their rights in respect of their children with special educational needs. A number of significant developments towards these goals have been described, all of which have evident applicability to special schools. There is scope for much more communication between schools, which are as vital a part of their communities as the families they exist to serve, and those families and other community networks.

Erstwhile rigid demarcations between pedagogy (in the school) and caring (in the home) are breaking down, with the advent of shared ventures, and complementarity of expertise. The notion of collective responsibility towards meeting children's special needs has been expounded elsewhere (Wolfendale, 1987c), in which key parts are played by designated personnel, including parents. In this model, support is given to teachers by parents for the specialised, responsible jobs that they do. Reciprocally, teachers manifest their concern for parents of handicapped children, and their awareness of the stress and awesome responsibilities placed upon them (Millard, 1984; Russell, 1986).

Opening education and schools in the ways described, encouraging schools to become accessible, can also pave the way towards realising the aspirations of many teachers and parents — namely, to inform the wider public about special educational needs, and thus safeguard their children's futures.

Chapter 11

INSET: The Role of the Special School
Mike Wright

INTRODUCTION

This chapter examines the changing pattern of in-service training and staff development in the field of Special Educational Needs.

The shift from full-time secondments towards a more modular pattern of activity arranged in levels of involvement is discussed within the national, regional and local context.

The role of the special school is examined in the context of the changing scene taking account of the needs both of staff within the institution and the local educational community. Consideration is taken of the grant-related in-service initiatives, of the TVEI developments and of the changing role of institutions of higher education.

Consideration is given to the potential central role of the special school in the emerging in-service training scene as more funding and responsibility is devolved to the school and new planning networks emerge.

TOWARDS A MODULAR PATTERN OF INSET (SEN)

It is recognized that an extra qualification is desirable for teachers of children with special educational needs, but only 30% of such teachers had had the opportunity to obtain such a qualification by 1981. It had been the aspiration that special school teachers should also have experience in mainstream schools, but the 1971 Education Act, which had brought mentally handicapped children under the aegis of the Education Department, had led to a number of special education courses being set up at initial training level and by 1980 it was not uncommon for special school teachers never to have taught in mainstream schools.

This situation led to a degree of undesirable isolation of both teachers and pupils in special schools from the mainstream of education, both in practice and theory. It would be untrue to suggest that there has ever been a universally accepted and coherent theory of special education, but one can identify some widely held beliefs which can be used to exemplify the thinking of special educationalists in this period. Most used what is now usually identified as a pathological model of learning difficulties, which saw the main focus of difficulties as being in the child or his family environment. There was often a strong emphasis on psychometric testing of children, with many using a contrast between Intelligence and Attainment Scores to produce relative concepts of Retardation and Backwardness, whilst others advocated the use of tests such as Frostig, ITPA and Bender to suggest a spectrum of Learning Disabilities which could be ameliorated by Ability Training programmes. What was common to both camps was a belief that diagnosis and remediation could only take place in special settings, supervised by experts. Thus at a time when schools in general were moving towards comprehensiveness and mixed-ability settings, special schools were becoming more isolated and claiming to be more specialized.

The one-year full-time Diploma courses were themselves both the product of this era which was special education as a treatment which could rarely be applied in the normal school, and also the purveyor of this philosophy. In many ways the situation of the courses and course tutor in the college was analogous to the position of special schools in the school system. The idea of special education expertise ensured that such courses were isolated from the mainstream, for few colleges could afford a range of 'experts'. Consequently the one expert was totally absorbed in running his/ her course, and had only minimal and token inputs with the initial training courses. This token presence was then justified by the theory that all students should have experience of ordinary children before they retrained, via the inservice course, for the teaching of the handicapped. The myth of an expertise different in kind from that available to the ordinary school teacher was not only reinforced by the isolation of both training and school, but was often further strengthened by expertise based on the pathological view of learning difficulties. Not surprisingly many such courses became propagators of the myth of the Hero-Innovator, seeing their role as one of taking the gospel of Special Education treatment to a hostile and uncomprehending world. However, for many teachers the cooperative learning experience — a significant element in the one year secondment course — proved to be the turning-point of their professional career.

The changes brought about by the Warnock Report and subsequent legislation as well as the changing pattern of financing INSET foreshadowed in the DES Discussion Paper 1986 has been such that there is a need to rethink the whole of inservice provision to take full account of the centrality of the special needs issue.

Among the major considerations are:

1. The failure of the one-year full-time model to provide sufficient numbers of qualified teachers. This argues that the basis of the new provision should be part-time rather than full-time.
2. The strength of the full-time course is that it provides time for reflection and a greater opportunity for objectivity. This argues that there should be a seconded element in the new provision.
3. The need for all teachers to be seen as teachers of all children.

A major weakness of the existing system of in-service training has been its piecemeal nature with a number of different providers and little cooperation between them. The new provision should illustrate transbinary cooperation between the LEA, University and Polytechnic, and College of Higher Education, and thereby provide a cohesive and coherent programme of training for special educational needs across each region, therefore making the fullest possible use of all available resources. It is suggested that a modular course will enable this to happen.

Any successful course in this field should concentrate on assisting schools as they develop a whole-school approach to special educational needs. This will mean that course members must be given the opportunity to develop skills which will enable schools to develop as a whole to meet special educational needs. The course must therefore be school-focused.

As previously stated, the major focus in the old-style one-year course tended to be on a pathological model of learning difficulties. This should be replaced by a curriculum focus in order that special educational needs can become part of the mainstream of education. The new courses will therefore be curriculum-focused and of an essentially practical nature.

The structure of training courses for teachers of pupils with special educational needs is somewhat idiosyncratic in that, for example, current reg-ulations require teachers of the deaf and the blind — in certain situations — to obtain a particular type of training but no such requirements exist in relation to any other type of disability. Only 30% of teachers of pupils with SEN in special schools and units have a 'recognized' post-initial teaching qualification. For the most part, such 'recognized' courses are one-year full-time (or part-time equivalent) certificate, diploma, Bachelor's or Master's courses.

Additional provision, arranged through the direct grant funding in-itiative, has increased slightly the number of teachers with post-experience training related to pupils with SEN in ordinary schools. Short courses on topics such as 'slow learners', 'exceptional children' and 'remedial reading' have always featured significantly in the INSET provision offered through advisory services, teachers' centres and DES regional courses.

While all these courses have been designed to improve the effectiveness of teachers — with varying emphasis on the balance between theoretical issues and practical skills — there has been no agreed pattern of training in relation to the different tasks that teachers have to perform at different levels within the education system or in relation to the different levels of responsibility at which staff are required to function. It is of note, however, that for the majority of teachers these courses constitute 'basic' training in relation to the teaching of pupils with SEN over and above the very general training that all teachers will now receive within their initial training course.

The current climate of opinion concerning in-service training suggests that such training should, for the most part, be carefully focused in relation to the actual tasks, roles and responsibilities that teachers are being asked to perform in order that they might be effective in changing and improving the quality of the provision made for their pupils. This implies a greater degree of involvement and planning on the part of heads and LEAs as well as a greater recognition by teacher-training institutions that courses should be planned to meet the objectives so identified.

Most importantly, there is a need for each LEA to establish a clear policy as to how it proposes to fulfil its obligations under the 1944, 1980 and 1981 Education Acts in relation to pupils and students with SEN, with respect to its provision in ordinary and special schools and the nature of its support services to schools and individual pupils (and students) wherever they might be placed. While the nature of the provision and the deployment of teachers will vary from LEA to LEA, teachers will be required to fulfil a number of functions which, in turn, are dependent on background experience, training and expertise. The new GRIST initiative is aimed at achieving a better match between local LEA needs and available training, thus enabling appropriate courses and training opportunities to be negotiated between LEAs and training institutions. Within this framework there is a need to develop, as far as is possible and practicable, some broad common forms of training across the country related to those functions that are common to LEAs and schools. In this way standards of provision may be set and maintained and the opportunity for a career structure for teachers wishing to specialise in the field of SEN offered.

There has therefore been the recognition that considerable teacher time has been involved in in-service activity and that hitherto opportunities have not existed for teachers to accumulate their experiences in a structured or award bearing fashion. Nor were clear pathways evident which would enable teachers to plan a course to suit their personal needs either professionally or over a variable time scale.

These various concerns have led to a range of developments across the country, each exploring the possibilities of the modularisation of courses in such a way as to facilitate award-bearing status. Such modular developments attempt to take account of the dangers inherent in such a process as well as the possible advantages. It is generally agreed that the modular units should exist in their own right and be of value irrespective of their accumulative potential.

In most cases the modularization process has begun with an examination of existing courses available in a region in order to explore the potential for creating a unified network of units available to teachers before commencing the design of any specific new ones. The process also offers the possibility of increasing the number of potential inset providers. Examples of the development are to be seen in the North West (centred around Manchester), in South Yorkshire (centred around Sheffield) and increasingly across the nation.

The prime aim has been to provide a modular structure which is flexible and which provides a range of levels of personal developmental opportunities suited to the new demands being faced by schools. Such a structure must be flexible enough to take account of the requirements of the GRIST initiative and to enable both LEAs and individual schools or teachers to use the finite resources to greater effect. Instead of 75% of the funding being spent on the support of a few teachers on long courses, many more teachers would have the opportunity to experience new training routes and opportunities — the queue for secondments is hopefully a thing of the past.

SPECIAL NEEDS MODULAR COURSES AS EVOLVING ACROSS SOUTH YORKSHIRE AND HUMBERSIDE

It is agreed that a major consequence of the 1981 Education Act is that staff of all mainstream schools will need to be aware of the problems of children with special educational needs, and that highly specialist training will still be needed for certain groups of teachers — i.e. those working with sensory handicap, severe learning difficulty, emotionally and behaviourally disturbed children, etc. It must, therefore, be seen as a priority that in-service help be provided to give staff the capability to undertake the responsibilities involved.

Each Local Education Authority has slightly different needs depending upon its administrative framework, its resource base and its general policy towards Special Educational Needs. This means that each authority will vary in its response to the new legislation but that a common core of requirements can be identified which can be modified to suit local conditions. If the higher education institutions can agree a common framework it will ultimately mean that LEAs may be able to share resources. At the same time, such a framework could provide teachers with a structure for their professional development, as well as a regionally recognised qualification.

As it is accepted the LEAs would neither wish to nor be able to cater for all of their own particular needs, the framework evolved must be of a modular nature, in which there is a core of compulsory modules and a range of options. The modular nature of the course not only gives LEAs the flexibility they require, but also allows the possibility that some course members will only be interested in certain modules, whilst others will be able to plan the timing of their own course, by choosing to do one or more modules in the course of one year. This flexibility, however, is not complete freedom as certain of the modules will be compulsory for those wishing to obtain a certificate or diploma.

The opportunities available for the teacher could be seen in the form of a tree, shown in Figure 11.1, growing out of grass-roots needs, which has a trunk of essential knowledge but which permits all teachers the opportunity to branch out from that core according to curriculum, career or management needs or interests; to set the pace according to the individual's own needs and provide the opportunity to follow the award-bearing route as far as the individual teacher wishes. The basic structure is exemplified as follows:

SUGGESTED COURSE STRUCTURE FOR FUTURE DEVELOPMENT IN HUMBERSIDE

Suggested modular pattern

Teachers wishing to follow this course pattern could be required to register with the validating body.

Level I (The basic core)

This consists of an integrated series of University/Polytechnic/Education Centre Units taught by staff from the LEA and in all three institutions. The aim is to provide a background to the whole course and set the pattern of work to be followed. The planning of this enabled the core teaching team to develop a common philosophy.

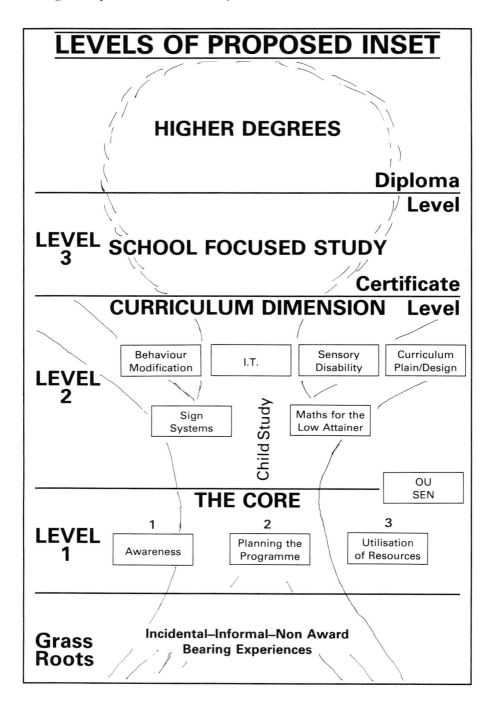

Figure 11.1: Levels of proposed INSET

This foundation course will provide in Humberside the major thrust for SEN coordinator and head of learning support training. These modules equate in time and content to DES direct funded courses (Circular 3.83 and later varients) and certain OU special education units (e.g. E.241).

Level II (Curriculum/Professional extension)

A planning group is looking at the possibility of jointly taught courses but it is accepted that the institutions (and LEA) at present run courses which could become option modules towards the award of a university validated certificate.

Possible modules which are available include:

Mathematics for Low Attainers in Secondary School — (3 units) — (Polythenic)
Severe Reading Difficulties — (3 units) — (University)
EDY Course (1 unit) LEA)
Instrumental Enrichment (1 unit) (LEA and Polytechnic)
Numerous LEA initiated Curricular Focused Courses

An effort will be made to use LEA modules based on Teachers' Centres as well as University and Polytechnic based modules. There will be an opportunity for one or more modules in which the student can devise an individual course of study for him/herself with tutorial guidance. The opportunity will exist for modules to develop around identified needs of specific schools or groups of schools.

Level III

Level III would include a taught linking module relating to research methodology and would essentially be delivered partially with an institute of higher education. Activity at this level leading to Diploma status would include a range of taught modules offered alongside particular school focused practical experiences. Cohesion would be brought to this level via the individual student's tutored dissertation.

In following the modular diploma route it is assumed that levels 1–3 will run sequentially and that certain modules at each level may be deemed compulsory in order to cater for specific interest groups (e.g. severe learning difficulties).

There are still areas of need which as yet fall outside the previously described pattern. The majority of LEAs may still perceive the need for specialist award bearing courses to be offered on a regional or national basis to serve teachers in specific areas of need such as sensory handicaps, severe learning difficulties and emotionally and behaviourally disturbed children.

The Warnock Report suggests that 75% of the teaching force will need retraining in order that the aspirations of the report be implemented.

Local planning for SEN training should take account of:

(a)   the need to coordinate INSET proposals for all aspects of special needs, i.e. primary, secondary, services and special schools, management;
(b)   the fact that SEN in-service needs to permeate all courses, i.e. subject focus, etc.;
(c)   the fact that all 'service' personnel are daily involved in incidental in-service and need to share a common philosophy;
(d)   the need to ensure that in-service should be offered at a variety of levels;
(e)   the need to ensure that opportunities are made available for teachers to experience and share good practice within the LEA and nationally;
(f)   the need for flexibility in course options and a balance between school time, extra-mural and residential courses.

HAS THE SPECIAL SCHOOL A PLACE IN THE CHANGING SCENE?

The issues to be considered by the special school

As previously indicated, the special school takes on a potentially greater role in the changing pattern and provision of in-service training. In particular the increased awareness of the value of school-focused in-service should affect the opportunities available to special schools.

The changed pattern of in-service funding influences the arrangements made by special schools in relation to both their internal organisation (school needs) and those of the external educational community.

Internal requirements

Each school will be expected to draw up an annual in-service proposal which takes account of the total needs of staff working in the institution. It is regrettable that no provision is made within the grant-related in-service proposals to include ancillary or non-teacher personnel. This is particularly unfortunate since the partnership between teaching and ancillary staff in special schools is so important. This currently remains a local in-service issue with no national recognition.

The school proposal needs to address initiatives affecting it at a community, county or national level as well as the on-going development of the school itself, its resources, management and its curriculum. As illustrated in Figure 11.2 the proposal needs to reflect the needs of the school and the service through the on-going development, both personal and professional, of the staff (short and long courses, etc).

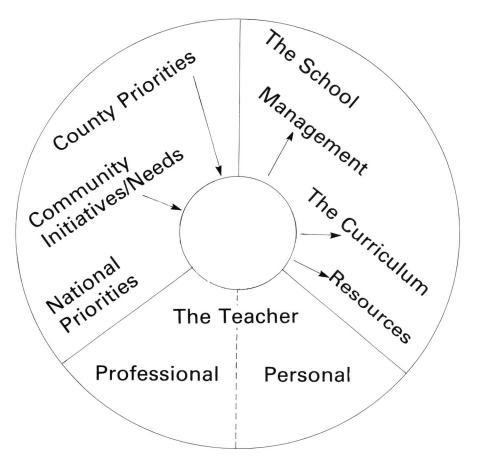

Figure 11.2: The School Proposal

In order to facilitate the process, consideration may need to be given to the identification of the Staff Tutor/INSET Coordinator. The evolution of such a position would increase the possibility of developing a whole-school strategy for identifying needs, selecting priorities/courses, arranging dissemination and appropriate feed-back, etc. A pattern developed by Riverside School, Goole, to illustrate this process is shown in Figure 11.3.

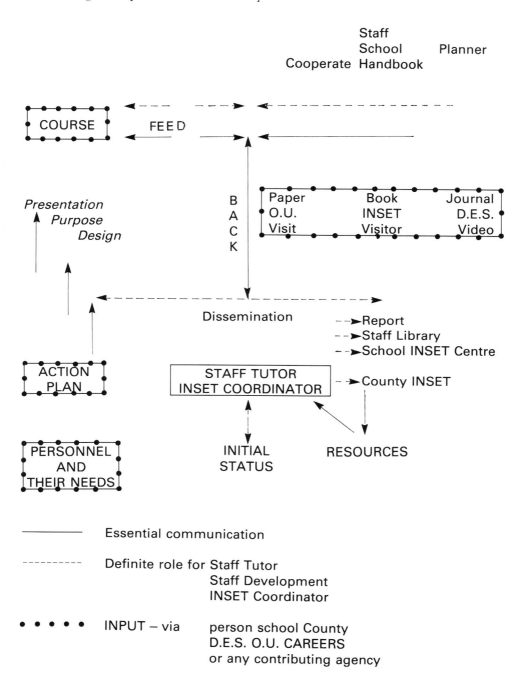

Figure 11.3: Staff Tutor/INSET Co-ordinator: A whole school approach

The internal in-service requirements relate to the on-going development of the school and its staff. It will take account of available courses locally and nationally to meet its perceived needs. Increasingly as more funding is devolved directly to the schools more control is available to meet these locally-perceived needs either through the school's own budgetary management or that arranged jointly with other schools identifying similar needs.

External opportunities

It is within the area of external opportunity that the special school is able to capitalize upon both the current high profile of special educational needs development in all schools and the devolved budgtary management of in-service training. It is vitally important that the LEA development plan is known to the school in order that appropriate training can be agreed.

The changing role of special schools highlighted in the Warnock Report and precipitated in many cases since 1983 provides a range of opportunities to engage in in-service work in mainstream schools and community groups. Increased levels of incidental in-service grow from every school contact and are fostered by the interest shown by schools in learning from one another.

The teacher consultant

The concept of the teacher consultant has grown considerably in recent years and many special schools are offering consultancy-style advice to other schools both within their local authority and wider afield. This approach has been developing for some years in the field of sensory and physical handicap and examples exist which have exemplified the potential of the information technology field for pupils with special educational needs, e.g. ACE Centres.

Some special schools have developed in-service training packages initially for themselves which they subsequently find are of value to other institutions. Under the new in-service funding arrangements both staff and materials are 'contracted out' to other institutions to share such materials — a process well developed in Cleveland and several parts of the Midlands.

More recently special schools have begun to develop the consultancy role in relation to TVEI initiatives. Such initiatives involve consultancy strengths in record-keeping, curriculum planning, teaching to objectives, continuous assessment and life skills courses.

This consultancy activity reflects the high profile of special needs providers across all phases of education from early years, through primary and secondary, to post-compulsory and adult education.

The school as a resource base

Elsewhere in this publication are descriptions of the role of the special school as a resource base. Where such a pattern of provision has emerged there has been the potential for the schools to develop as local in-service centres. In such cases the schools are involved in a variety of ways as providers of:

- courses on specific themes
- venues for courses arranged by local INSET committees
- venues for interest groups (NARE, NCSE, Spastic Society, APHASIC, etc.) meetings
- venues for resource development workshops
- venues for parent support groups
- venues for adult literacy activity
- venues for community activity classes
- venues for inter-agency activity.

The staff as INSET providers

As special schools engage in and develop their support role they automatically become involved as change agents and in-service providers as they collaborate with and negotiate a working relationship with the host school and/or class teacher.

The range of possibilities for staff to be involved as INSET providers has been growing since 1983 with the development of the DES-funded short courses. The school-focused nature of these courses meant that many institutions involved practising teachers in specific elements of the courses as tutors or in some cases as course tutors seconded from the LEA for the total duration of the course. Such teachers were generally seconded from special schools or services in the region to be responsible for the day-to-day running of the course. This could become a feature of the modular developments.

Many LEAs also took advantage of fellowships offered by institutions of higher education in order to develop specific curricular initiatives. These were often taken up by special school staff and subsequently led to regional or national in-service opportunities, e.g. Hill Top School, Maltby — information technology and the profoundly handicapped and the development of regional networks including a special educational needs information data base by teachers from Sheffield and Humberside. The latter project has involved the establishment of groups of readers, attracted from all types of schools in each area, the coordination of this activity and the maintenance of a data base. This is available to a wide range of schools and institutions who might require information on recently published articles in the special educational needs sphere of education.

Staff from special schools and services (e.g. sensory and physical handicap) are increasingly involved in local and county courses both for and with mainstream institutions as they take advantage of the revised budgetary arrangements and appreciate the need to increase their staffs' expertise in the area of special educational needs.

Modular courses, as described at some length earlier, again offer a range of opportunities for special schools and their staffs to be involved as identifiers of need, as course planners, and frequently as course tutors.

Schools will inevitably change and be reorganized but pupils with special educational needs will still have to be appropriately catered for. Teachers and schools with particular expertise will be needed and indeed will be expected to share knowledge and skills with an increasingly wider audience. New strategies will have to emerge if the Warnock aspiration is to be realized — 75% of the teaching force would need to be retrained if the aspirations of the report are to become a reality.

There can be little doubt that during times of change new opportunities emerge continuously to replace what may appear as lost causes. The next decade offers teachers in the special schools and services an exciting challenge within the rapidly changing in-service scene.

Chapter 12

Special Schools: A Setting for Initial Teacher Training

Morag Styles and Catherine Pearce

In the summer of 1986 the English Department at Homerton College, Cambridge, decided to mount a course on Language and Special Needs in the Primary Curriculum which would be offered as an option to Year III students, and contribute to the first part of the Education Tripos. In the English curriculum courses in Years I and II, attention is paid to ways of helping those with problems in reading and writing, but we intended this course to focus on the wider issues of Special Needs, to give students the opportunity to respond to the needs of those children whom they were meeting on teaching practice and on leaving college. Two examples may illustrate the causes of our concern.

A former student on her probationary year wrote: 'I have a spina bifida child in my class. Nothing at college prepared me for this.' A current student had a boy with a hearing aid and amplifier in one of her secondary classes. No one had given her any guidance; he reminded her to put on the radio mike and placed the amplifier at her feet. Clearly he didn't want to be a nuisance; he coped with a partner in small-group work, but when the groups were performing he probably heard nothing.

We planned that this course should from the beginning involve cooperation with local schools and teachers, and were grateful to them for attending meetings at the end of busy school days. We decided to devote half of the course to lectures followed by seminar discussions. The second half should involve practical work in school, helping a child with language and learning problems. We hoped to place the students in local special schools, units and mainstream classrooms, so that they could make visits regularly. Since neither of the tutors concerned felt themselves to be experts in the field, we invited the teachers to guide and assist the students. We discussed with teachers the kind of work that students might do, received suggestions for the reading list, and agreed on what would be an appropriate assignment. It was a true collaborative enterprise.

The assignment, written up over the Christmas vacation, was to be a 3,000 word case study of a child's strengths and weaknesses. The students were urged to focus on a small area of learning difficulty, in the hope that this might ensure success. This case study was a departure from the work normally required of students: essays, files and seminar papers; it had two areas of focus: the first was the planning and evaluation of the work undertaken with the pupil. This should be a small-scale scheme of work where the pupil should be able to make at least some small improvement. The student was invited to analyze both the pupil's response to the work and her own reactions to it. In fact the emotional impact of the experience was considerable for most students. Secondly this scheme of work was to be put within the context of the child's needs and aptitudes, and involve observation of the child as well as teaching, thus dignifying the students' endeavours as mini-research. Students took this assignment very seriously — there was a real child involved, and a strong personal commitment to the pupil was often evident.

Students made contact with the schools early in the course, and discussed the work they were planning with college tutors before they actually began the sessions with the child. The 'Needs' encountered varied from children who were slow, with poor concentration, whose language or hearing was limited, who hadn't mastered reading, to a brain-damaged girl who had no speech. In some cases, teachers suggested specific objectives, sometime very limited, such as teaching 'several words of sight vocabulary'; others left the general development of skills open to the student.

What struck all who read the assignments from the course was the enthusiasm and commitment of the students. The analysis of problems, often made without access to the children's files, was remarkably mature. Some students were actually able to record a breakthrough with poor or reluctant readers, by establishing that reading and books could be enjoyable, not just a source of repeated failure. Others could honestly claim only a partial success.

All the students gained a great deal from this experience; they certainly learned a lot about teaching. In a one-to-one situation with a child with difficulties, the student is forced back on her own basic resources as a teacher. One or two found this threatening: most found it challenging. You cannot fool yourself that you are teaching successfully if the child in front of you is struggling with the task you have set, bored, unmotivated or refusing to work. Inevitably students' understanding of how children learn and what gets in the way of learning (including teacher expectation and teacher materials) increased when they were forced to spend periods of time with a single pupil.

We also encouraged the students to observe their pupil in his or her ordinary classroom setting. This immediately offered insights into the child's attitude to work, relationships with the class teacher and other pupils, personality, level of engagement with the task in hand and such like. In the busy round of classroom life, how often is a teacher able to observe a single pupil in this way?

Some of the practice adopted by the students was quite simply inspirational — they found the key to helping a child progress. This often involved personal qualities of non-judgmental warmth and affection for the pupil (not always immediately achieved — some pupils understandably put up barriers which were hard to overcome) as well as qualities associated with teaching, like patience, positive feedback and the ability to excite a child's interest by the use of attractive and meaningful materials. We were most impressed by the high standards reached in these case studies: they were more than academic exercises for the students — they were about a relationship between two people where the more mature helps to guide the understanding and increase the confidence of the less mature.

What follows are extracts from students' assignments which we have commented on to highlight significant issues for the purpose of this chapter. The students' names are genuine: the pupils' are not.

GILLY BAYES AND 'JASON'

Jason's class teacher described his parents as 'care-worn and passive with two demanding and needy children'. She said they seemed to discuss him in an objective and detached way as though he were a stranger. As a baby he had been 'undemanding and placid' and his mother only noticed he wasn't talking when people said he 'wasn't normal'. Most of all his class teacher observed that his parents appeared to live side-by-side with Jason rather than to be involved with his life. (I noticed that when he was in the playground, on the climbing frame, he played alongside the other children, not with them. The children did not ignore him, they just moved round him). Hence it seemed apparent that a major factor in Jason's speech delay was the marked isolation and lack of conversation during his time at home. He was physically well looked after and there was plenty of toys and games, but little of the social interaction that is necessary to stimulate his speech development.

My observations seemed to show these problems. I observed Jason whilst he was attempting to write his news. He sat at the front of the class facing the blackboard, but he kept turning round to look at whatever was going on behind him, and when his teacher asked him how he was doing, one of the other children replied, 'He's too busy looking round'. His concentration was obviously very limited. When he started to write, at first he used the wrong paper. He could not spell the word 'and' and only wrote 'a'. When the teacher asked him to make it say 'and' he wrote 'a' 'e'. He had problems with every word that he wrote and put fullstops after each word he attempted. I was not surprised then that his motivation was so low — when every word was wrong and it was so difficult to write anything down correctly.

Watching and helping him in a maths lesson, I saw that he became very excited when he was able to read the simple instructions and measured lines with his ruler correctly. He was so pleased and satisfied with himself when he succeeded that I knew then, I would have to find something to work on with him where he could *only* succeed. Jason's spoken language, I found, was very limited, and he would leave out words and the ends of words just as his parents do. His teacher reported that they spoke quietly and rapidly so that it was often difficult to distinguish meaning.

His teacher had been trying to teach Jason his letter sounds but felt that even though he was not quite ready, she would see if he could read a simple story. He snuggled up to her to begin reading, seemed to recognize certain words and made good guesses about the story-line. With encouragement he used the pictures as cues and managed some phrases. However, when he was corrected, he often refused to accept the correction and repeated the word he had uttered first. He had great problems with basic but abstract words such as 'was', 'but' and 'you'. His teacher always asked him if he thought he had done well, hence encouraging self-assessment. I realized that it is important for all children to be able to judge their own performance and feel pleased with a good result as this will lead them to rely less on outside praise.

Therefore I felt that isolated exercises would be meaningless to him without a context and would not help to build up his confidence. As a result, I decided to concentrate on building up his communicative competence, specifically by using contextual picture cues. I thought this would aid his reading and also give meaning to the written word. I thought that perhaps if he realised that words and sentences had a purpose he would be more greatly motivated and would see that reading and communicating were necessary and important for meaning only, not as an experience isolated from meaning.

As a result, I devised four lessons which would endeavour to encourage Jason to communicate. I decided he would benefit most from building up his own story based on a sequence of pictures, in order to develop communication, enlarge his vocabulary and create something meaningful for him to read — meaningful because they were *his* words and he would know where they had come from.

In the first lesson I used a little pictorial story drawn by Heath Robinson, since the story was simple but the pictures had been drawn for adults. I wanted to see how Jason would react to the story and whether eventually writing a book based on picture cues would be a viable proposition. Together we looked at each picture in turn and after some small discussion I wrote down exactly what he wanted to say. At the end, with help, he read back what we had written.

The lesson was successful in that Jason enjoyed it and found the story amusing. He felt he had achieved something by seeing all the words I had written down and knowing they were his words. But most importantly, although he had had great difficulty finding the right words and I had to prompt him fairly often, he had had the opportunity and had used it to create.

I decided to use *The Snowman* by Raymond Briggs next. It seemed ideal because it was deliberately designed without words and would appeal to a large variety of ages. I was able to edit it to half its original length without losing its magic. I photocopied the relevant pages, cut out the pictures, coloured them and arranged them on card in a book form: a book to be written by Jason, for him, with his own words. I aimed to use *The Snowman* as a springboard for talking and communicating, giving him the opportunity to analyze the pictures and describe the events. I also wanted to boost his confidence by completing a piece of work created by him over a period of three one-hour sessions. I planned to write down exactly what he wanted to say and then to read it back to him, or let him read, so that he could change anything he was not happy with. I also taped all the lessons so that I could transcribe and evaluate them closely later. I typed up his words to go with the relevant pictures, but since the completed 'book' would be for Jason to keep, I decided to correct his tenses so that it would make grammatical sense and be a good example for him to refer back to.

I was worried that an hour would be too long and I would not be able to hold his attention for that length of time, but the excitement, particularly in the first lesson, of producing his own book and seeing his ideas on paper and then in print motivated him sufficiently. I was also determined to remain aware of the types of question I was asking Jason, varying them from 'What colour is his jumper?' to 'What do you think happened next?' and 'What do you think he's saying?' in the belief that they might provoke him to express himself.

In the first lesson using *The Snowman* I explained to him that we were going to look through the story and he would tell me what was happening on each page so that when I had typed up what he dictated to me, he would have written a whole book which would say 'By Jason' on the front cover. He seemed very pleased by this. It was important that the pressure was not on Jason to have to write, and that was why *I* wrote so that he just had to concentrate on talking.

Soon after the lesson began it became apparent that Jason had seen the film of *The Snowman* and often, as a result, he drew on his knowledge about the film to describe what was happening, including information which could not have been extracted from the pictures themselves. He also used words from the limited reading he had experienced in the two previous weeks. He called the boy in the story 'John' (the name of the main character in his reading book). He also took phrases from the work we had done the week before, describing the wheel in Heath Robinson's pictures and the snowball in the same way: 'It got bigger and bigger and bigger.' I was extremely pleased about this because I thought that if he naturally drew on his previous experiences, however limited, as these experiences grew, and given the opportunity, he would be able to do so more and more, thereby enriching his vocabulary and building up his communicative competence very naturally.

When I played back the first lesson, I realised just how much I had had to initiate the conversation and how much I had spoken. I had had to work very hard at times to gain responses from Jason, and when I did, many consisted of one word answers or underdeveloped phrases. Hence, in order to extract a whole sentence, I often had to ask a series of questions. Often Jason would opt out of answering by replying 'Don't know!' and I had to be very firm with him.

Later when I was able to examine Jason's story in detail, I realised how long it took to build a single sentence. Seeing the transcripts helped to illustrate for me the complex process our brains must go through each time we utter a phrase and the opportunity to see the process slowed down was fascinating. Jason often had the ideas and had interpreted the pictures quite successfully but he found it such a struggle to sort the ideas into a coherent form. At times he found it so difficult to call on the limited vocabulary that he had, that he would opt out. However when he did discover the correct word he was delighted, and this gave him a great impetus for continuing. I also found that because I always repeated what he said, and had to write it down, this helped him to clarify some of his muddled, haphazard thinking. It also gave him the opportunity to hear the sentences he had created and to alter them if necessary.

Having listened to all three lessons on tape, I realised how much of an improvement Jason had made by the end of the third. In this lesson, when I asked him questions his replies were longer and more coherent. He self-corrected more and his descriptions and discussion were more exciting. Jason knew he had improved. He described John trying to sleep beautifully (extract from the tape-recording): 'The boy can't go to sleep...he's thinking...about the Snowman...he turned over this way and that way...he went under-cover...John did...to try to sleep...he turned over and backwards...no! back and front...this way and that...Can we show it to the class?'. With help from my questioning Jason really created the restless sleep which John, in the pictures, was having. Perhaps he had been able to describe it best because it was something he had also experienced: it was almost poetic in form as well as logical and coherent. He had self-corrected and described the action meaningfully. When I asked him what he thought about the work he had done he said, 'It's good!' and it was. He was proud of it, and when he showed it to the rest of the class, they all reacted delightfully. One of the boys asked, 'Did you do this, Jason? It's really good!'. Jason grinned from ear to ear. He felt he had really achieved something and his ego had definitely been boosted.

I very much enjoyed the time I spent at the school. The class teacher was a great inspiration to me and I learned a lot from Jason as well. I think that if possible every student should have the opportunity to work with children with special needs and to understand how this kind of teaching compares with that of mainstream education. Most of all we should learn how to 'slow the system down to make the children shine'.

★★★★★★★

These extracts from Gilly's file provide apt evidence of her appreciation of the teachers with whom she was working and how she learned from them. It is an example of the painstaking preparation students were prepared to undertake to help their pupils gain success. Gilly seeks to understand her child from the inside out — to relate to him first as a person and only then to concentrate on his academic progress. Her sensitivity to his needs is moving to read, as is her delight at his achievement.

ANNE-MARIE WALKER AND 'PHILIP'

The Warnock Report's statistics of 'one in five' took on human form for me when, on my second-year teaching practice, I was confronted with over a fifth of the class requiring special educational provision. Allowance made for a predicted ability range did nothing to prepare me for the degree of difficulty experienced by these children, and it was with this background that I opted for the third-year special needs element.

I chose to work within an ordinary, maintained school, and was introduced to a 10–year-old boy who, for the purposes of this paper, I shall call Philip. Philip had a long history of academic difficulties throughout the curriculum. Reading was highlighted as the primary cause for concern, being last measured as a thirty-two month deficit to his chronological age.

During assessment I established a wide sphere of reference, employing miscue analysis, comprehension and recall questions, and a reading questionnaire in an informal setting. From this, I was able not only to identify a specific weakness, that of sequencing, but also to build up an overall picture of Philip's strengths and attitudes which could counterbalance his problems.

From this standpoint, I set about devising a personalized scheme of work to address his sequencing difficulties, particularly with regard to reading comprehension. I soon found published sources to be inadequate, making too many assumptions and missing significant bridging stages. I was thrown back on my own resources, and through trial and error in a mutual learning experience, the clear stages of a scheme evolved, comprising:

Concept — pictures — pictures and sentences — sentences only.

The scheme built on Philip's positive strategy of looking to pictorial cues, using this as a 'way in' to the sequencing of sentences. This factor also influenced my choice and production of material, which originated from a wider range of sources than I had initially anticipated. For example, P. Woolcock's *Busy Days,* a book on time, provided sentences clearly indicative of order, in addition to animated pictorial accompaniments.

I was able to chart Philip's progress by means of continual assessment, and working on this stage-by-stage individual basis brought to my attention a number of points about the way in which learning occurs.

Firstly, the *ad hoc* nature of the learning process became obvious when we followed up natural digressions, enabling Philip to learn whatever he needed to know and seemed relevant to him at the time. Secondly, the way in which learning occurs incrementally meant that some of our most profitable work on reading also assimilated the aspects of talking, listening and writing, with the sequence topic becoming the common nucleus which bound these aspects together. Thus, in our culminating activity — the production of a book — the germinating idea was a discussion of a picture sequence which then provided a framework for writing. Finally, one of the most frustrating aspects about trying to elicit learning must surely be an inability to make oneself understood. No matter how straightforward a statement may appear to be or how clarifying an example, there will be times when the teacher and pupil seem to be on 'different wavelengths'. Presenting Philip with a picture designed to reinforce the sequencing concept, I gained an insight into the root cause of this, since he did not perceive the dimension of the picture in the same way I did. This indicates the very different world picture the child possesses, and which the teacher must aim to address.

The intensity of the one-to-one situation instigated innumerable instances of success, failing and re-thinking. In the same way as I valued Philip's more general improvements in terms of class presence and motivation, I sought to derive from the experience wider issues applicable to the classroom situation. The common platitude 'Begin with the child' had taken on renewed meaning. Merely presenting the same material at a lower level no longer seemed a viable manner of working, but by taking the lead from the child, his motivation and needs, I had found that more personally relevant and potentially successful learning could take place.

★★★★★★★

Again, impressive documentation of a student's determination to carve out the best strategies to help her pupil by providing materials and activities she thought appropriate to his needs. It is a pity that we cannot include some examples of the very large amount of beautifully made materials which Ann-Marie produced for Philip. Moreover, she became aware that he was uneasy at apparently being singled out for help, so she included another child in her work, thus giving Philip a sense of security and normality.

JANE CLARKE AND 'LISA'

During the preliminary visit, I initially observed Lisa at work on a comprehension. It was immediately clear that her concentration was so low as to be almost nil: she would glance at the passage and then into space, perhaps write two or three words and then, more than likely, rub them out. When I asked her if she would like to read the passage to me, she refused, saying, 'I've got to get on with my work.' She had her exercise book directly below the line she was trying to read and she actually fought me when I tried to move the book further down the page, suggesting she would be able to read the passage more easily. Her spoken language was very aggressive, most of her answers being sharp retorts of one-word answers. I found this very interesting as, in my experience with children of all abilities, there are very few who do not enjoy telling you what they are doing. This lack of concentration and confidence, shown by the continual rubbing out, dominated Lisa's work. It was difficult to judge her actual ability as regards reading or writing because she really did very little of either. However, it was clear that Lisa was unable or unwilling (unable because she was unwilling, or vice versa?) to read the passage in front of her: she needed help with every word, and would frequently turn the card with the passage on it over, saying she did not need to read the passage to be able to answer the questions. It was this that suggested to me that it was Lisa's difficulties with reading that were at the heart of her language problems. It was also clear that Lisa's attitude to her reading was playing a major role within these problems.

I felt it necessary to give consideration to *why* Lisa's emotional state was getting in the way of her successful reading, to decide if my work with her could be based around her reading, and if so, in what specific area. It is perhaps to Lisa's disadvantage that the school she attends engages in a large amount of very factual work and has a high number of bright, highly-motivated children. When I observed Lisa initially, the comprehension passage described the migrating habits of birds, and it clearly had very little meaning for her.

It was in this word 'meaning' that I felt Lisa's problem regarding her attitude to reading lay. It was because she was gaining no meaning or understanding of the passage in front of her that she could not concentrate sufficiently to be able to answer the questions. I was interested to receive confirmation of this view in a fascinating study called *Achieving Literacy* by Margaret Meek. It seemed obvious that Lisa's lack of confidence, fuelled by her own feelings of inadequacy, came at least in part from the unsuitable — for her — material she was working with. It also seemed clear that to work with Lisa on a series of word games, concentrating on a specific skill, would be a waste of time. It was her fear of reading and reading material that had to be tackled first.

I went into my first session having in mind the possibility of eventually narrowing the focus of my study to reading for meaning. However, I needed firstly to pin-point her needs more definitely within the area and assess her current strengths and weaknesses in more detail.

Lisa was obviously not enjoying her reading: she could not remember the title of her reading book, or any detail of what it was about. She was not familiar with the word 'author' or even 'writer' or favourite characters. Conversation with her was once again difficult:

ME: Do you have any books at home that you like to read?
L: No...don't know.
ME: None at all?...If you did, you could bring them into school and we could read them together.
L: Well — me and my sister — me sometimes read Winnie the Pooh with her.
ME: Do you — which Winnie the Pooh have you read?
L: Mmmm...me no know, me don't (bubbling noise with mouth).
ME: Was it *The House at Pooh Corner*?
L: No! (aggressive).
ME: You don't have to shout. Was it *When we were very young*?
L: Mmmm...might of...dunno.
ME: There are some good poems in one of the Winnie the Pooh books. Have you read any of those?

L: No...don't like poems.
ME: Why not?
L: (No answer)
ME: Why don't you like poems, Lisa?
L: Dunno (shrug, giggle).
ME: Do you ever write your own poems in class? Sometimes you can write
       a poem instead of a story in class. Do you ever write a poem?
L: Me...no...me don't like poems.

I decided finally on reading for meaning as my focus narrowed. After advice from my college tutor, I felt that I would endeavour to do this through giving Lisa, as best I could in such a short time, an interesting and varied reading experience, including both poetry and stories, and involving the skills of listening and spoken communication. I wanted at least to begin to break down her wariness of written material, which I am sure is central to her competence in language. In short, I intended to take the positive factor of Lisa's language position and capitalize on them.

As far as the scheme of work for Lisa was concerned, my most necessary task was to have a definite aim for each session, even if this had to be changed. For the first session, I intended to try to get to know Lisa more, and also to allow her to get to know me: I set up a casual, informal situation, whereby we could discuss her feelings about reading. The first session was difficult as I found it hard to warm to Lisa. Her lapses into baby talk were intensely annoying, and I corrected her too much for this which was, of course, her intention.

I planned for the second session with this in mind. She had a toy owl with her at the first meeting and so I decided to try taking in some owl poems and really concentrate on what the poems are saying. Although it was not directly relevant, I planned to get Lisa to compile a selection of words which she felt described an owl, based on her own owl and the owls from the poems we were going to read. I wanted her to think about the words and put them in her own context. I was delighted to see that the owl poems had her attention immediately: 'Owls! Me got an owl — he came to school with me last week'.

I had brought in several poems, and I probably pushed her attention to its limits. Despite this, she read the poems — I read them first — with amazingly good expression and a vague awareness of punctuation. Her actual reading was better than I had heard it before, though her word recall was poor. Her enjoyment of the poems was clear and she even asked to read one again. She was not very keen to write any words, so I wrote several to start off, and she soon joined in with her own. When the list was complete, Lisa arranged the words in an order she liked. It was fascinating for me to see her actually using words to create a visual picture, and also to see her so proud of her work. It was clear that Lisa was still very wary of reading, although she has proved easier to motivate than I had anticipated. She was still using the baby voice, but I found it slightly easier to cope with. I hoped that if I ignored it, she might possibly stop using it.

Having broken down Lisa's initial hostility towards me, I felt that the next session could be concerned with listening and talking as well as reading. I prepared a session around the tape of the story by Raymond Briggs, *The Snowman*. As I also have the book, which has pictures but no words, I wrote out captions onto cards which came from the tape and the idea was that Lisa should ready the captions and fit them to the pictures in the book. By doing this, I felt that she would have the help of both tape and pictures to aid her reading, and because the captions were very simple, she would generally be successful. The session began badly as Lisa had an ulcer in her mouth which she was determined I should be made aware of. Due to this, my idea of talking about cold weather and snow fell very flat. I decided it was better to proceed with the tape. Lisa loved the story of *The Snowman*: she was totally caught up in it. She was keen to read and fit the captions to prove she knew what the tape had said, and she read the words on the cards intelligently, searching the pages of the book for the picture that would fit: 'The boy ran down the stairs'; 'The snowman put on a big hat'. Here was a child who, despite her fear of reading, was enraptured, to quote Meek, by 'an author who genuinely wants to tell a story'.

This was the first session where I felt that Lisa had done more work than me! She was really putting a lot of effort into listening and converting what she had heard into words. Due to the success of this, I carried it on for two sessions, and even after this, Lisa still wanted to hear the tape again!

I planned to read *The Owl and the Pussycat* with Lisa. I found a beautifully illustrated copy (by Gwen Fulton) and felt that an initial interest could be aroused by the familiar presence of the owl. I wanted to show the book to Lisa first and find out if she was familiar with the poem, and if so, what she knew about it. I wanted her to look at the pictures and try to say what they were showing.

This was the first time that Lisa showed an interest of her own accord in what I had brought. She picked up the book while I was taking off my coat and began to look at the pictures. The discussion went better than I had hoped:

ME: This book has some really lovely pictures...
L: Mmmm...like that one (laughs).

ME: Can you...
L: Oh...he's playing a...um...a glittar.
ME: A guitar, yes he is.
L: My owl can't do that.

Her reading of the text was of a very good standard. For the first time, I noticed that she was more prepared to try correcting her own mistakes, something she had never done before. She did not always get it right, but the effort was certainly there. It was at this point, I think, that Lisa actually began to enjoy reading a text. Although her interest in the book waned about half-way through, it had definitely been present. She drew a picture from the book and she searched through to find a good view of the owl's face. When she found what she wanted, she used it for the owl's features and then disregarded the rest of the picture to draw him with a guitar, an image which had clearly stayed in her mind.

I used some of my allotted time to observe Lisa within the classroom. It was a maths lesson, and I made sure I did not have any contact with her. Once again, her concentration was very low. She had a rubber with her which was in the shape of a pair of glasses, and her main aim was to use this as much as possible. She did not just use one part of the glasses to rub out — she had to take the whole rubber to pieces, rub out what she wanted, and then re-assemble the glasses. She spent literally ages engaged in this as she followed the same procedure every time. She was sitting by a dominant, bossy girl, who interfered with her maths frequently: 'No Lisa, that's wrong — you *always* do that wrong!'. Lisa seemed aware of the girl next to her but gave no real response, apart from changing her maths answers. She had no real communication with any of the children on her table: she seemed to listen to their conversation, but rarely took part in it. Most of her time was spent gazing into space, chewing her pen or playing with the toy glasses.

The final session had a difficult start, when Lisa was very negative. Then she showed me a story she had written at home. It was about keeping a dog as a pet. I asked her if she would like to read that to me and she agreed. Although the actual written words did not make sense, Lisa read it as if it did, and it sounded coherent and interesting. Following this, we discussed some of the ideas in her story — what sort of dog she would like, and she also talked about her grandmother's dog, of whom she was clearly very fond. After this, she was far more relaxed and the book of nursery rhymes I had brought worked well, though we only had time to read one or two.

Despite the patchy start to the final session, I felt that from Lisa's point of view the course had been successful: I was sure she enjoyed the reading we did, and she became more responsive, both to me and to the reading. She is an unpredictable child: her attitude can change from minute to minute. It would be foolish to be confident that I had been able to open the wide doors of literature to Lisa. I do not feel that is so, but I do feel that I was able, just a little, to allay her crippling fear of reading by showing her that words in themselves could be fun and could be enjoyed. I do not think she will ever be a reader for pure pleasure, but if all I did for her was to show that books and poems are not to be fought, not to be hidden away from, then it was worthwhile.

From my own point of view Lisa was a valuable challenge. It was marvellous when she did respond to words and it was clear that she was reading for meaning. It was excellent experience in selecting materials and a good opportunity to see exactly what is available for teaching in this important area.

★★★★★★★

It isn't always easy to help a child with learning difficulties, as Jane's honest account makes clear. Once again a student demonstrated patience, tolerance and persistence, refusing to accept the child's negative self-image and gradually aiding that child towards a measure of success and pleasure in reading.

CLARE PIGGOTT AND 'JOE'

I first observed Joe working as part of a SERC group on a combination of listening and writing skills based around a tape recording. This was supervised by one of the three special needs teachers within the unit. Joe appeared to participate fully in the group discussion and showed no lack of confidence in answering the teacher's questions. As I concentrated on Joe's speech patterns I noticed that his speech was unclear (by that I mean difficult to understand), especially when he became very eager to answer, and that he did not use complete words or sentences when he answered.

These speech observations became more detailed once I was able to speak to Joe alone. I was struck by his difficulty in discriminating between different sound clusters in isolation and within words. For example, 'struck' would be pronounced as 'druck'. The st, sk, str sounds were particularly difficult for Joe to produce. He never used plurals and he could not predict, which meant he could never make use of past or future tenses. I had to concentrate at all times on what Joe was saying to me because the mispronunciation of certain words meant I could lose his train of thought and make him self-conscious by asking him to repeat himself. At the same time he would skip over words making little effort to complete what he was saying. Joe is able to conceptualise but 'something inside his head' (for want of a better expression) stops him, or rather limits his means of communication. Joe knows what he wants to say, but has difficulty in saying it. The frustration this causes him must be enormous.

During the first session I spent some time talking generally to Joe. I felt this was necessary not only to try to identify more detailed speech difficulties but also to discover more about Joe himself: his likes, dislikes and interests. I thought that in doing this we would be getting to know each other better, and he would feel confident enough to make mistakes and not feel too self-conscious about corrections we would then make together.

I started to run into difficulties almost straightaway. Joe showed me a picture of a football match he had drawn. Pictures were to become the most important launch point for all my work with Joe. He is a keen footballer himself and a member of the school team.

J: Half time we break up and get some grink and er...
C: What kind of drink?
J: Cocoa and lemerlade
C: Mixed together?
J: Yer.
C: Mixed together. Ooo! Does that taste nice?
J: And er...and er...some, a bi-tit, two bit-tits, and then we start playing. So. We win.
C: What kind of biscuits do you have?
J: Um...Chocolate bit-tits.
C: Chocolate biscuits.
J: And we win.
C: You say biscuits for me. Biscuits.
J: Bib-tits.
C: Biscuits.
J: Biss giss.
C: Biscuits
J: Bits iss
C: It's a difficult word isn't it?
J: Bit-tits...and er...we...
C: Biscuits.
J: Bi...
C: Biscuits. Say Bis.
J: Bis.

C: Gits.

J: Gits.

C: Biscuits.

J: Bit–tits. And...er...we won two nil.

I am not a qualified speech therapist and I feel the way in which I 'split' the word biscuits was not effective and of no probable use to Joe. It only seemed to confuse him more. Biscuits is however a difficult word to say. Perhaps 'buss–kits' would have been more effective.

However the transcription as a starting point is of considerable value. It illustrates Joe's disordered phonology and problems with auditory discrimination between different sound clusters, e.g.:

drink = grink;   chocolate = chotox;   lemonade = lemerlade;   biscuits = bissgiss.

I realised from this that I needed to speak very clearly and make use of repetition to help Joe produce more difficult words. Following Joan Tough's 'uses of language' technique proved very useful in assessing Joe's progress. When he and I talked about football, his use of language was in *reporting on a recalled experience*. The strategies he employed were those of:

1.   Labelling: he identified positions on a football pitch.
2.   Referring to detail: he noted team colours.
3.   Referring to incidents: he talked of the walk from the changing area onto the actual pitch and what it felt like, using the present tense.
4.   Referring to the sequence of events: the way the game was played and its outcome — present tense.
5.   Reflecting on his own feelings: what the winners felt — present tense.

From this short analysis I hope it is clear that Joe's limitations do not affect his imagination.

For the last session, I decided to base the discussion on Joe's own picture about an underwater adventure. He was keen to tell me about it.

J: That diver that me. I dive down and get the measure.

It was surprising to me that he should so suddenly and so easily become the diver, as he had shown little evidence of entering into role during the past weeks. He explained that the water was warm because of his air bank and that he was also warm because of his clothes. He even cut me off in mid-sentence to tell me what happened while he was diving. I was delighted by this as it added to my growing conviction that he was improving his communication skills, and will continue to do so. 'Suddenly shark bit Joe on the hand and leg.'

C: What did you do to the shark?

J: *Killed* him with my spear.

Joe was visualising himself, spear in hand, attacking the shark. He even made the sound effect of the spear biting into the shark. But the shark did not give up easily and it was only after he had hit it with a piece of metal from the ship which contained the treasure, and enlisted the help of a dolphin, that the shark actually died.

C: Did he get away?

J: She/he did.

C: He did?

J: No.

C: He didn't get away?

J: He ded.

C: He did get it out?

J: No. He's dead.

Because of my slowness in identifying the word 'dead', Joe corrected himself, and did so very clearly indeed.

This was undoubtedly the most successful story discussion Joe and I had. He showed himself to have little need of my assistance, and perhaps more importantly, he used appropriate tenses and completed many of his words. It was an excellent note on which to end our work together, and I hoped that Joe would retain something of what we had shared in learning.

This case study has been invaluable to me as I have had the opportunity of working on a one-to-one basis with a child who has communication difficulties. I have learned a great deal about the very nature of communication and the ways in which a teacher can promote an environment in which a child feels confident enough to learn to verbalize effectively. How much Joe learned is however questionable; it is far easier to note his difficulties than to assess the impact of my teaching. But I have at any rate come to realise that apparent inability to express oneself does not mean that the language is not actually there.

****

Here we see another example of a student moving from 'corrector' to 'enabler', while using careful analysis to try to understand her pupil's difficulties and capabilities, and so develop strategies to help him achieve some success, however limited. It is edifying to see Clare's growing belief in Joe's abilities, which must have communicated itself to him, and so contributed to his success.

ANDERLEY KNOWLES AND 'MARTIN'

Results of the COP test taken in 1985, when Martin was 7 years old, showed him as having poor sight, poor communication skills, a poor memory for letter sequences, little phonic knowledge and generally a low reading and writing ability. Up to February 1987 he had also missed approximately a term's worth of school time as a result of short periods of illness, had frequent tests for astigmatism, short sight, dyslexia and possible hearing defects and is further handicapped — according to his parents — by a family history of spelling difficulties. Class work and participation also suggest an inability to form continuous curves on paper, poorly executed letter formation using wrong stroke directions, poor general coordination, a strong tendency to be a loner and, most importantly, a low self-image.

It would appear from the above information that Martin severely lacks many of the vital characteristics associated with the child that fits in well at school, makes good academic, social and emotional progress and takes the skills of reading and writing in his or her stride. To a certain extent this deduction is true, yet work with Martin has shown just how dangerous such assessment would be, as Martin, in fact, shows many positive qualities and abilities which emerged more and more in each session. Martin has a great deal more potential than may at first be apparent.

If Martin was clearly backward in all aspects of learning then his low self-image in terms of reading and writing would be immediately understandable. However, there is substantial evidence to show that Martin is an intelligent child with a vivid imagination and desire to learn and understand. When assessed against the British Abilities Scales and British Picture Vocabulary his visual IQ was only 65–73, but his verbal IQ was above average at 115–123. This verbal ability is always apparent when talking to Martin as his sentences are well formed and often fairly complex in structure, and he has a varied vocabulary. That he enjoys putting his ability to use was also shown by the fact that when given the chance to dictate, and relieved of the practicalities of spelling and writing, Martin produced an excellent piece about sea creatures and his own imaginary monster. The opening not only contained a wide variety of different creatures but showed evidence of both imagination and factual knowledge at work. It was also very noticeable that as the dictation progressed, so his speed decreased as he watched me and appreciated that words could not be written as fast as they were spoken. This shows him observing the difficulties of writing, taking them into account and understanding the problems of another. Martin realised that he was not the only one to struggle and that nothing 'superhuman' was expected.

After the piece about the sea creatures Martin could not wait to dictate another passage about his own monster. The danger of his becoming passive and exploiting the situation arose as, after being allowed to dictate, he was very unwilling to struggle with writing for himself, but we came up with a mutually satisfying compromise.

I thoroughly enjoyed working alongside Martin and attempting to get to the source of his problems. I feel that the most satisfying result of my time with him came from watching his confidence increase and with it, his trust in me. This led to a greater willingness to participate and to try where he had always failed before. Although physical problems appear to have been concentrated on a great deal, the session suggested that the greatest stumbling block is in fact to be found in Martin's own self-image. With increased confidence, progress at his own rate and opportunities to read for meaning and to experiment with varied activities that offer frequent yet earned success, there can be no doubt that Martin could make extremely satisfactory progress.

****

Anderley's description of her work with Martin demonstrates the careful attention the student gave to her pupil:

'Martin has shown just how dangerous such assessment (low achievement) can be, as he shows many extremely positive qualities and abilities which emerged more and more in each session.'

'Martin has a great deal more potential than may at first be apparent.'

'This verbal ability is always apparent when talking to Martin, as his sentences are well formed and often fairly complex in structure and he has a varied vocabulary.'

It also shows her determination to form her own opinion of her pupil and her wariness of a general negative assessment. She was on his side, looking for his strengths.

She is sensible enough to be aware that the advantages for the pupil of the teacher acting as scribe can lead to a reluctance to put pencil to paper, and she takes appropriate action. Most importantly, perhaps, Anderley discovers for herself what Margaret Meek so insightfully documents in *Achieving Literacy,* that the pupil's self-esteem is the single most significant factor in the whole enterprise: 'The greatest stumbling block is to be found in Martin's own self-image...'. Widsom indeed from a student at the beginning of her third year of training.

ELIZABETH GRIFFITHS

This short final piece was written for this chapter by a student who was in great pain from a back injury and had to stand up while writing. Despite her discomfort, she put great energy into her work with her child and even went swimming with her class every week in order to build a relationship with him outside the teaching situation.

Special needs from a student point of view: Elizabeth Griffiths

My experience of special needs children began when on teaching practice in Year one. During the away-based practice I was only allowed by the class teacher to work with the three children in her class who had special needs. The result of two weeks' work with these children was not very favourable, as I felt ready to give up with them and teaching, feeling I was getting absolutely nowhere. This resulted in my giving them little help and encouragement, as I was not enjoying what I was doing.

Because of this experience, when I went into my second year practice and was informed that I had another three special needs children, I was immediately daunted. However, after some thought, I was determined to make an effort to learn about them, what they were working on with their helper, and therefore how I could work with them in the classroom. Slowly I recognized that I had been totally wrong, and with help and encouragement, and treating them as I would any other child in the class, they would produce some very good work. Over the six weeks, I found they could do similar work to the rest of the class, but at first with a lot of help. Where their writing proved to be a problem — it didn't look as good as the others' — I used a computer with a printer (something I had to learn about myself!) so that they could proudly display their work as well, but I found that with encouragement their written work improved dramatically, and they wanted to spend extra time working on presenting good work for me. Time and effort gained their confidence, and with this they gained self-confidence.

This experience persuaded me to opt for the Special Needs courses in Year Three. Here I worked on a one-to-one basis with a child with severe learning difficulties, who could not even recognise letters of the alphabet.

****

Elizabeth worked very hard to find materials to interest her pupil. As part of her work, she devised a pictorial alphabet to help him learn some letters and words, and since he took pleasure in this, as something made especially for him, she made a complete picture alphabet during the vacation and gave it to him the following term. She, like many students, was concerned about the depth of the emotional relationship that had developed, and was worried lest the loss of that and the personal attention which had been so encouraging, should prove detrimental... One can only hope that some of the confidence he has gained will remain with him.

CONCLUDING REMARKS

Some students worked with older children whose hearing was severely impaired. They often had to learn to question their own attitudes to learning, particularly in fostering communication without insisting on correctness, as did Clare with Joe, a point made by Webster in *Deafness Development and Literacy* (1986). One became aware of the confusions between the concepts of deaf children and 'normal' language, and the need to modify vocabulary accordingly: 'What type of cereal do you like?' caused confusion because 'type' is to write with a machine. They realised the need to develop their pupils' social skills, taking them shopping, and finding strategies to promote some independent choice, for those who seemed over-protected, even if this only meant choosing an imaginary wardrobe from magazine advertisements.

Our extracts from students' case-studies perhaps give an impression of unqualified success. Students did not however underestimate their own difficulties, and one described working with a special needs child as 'challenging, frustrating and often depressing'. One of the most interesting studies was an analysis of what seemed to have been an unsuccessful attempt to teach a child simple ordering and categorising. The student reviewed her attitudes and strategies, reflected on how it must have seemed to the pupil, and decided how she would approach the task another time. What all seemed to have learned was the importance of building a relationship, and, that achieved, 'to learn to trust one's intuition', perhaps a remarkable statement from a third-year student in this age of universal testing.

During this course we worked with a good number of mainstream schools, some of which had specialised units, and several special schools. We were particularly lucky to include in that number the headteacher of a local special school who welcomed our overtures with enthusiasm, agreed to accept twelve students and supported their endeavours, with his staff, with generosity. This headteacher is one of the co-editors of this book, and it seems fitting, therefore, to touch on our relationship with his school in the final section of this chapter.

Until our course began, Homerton students' acquaintance with special education tended to be in terms of whistle-stop tours of Special Schools. However well-intentioned the tutors, Special Schools were seen as 'special' or 'different' and their pupils similarly categorised. Of course, most of our students took great interest in, and felt great sympathy for the pupils of Special Schools. However, in the light of new thinking about 'special needs' the old method did not seem very healthy or enlightening. Nowadays a great many of our students gain experience of pupils with special needs in mainstream classrooms, and soon realise that they have strengths and weaknesses, as all children do, the latter often being physical, not mental disability.

The headteacher and a number of staff of the Special School in question, the Lady Adrian School, visited Homerton on several occasions to discuss this course with us. Busy professionals took the time and trouble to try to meet the needs of our students. This was a genuine collaboration: we could not have run the course without them, and we needed their support and their suggestions.

Twelve students over six weeks visited the school roughly once a week to work with a child. Instead of taking a superficial look at a 'special school', the students became part of that school, got to know pupils and teachers, and were able to offer something back to the school — their serious attempts to help pupils learn. By the end of the course, the students were familiar with the working of a Special School, surprised how similar it was to an average Primary School, and aware of the type of child it catered for. The Special School had indeed become ordinary!

.

Section 5
Specialized Views

Chapter 13

The Special School as Part of a Whole-Authority Approach
Jim Muncey

Special schools are under siege. Much has been written about the problems they present in terms of both educational philosophy and practice (e.g. Booth, 1987; Tomlinson, 1982), so that the efficacy of an education separated from the mainstream is questioned. In such a climate do special schools have a role to play? If they do then what is that role, and if adaptations are required to the present style of provision can special schools make the necessary changes? Indeed, with the introduction of the Education Reform Act will it be necessary for special schools to change at all or will there be, as some writers suggest, a significant increase in demand for pupils to be formally assessed under the 1981 Education Act, with a view to being placed in special schools (Swann, 1987)? Whatever the outcome of legislation it can be agreed that significant changes are afoot for pupils with special educational needs. This chapter addresses some of these issues by examining the role that special schools have within the context of a Local Education Authority.

The majority of special schools are run by Local Education Authorities, primarily for pupils within the Authority. The provision that an Authority makes is inextricably linked with the policy of the Authority, so that it is necessary to consider developments within schools in the context of the controlling Authority. Indeed, it is felt that there is considerable inter-relationship between the provision made in any educational institution, the in-service offered to the teachers within that institution and the development of Local Authority policy. This inter-relationship is illustrated by Figure 13.1, which also indicates the factors which impinge upon these three major variables.

Some of these factors are local in their effects; some are national. Nevertheless the manner in which they affect developments in an Education

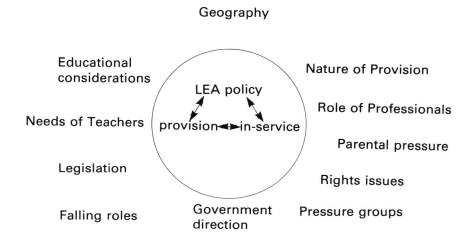

Figure 13.1: Policy, provision and in-service

Authority means that inevitably the developments within each Authority will be unique whilst there will also be some common threads between Authorities. This explains why, for example, an in-service programme developed in one Authority does not readily transplant to another Authority unless prior consideration is given to the differences, as well as the similarities, between Authorities. Some examples of the manner in which the different factors shown in Figure 13.1 affect the responses of an Authority will illustrate these points.

The last decade has seen considerable development in the 'rights' movement in special education so that now the education of pupils with special educational needs is viewed as one aspect of equal opportunities (Fish, 1985). Academics and formal representatives of this movement have expressed concern about the manner in which children with special needs are assessed and educated (Tomlinson, 1983; Newall, 1985), and parents have become more vocal, both as individuals and as groups, in stating their views about the education of their children (Family Focus, 1983). Activity by individuals and groups has been greater in some areas than others, as has the response of Local Authorities to their requests. Some Authorities have responded by examining their policy regarding provision for pupils with special educational needs and as a consequence have offered resources to support some individuals in mainstream schools. In other cases there has been an impact on in-service training which has focused on specific groups such as governors (Muncey and Winteringham, 1987).

Another example of the impact of different factors on Education Authorities is shown by considering some of the major educational considerations that have affected Authorities. Possibly, in the last decade, the greatest influence in this country has been the Warnock Report (DES, 1978) which made a number of recommendations about the education of children with special needs. The report itself was based on a review of both the national and international research carried out into the integration of children with special needs into ordinary schools (Cave and Maddison, 1978). The report stimulated much debate as it introduced a number of assumptions about the education of children:

- Any child, whatever his overall attainment level, may experience a difficulty at some stage in his school life.
- As the handicapped and non-handicapped do not present two discrete groups, special help and support must be available to all pupils when necessary.
- Educational difficulties result from an interaction between what the child brings to the situation and the programme provided by the school. The focus of concern therefore needs to move from within-child variables to examining the interaction of variables.
- Because it is now recognised that up to 20 per cent of all children have special needs at some stage in their school careers, all teachers have to be teachers of children with special needs.
- Support must be available to staff in mainstream schools to help them fulfil their responsibilities.

These assumptions have impacted on all Education Authorities, to a greater or lesser extent, and have affected policy-making, provision and in-service training of teachers. The legislation which then followed added extra impetus to the changes (DES, 1981a) although the caveats within the 1981 Act provide plenty of excuses for Authorities which do not wish to make any significant changes. Perhaps it is not sufficient to argue whether placement in an ordinary school is compatible with the child receiving the special educational provision that s/he requires, the provision of efficient education for the children with whom s/he will be educated, and the efficient use of resources; but whether or not placement in an ordinary school can be *made compatible* with these statements. If this is not taken to be the spirit of the legislation then the 1981 Education Act cannot be regarded as an instrument for change, as it requires Authorities to do little that is different.

Whilst such factors do affect provision, policy and in-service in a local Authority, it would be naive to assume that the relationship is as simple as is implied above. Influences on an Authority are frequently multifactorial and their impact is dependent on the state of play within the Authority. Change within an Authority has many of the characteristics of change within any institution. What can be relied upon is that to affect change within an

Authority is difficult, particularly if that change is to endure. However, to attempt to change institutions, such as special schools, while neglecting the relationship between the Authority and the institution, makes it exceedingly difficult to bring about significant changes. It can also lead to a conflict of interests between school and Education Authority.

These sorts of difficulties are seen when the relationship between the process of identification of pupils with special educational needs, and the support of such pupils, is examined.

One of the effects that the heightening of awareness of special needs through in-service training has had is that schools have become more adept at identifying pupils with special educational needs, with a view to offering appropriate support. The process can be considered to be a cyclical one, as illustrated in Figure 13.2.

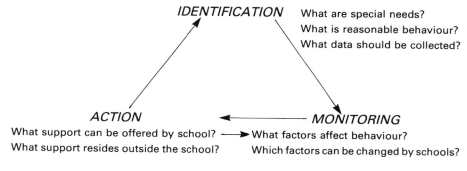

Figure 13.2: Identification, support and review

When considering the identification of pupils with special educational needs schools need to consider the following questions:

1. What is considered to be reasonable behaviour, both in terms of academic achievement and conduct? This needs to take account of the context in which the pupil's performance is being judged. So, for example, it would be reasonable to expect a child of 7 years to have acquired a significant sight vocabulary, but not a child of 4 years. Similarly, it is reasonable to expect that a child in a secondary school shows a regard for others by not fighting them or destroying their property. Such judgments are, however, rarely clear-cut, particularly when conduct is being considered rather than just academic achievement. For example, one child hitting another may be justified as reasonable by some people in certain circumstances. With conduct it is generally most useful to attribute problem status to a behaviour, on the basis of its implications for the development of the pupil and those with whom the pupil interacts.

2. What is a viable definition of special educational needs? Because special educational needs are related to context, the definition of a pupil's needs must take into account that context. Schools which have developed a policy for the identification of special needs generally seem to have evolved definitions along the following lines: with educational performance consideration is given to the schemes of work in operation, so, for example some schools have formulated a definition as follows:

— A child has special needs if extra help is required to allow that child to access the curriculum.

Similarly, context-related definitions exist for conduct, for example:

— A child exhibits problem behaviour if that behaviour interferes with the process of education.

When such definitions have been formulated it is generally after much discussion and debate about issues such as 'what is the process of education?' or 'how do you know if a child has access to the curriculum?' Nevertheless, the process of discussion that precedes the definitions should not be underestimated in its importance.

3. What observational data acts as evidence to support the view that a pupil has special educational needs? This data ranges from specific test results through to information about a child's performance or examples of particular types of work.

Once a school has gone through this process of identification, then the staff must look at the establishment of some form of monitoring process. This necessitates reviewing the factors which are affecting the attainment or behaviour of a pupil , and then deciding which of those factors can be readily affected by the teachers.

In many schools this process of identification and monitoring has been developed to a fairly sophisticated level. However, there is a third element to the cyclical process of providing for special educational needs in mainstream schools. This third element is the action which a school will take to support pupils with special educational needs. The particular course of action chosen will depend on a number of factors, some of which teachers will be able to affect within the classroom and some over which they will have little control. An important factor in this area is resources. This particular factor is both within the control of the teacher and also outside their control, depending upon the particular resources being considered. Schools have still some way to go in mobilising their own internal resources to be more effective, as well as capitalising on the resources in their Local Authority which are lodged in support services or special schools. However, in those schools which have relatively sophisticated support systems there remain difficulties in providing adequately for a number of pupils who are identified as having special educational needs. When this happens, the school resorts to the policy of the Local Authority.

This policy is frequently embraced in the 1981 Education Act. When this is invoked to look at what is necessary to support a pupil with special educational needs, then it is used rather like a blunt instrument and results in the pupil being ascertained as being in need of specialist provision. If this provision resides within a special school then frequently the pupil is transferred from mainstream to special school rather than the appropriate resources being transferred in the opposite direction.

Thus, in summary, after a period of identification and monitoring the school moves into a phase of action. Initially this action will be school-based and will be closely linked to the monitoring process. Whether or not the intervention is successful will depend on whether a high proportion of the factors affecting the pupil's educational needs are under the control of the school, and how well the school is organised to examine these factors. If the school affects no change, then other responses must be resorted to which ultimately involves the Local Authority. The Authority can then examine the case made by the school with a view to providing:

- support and advice on possible reorganisation;
- extra resources in terms of staff, facilities or materials;
- special education outside the school.

The less effective the first two factors are the more likelihood there is that the pupil will be sent to a special school.

The relationship between mainstream schools, special schools and the Local Authority is enhanced if all schools embark upon the development of a whole-school policy for pupils with special educational needs. This would appear to be more easily achieved in special than mainstream schools although one of the problems often encountered in both is that certain aspects of a whole-school policy can often be defeated by the operation of a whole-school policy in another area. This is because the inter-relationship of different policies is often poorly understood and is rarely the subject of analysis by the support services, the senior management of a school, or the whole school staff.

To illustrate this by an example it is useful to look at the manner by which many pupils are now being supported if they have special needs. Schools are examining how they can offer more in-class support to enable the pupils to access all aspects of the curriculum. Thus, whilst withdrawal still has its place, the notion of a separate remedial class is regarded with suspicion. This whole-school policy of offering in-class support to pupils with special needs may run alongside a policy for dealing with children whose mother tongue is not English by operating a system of withdrawal of pupils for special teaching.

When this happens staff (and pupils and parents) will start to ask questions such as:

- whose responsibility is it to educate the children?
- what is an equitable distribution of resources?
- are resources available to everyone?

While schools have no well-developed mechanism for collating the formation of policies in different areas this will continue to happen, as more cross-curricular initiatives develop and become subject to discussion at a whole-school policy level.

What then does a whole-school policy in special needs mean? It is suggested that it arises out of consideration of current educational concepts which are themselves influenced by society's attitudes and the needs of children. This initially becomes embodied in a policy which relates specifically to an identified group and suggests specific responses to this group. At a later stage there is recognition that a response to special needs is just one aspect of a school's response to individual need. This becomes embraced by a whole school policy, which is ultimately reflected in the ethos and traditions of the school. This process is shown in Figure 13.3.

Thus a whole-school policy is a policy which is understood by all and reflects educational principles which have been built on social philosophy. It in turn affects the whole school community as its purpose is to guide practice

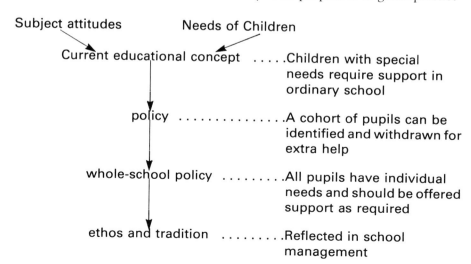

Figure 13.3: Development of school policy

and influence attitudes to achieve a school ethos consistent with the philosophy. The effects of the whole-school policy will be reflected in the management of the school in terms of:

- curriculum;
- school organization;
- classroom practice;
- attitudes and relationships;
- the physical environment;
- communication.

If special schools are going to become more prominent in supporting pupils with special educational needs then it is important for them to review their policies by examining where they overlap with the policies being developed in mainstream schools, and, in turn, how the policies relate to the policy of the Local Education Authority. The management of the school in terms of the factors mentioned above form a useful starting point by asking: what do special schools have to offer in these areas?

Possibly the most important area to consider is the curriculum as this is central to much of what goes on in school, and with the introduction of the Education Reform Act will undoubtedly become more prominent.

It is evident that the Government is keen to get agreement on:

- the purposes of learning;
- the contribution of each subject area;
- the organization and content of the curriculum;
- levels of attainment.

With respect to the purposes of learning, reference is made in *Better Schools* (DES, 1985a) to the purposes of learning stated in *The School Curriculum* (DES, 1981b):

1   to help pupils to develop lively, enquiring minds, the ability to question and argue rationally and to apply themselves to tasks and physical skills;
2   to help pupils to acquire understanding, knowledge and skills relevant to adult life and employment in a fast changing world;
3   to help pupils to use language and number effectively;
4   to help pupils to develop personal moral values, respect for religious values and tolerance of other races, religions and ways of life;
5   to help pupils to understand the world in which they live, and the interdependence of individuals, groups and nations;
6   to help pupils to appreciate human achievement and aspirations.

The priority accorded to these statements, and the inter-relationships between them, is left to decisions at a local level. However, it is such statements which are informing the development of the National Curriculum and which will therefore be of great relevance to special schools.

Whatever developments take place in the curriculum it is necessary for them to reflect the following principles — the curriculum should be broad, balanced, relevant and differentiated.

One of the interesting factors is that although special schools initially set about developing their own 'special' curricula for each group of pupils it is now widely accepted that, because all pupils deserve similar opportunities, special schools should have curricula that are not essentially separate or different from the curriculum found in mainstream schools. This view is reflected in a number of HMI reports which make reference to the limitations, rather than the differences, that exist in the curricula of both special and mainstream schools. It is therefore not surprising that it is proposed that the new legislation embraces the notion of a National Curriculum for all. Indeed, would it not be divisive if it proposed different experiences or access for different groups of pupils?

If there are now considerable similarities between the curricula found in special and mainstream schools, what then can special schools offer to colleagues within the mainstream?

In recent years many special schools have pursued the development of their curricula by examining the contribution that can be made by a behavioural objectives approach. Without wishing to explore the relative merits of this approach in curriculum planning there is nevertheless evidence to suggest that a systematic approach to the development of the curriculum is particularly important for pupils with special educational needs (e.g., Becker and Englemann, 1977). This is perhaps best summarised by Brennan (1979), who commented that the following weaknesses were apparent in a number of schools, which were examined in an attempt to describe the best practice in the country:

(a)   There was little evidence of attempts to plan the curriculum in terms of precise objectives, indicating the knowledge, skills, attitudes, values and sensitivities which pupils are expected to achieve.
(b)   Procedures for recording and evaluation were found to be inadequate.

If special schools have pursued a curriculum based on behavioural objectives then they are in a strong position to offer support with the following:

- the selection of appropriate targets for pupils with special educational needs that can be regarded as real, relevant, rational and realistic;
- the systematic analysis of such targets by the application of task analysis;

- the relationship of special programmes to other aspects of the curriculum, particularly in terms of the learning hierarchy (Haring *et al.*, 1978);
- the maintenance of skills acquired through systematic teaching;
- the development of appropriate assessment and recording techniques which can be used to monitor progress.

In addition to expertise in the curriculum, both at the level of the development of a whole-school policy and individual programmes, special schools have a wealth of experience of responding to the needs of individual children; that is, the schools are generally characterized by being pupil-centred, rather than, like their mainstream counterparts, curriculum-centred or even teacher-centred. Obviously, special schools enjoy some advantages which mainstream schools do not, such as being less constrained by external pressures like examinations, which allows greater flexibility in terms of the development of teaching approaches. This experience of dealing with individual needs is something that can inform the practice of all teachers to the benefit of all pupils. Certainly it can be argued that the difficulties experienced by some children throw light on general problem areas in education (Hart, 1986), and that developing strategies to respond to those with special needs can improve the quality of education for all (Hanko, 1986). In other words it is frequently the case that the principles of good practice for pupils with special educational needs are the principles of good practice for all children.

Alongside the pupil-centred approach to learning have developed strategies for involving pupils directly in the negotiation of their own learning. For example, in schools for children with moderate learning difficulties pupils may play a major role in selecting appropriate educational objectives to work towards; while in schools for pupils with emotional and behavioural difficulties the pupils may be involved in negotiating contracts which are aimed at bringing about changes in their behaviour. Whatever the strategies employed the teachers in special schools will have had useful experience of implementing them in educational settings, and it can be argued that where pupil progress is concerned the experience of the teacher is an important factor (Gray, 1979).

One of the encouraging things that can be noted on a visit to a special school is that the staff spend a lot of time talking to the children. They value what the child brings to the situation and will often be seen to demonstrate a flexibility in lessons which capitalises on the child's experience and interests. This attitude to learning in the classroom is also reflected at a whole-school level where, in many schools, a pupil's difficulties will be the concern of all the school staff. Although this is facilitated by the smaller size of special schools it is not the sole explanation, as is demonstrated by the effects of reduction in pupil numbers in mainstream schools. Here a decrease in size is often accompanied by the staff feeling threatened and less able to respond in a flexible child-centred fashion.

If special schools have some of the advantages mentioned above, why is this? Firstly, the schools are generally better resourced in terms of staffing, buildings and capitation. In addition to providing greater flexibility this also helps the staff accept their responsibility towards pupils with special educational needs. This is often an issue in mainstream schools, particularly secondary schools, where staff may feel that they are primarily a teacher of a subject rather than a teacher of children. Of course, mainstream teachers have also been led to believe that they do not always have the expertise to cope with pupils with special needs, and therefore that they would be doing them a disservice to try and provide for them within the mainstream. This is particularly the case where there is a flourishing special school sector, which was established before the change in philosophy towards the education of children with special needs. A high level of special school provision is also frequently accompanied by a plethora of support services, who as experts may also feel that they have an interest in supporting a view that ordinary classroom teachers cannot accept responsibility for the education of pupils with special educational needs. This notion of expert and separateness supports teachers in the view that when a pupil is transferred to a special school the special school is better able to deal with the child's needs. Whether this is, or is not, the case in terms of the curriculum, teaching methods, etc., it is the case that the teacher is more prepared to accept responsibility for the pupil. Thus, schools which cater for pupils with emotional and behavioural problems will have a higher threshold of tolerance to difficult behaviour than mainstream schools because the staff are employed to accept this role, and are paid to do so with the guarantee of a higher allowance.

Another important feature about the higher level of resourcing in special education is that it adds to the flexibility of provision, and makes it more likely that individual needs can be met. Indeed, the basic reason for embarking on assessment under the 1981 Education Act is that it makes it more likely that extra resources will be provided as the resources available to meet the pupil's needs at that point are regarded as inadequate. If mainstream schools were resourced at a similar level to special schools would there be anything that was then different about special schools? It is suggested that the following features may still be lacking: a child–centred approach, specific training and style of management.

It has already been mentioned above that because special schools are not subject to the same external pressures that affect the curriculum of mainstream schools they can afford to be more child-centred. This is reinforced by the teachers' view of their role as being able to respond to individual needs. In addition, many teachers have received specialist training in the education of pupils with special needs. This not only provides additional skills but also adds to the view that the teacher is charged with the responsibility of providing something additional. The size of the institutions also facilitates a consultative approach to management which may facilitate team-work, or a whole-school response to specific issues. The fact that there is a headteacher and recognised school structure, also adds to the status of the placement as well as the individual staff. Even a sophisticated staffing structure in the special needs department of a mainstream secondary school is unlikely to afford its members the same level of status as the senior management structure in a special school, despite the fact that salaries may be comparable.

All Local Authorities currently have specialist facilities, and many Authorities have started to review the place of these facilities in the overall structure of the Authority. What is it then that will facilitate the evolution of special schools?

First of all there are practical issues such as the deployment of resources and the effect of falling rolls. As numbers decrease in mainstream schools so there is a knock-on effect in special schools, although not necessarily in line with the drop in the mainstream (Mar Molinero and Gard, 1987). This may be due to a decrease in the flexibility of mainstream schools as staff are cut in line with the drop in pupil numbers, or it could be to do with the development, or lack of development, of Local Authority policy, as discussed earlier. Nevertheless, if numbers do fall within a special school then it is likely that this will increase the likelihood of staff wishing to diversify in order to protect their jobs. How may outreach programmes in special schools have been facilitated by a change in staff attitudes as a result of a drop in numbers?

Another factor that will affect the role of special schools is that there is a greater emphasis on support in mainstream schools, which is accompanied by a move towards the view that all teachers are teachers of children with special educational needs. This move towards support in mainstream is a result of a number of influences, which have an effect not only on provision but also Local Authority policy and in-service training, as was shown in Figure 13.1. These factors become even more influential if it is believed that the existence of special schools for some pupils is a statistical phenomenon. For example, why should 1 to 2 per cent of pupils with moderate learning difficulties be placed in a special school and not 0 to 1 per cent or 2 to 3 per cent? A small variation in the percentage recommended for such placement would have a dramatic effect on the roll of a school.

As numbers fall in Education Authorities so there has been a change of role in the support services, with a move towards a more advisory role, and less of an individual case-work model. Whether this trend can be sustained in the face of the new legislation remains to be seen, but at present it does lend itself to a model where the advisory function of support services is supplemented by the work of staff from special schools. Besides being practising teachers they also have the advantage of not being regarded as possessing expertise that cannot be easily acquired by teachers in mainstream schools.

Lastly, another factor that will impinge upon the development of special schools is that special and mainstream schools have resources, expertise and opportunities that could be viewed as complementary to mainstream schools. Special schools can offer resources and expertise which take the form of staff, materials and processes, and yet they lack some of the resources and opportunities of mainstream schools. For example, it is very difficult for a special school to offer the same degree of breadth in the curriculum, although it may be good at devising a curriculum that is relevant and differentiated. Again a number of initiatives are developing in mainstream schools which can be very relevant to the work in special schools. As an example, Technical and Vocational Education Initiative embodies a number of principles which are important for many special school youngsters, as is shown by an examination of the basic aims of the initiative:

- to allow students to achieve qualifications and skills which are of direct value at work;
- to help students to be better equipped to enter the world of employment;
- to assist students in understanding the practical application of the qualifications for which they are working;
- to help students become accustomed to using skills and knowledge to solve real problems;
- to emphasize the development of initiative, motivation and enterprise, as well as problem-solving skills and other aspects of personal development;
- to provide a bridge from education to work through planned work experience;
- to facilitate close cooperation between Local Authorities, industry, commerce and the public.

If special schools are to evolve then it is necessary for them to develop within the context of Local Authority developments. Dessent (1984) goes as far as arguing that changes in special schools are totally dependant on what happens outside special education, and that the future of special schools as resource centres, for example, will depend on the pattern of developments in the mainstream sector.

Some of the reasons why special schools need to look at developments within this context of the whole Authority include the problems related to change, the pattern of change within an area, the differences between managing resources and managing individuals, the role of support services, and the distribution of resources.

The problems of managing change are well documented and the myth of the hero innovator almost legendary (Georgiades and Phillimore, 1975). For an individual, or even a whole school, to try and bring about change in a large system like an Authority there has to be a receptive structure. If the Authority has already sanctioned the change through policies, both formal and informal, and its in-service training, it makes it considerably easier to work within the Authority to bring about change in the direction indicated by the policies and in-service. The DES (1985a) urges a consultancy model as one way of developing expertise, and yet there are very few large Local Authority-based in-service programmes aimed at facilitating the development of this consultancy model. Locally, the Special Needs Action Programme has tried to develop this model at primary school level by establishing a coordinator for special needs in each school, and involving the support services, including special school teachers, in the task of supporting the coordinators. The role of the coordinator is then to act as a consultant to colleagues, and support them in carrying out their responsibilities in meeting the educational needs of their pupils.

Thomas (1985) argues that the issue of integrating special sector resources and special sector personnel must be addressed by examining ways of moving from methods of helping individual children towards methods of managing resources, time and personnel within mainstream classes. Thomas goes on to suggest that what is needed is a method by which individual help can be offered to pupils with special needs in mainstream classes and that this can be done by investigating the use of room management techniques and zoning. Special school personnel are well placed to help with the development of such approaches, as many schools for pupils with severe learning difficulties, in particular, already have some training and experience which is of relevance.

The role of support services has already been touched on. Because of the key role played by these services in special education it is particularly important that they feel they are party to developments and have a role to play. Without this there is every possibility that they will be antagonistic to developments, or different services will rival each other for positions of authority and control over developments. This is particularly so when the question of resources is at stake. As special schools constitute a major resource within an Authority it is not surprising that support services are keen to control them, by, for example, regulating their supply of customers. Any change that is proposed has to take account of this. For example, if an outreach policy from special schools is developed, with the aim of supporting colleagues in mainstream schools, then it is necessary to involve relevant support services in both the development of the policy and its operation. Failure to do this is likely to result at best in those services that are excluded from the developments not supporting the developments, and at worst actively undermining progress that is made.

If special schools are to develop their role then how can they do so? They need to examine what is transportable; this includes the pupils! Currently the provision made for the majority of pupils in special schools means that they enter a school full-time, and almost invariably remain at the school for the rest of their school career. This is hardly surprising as the mainstream school which was originally not meeting their needs is unlikely to develop new strategies to do so, so that if a return is to be successful the onus is on the pupil to change. Other alternatives to full-time, permanent admission, should also be considered. These could include:

a)   The pupil is placed in the school with the specific objective of returning them to mainstream within a set period. This necessitates a detailed analysis of the objectives for the placement and for the special school to offer an approach which is likely to meet these objectives.

b)   The pupil is placed at the special school full-time, but for repeated short bursts. This requires the special school to offer a specific programme that needs to be repeated periodically in order to boost the achievement of the pupil or teach them new skills.

c)   The pupil is admitted to the special school on a part-time basis. This should theoretically allow the pupil to obtain the benefit of both the special school and the mainstream school, although there are frequently significant problems in terms of timetabling. However, with careful planning some of these difficulties can be overcome.

d)   Movement of the whole class of pupils into a mainstream school whilst keeping them together as a group. The merits of this approach include being able to make very specialist provision whilst giving the pupils access to a wide range of curricular experiences. The danger, however, is that the pupils end up being stigmatised, as were pupils placed in remedial streams.

A number of writers in the area of special educational needs claim that the most effective form of provision that can be made for pupils with special educational needs is in mainstream schools. This can only be done by increasing the resources allocated to mainstream schools to allow them to make adequate provision. Obviously, such provision can be very expensive and should not be viewed as a cheap alternative to making appropriate provision in segregated special schools. A compromise might well be to identify a cluster of schools and to make provision within these schools for specific pupils with special educational needs. Such a process might include the following:

a)   A comprehensive school and the feeder primary schools are identified as a *unit* for the allocation of resources.

b)   The comprehensive school is established as a resource centre for that unit.

c)   The Head of Department of that comprehensive school is given the responsibility for the coordination of the allocation of resources within the unit.

d)   A specific special school is attached to the unit to advise on the development of programmes/approaches for individual teachers.

e)   A named teacher for pupils with special educational needs is allocated to the unit to advise on the development of suitable resources for such children.

f)   A supply teacher is also allocated to the unit to work in feeder Primary schools to release the class teacher to work with the children with special educational needs.

As well as looking at provision for pupils it is important to examine how staff can be employed to maximum advantage. Possibilities include:

- the secondment of teachers to other phases of education, or other institutions catering for different special needs;
- appointing specialist staff to a cluster of schools;
- the interchange of staff for specific subjects or lessons; and
- the involvement of staff in the extra-curricular activities of other schools, or school-based staff development.

One way in which staff from special schools can be used is in the role of 'teacher consultant' (Jones, 1985). This role can be developed to avoid some of the pitfalls of 'the expert', and as explained by Jones can embrace the following four elements:

a)   acting as a consultant or enabler with subject teachers and class teachers in order to allow access to a broad curriculum, by means of the modification of objectives and resources;

b)   acting in a face-to-face teaching role with children who are in need of specialised teaching in the communication skills;

c) acting as an enabler in team teaching situations which may result from functional integration; and

d) acting as a consultant or enabler to parents of children with special educational needs.

The last aspect of development is the development of special schools as a resource base, as suggested in the Warnock Report. One of the advantages of using special schools in this way is that they are frequently very adept at attracting additional funding from commerce, industry and charitable sources.

In summary, some of the advantages that special schools have which can be used to good advantage within an Authority include:

— practising teachers who are well versed in the use of different approaches ranging from specific methodologies to management techniques;
— teachers who do not have the mystique of experts but who nevertheless can contribute much in the role of consultant;
— a child-centred approach which capitalizes on what the child brings to the situation;
— a concentration of resources which can be used across the curriculum;
— the possibility of offering a continuum of provision ranging from an alternative school to some form of part-time admission, or outreach provision within mainstream schools.

When looking at these developments it is useful for special schools to address the issues by discussion involving outside agencies, including education officers, as major developments are only likely to occur within the context of developments in the Authority. To facilitate this it is suggested that special school staff could address the following questions:

1. What professional skills do I have and how could they be used in other contexts?
2. How could I best support colleagues in mainstream schools?
3. How can I best complement the work of mainstream teachers?
4. Is it likely that our attitudes to meeting special needs is similar? If not what are the differences and why?
5. Is the timetable of the mainstream school and my school flexible enough to allow support?
6. What specific aspects of the curriculum I offer would enrich the educational diet of pupils in mainstream schools?
7. Do I possess particular knowledge, for example, of the range of support available, which would be useful to mainstream colleagues?

8. What interchange and communication is there between my school and other schools? How can it be improved?
9. Are there reasons for making provision more flexible? If so how can this be achieved?
10. What material resources do I possess that can be used by other teachers?
11. Are there specific initiatives in my school which would facilitate developments in other schools, or at least provide an example of an alternative approach?

Many of the developments referred to above are facilitated by appropriate policy development within an Authority. As explained, this policy not only affects provision, but also in-service training, just as the provision currently in existence, and the nature of in-service being run, can affect policy formulation. It is this relationship that makes it so necessary for developments in one sector, or phase of education to take place in conjunction with, and in the knowledge of, changes that are occurring in other areas. Failure to do so leads to developments taking place in a piecemeal fashion, which is unlikely to capitalize on the strengths of institutions, and the people in them, and is unlikely to endure.

Chapter 14

The View from the Education Office
Tom Peryer

If special schools did not exist would we now feel the need to invent them?

> Ah, solving that question
> Brings the priest and the doctor
> In their long coats
> Running over the fields.

It's a question which is not one that primary and secondary schools have to face; they can feel confident that there will always be a place in the scheme of things for them. That confidence is not one that even the best special schools can assume for themselves. They are under challenge and their response to that challenge will vary from enthusiatic acceptance of it, through to extreme defensiveness and hostility, or perhaps a hope that early retirement will come before the enemy actually reaches the gates.

It is now a commonplace of educational comment that the education service generally is inundated with an unprecedented series of initiatives, criticisms, demands and developments. The list of them is daunting and their acronyms bewildering. Somewhere on that list is special educational needs. That it is there is largely due to Warnock and the 1981 Act. Consequently, there has been a flourishing of research projects, conferences, publications and local authority reviews. At the same time, the voices of parents and pressure groups have grown louder and more insistent. Principally, the issue has been one of integration, but other examples include services for pre-school children, special educational provision in further education, speech therapy, etc.

An increased profile for special education is mostly to be welcomed, especially as so often in the past there has only been a superficial understanding of what happens in special education and special schools. With a heightened public awareness, the opportunities for improving the quality of education are more likely to be increased. At the same time the prospect of growth and development inevitably means change, and change is threatening, especially if it is initiated from outside. Even worse, if it comes from the Education Office! A sharpened awareness means greater scrutiny of what is actually on offer at the special school, as well as a knowledge of what other schools and authorities offer.

Expectations of what schools should offer is increasing all the time. Quite rightly, parents, psychologists and schools themselves require more than warm, secure environments which protect pupils from the rigours of ordinary society and schools, but provide only a basic curriculum with low expectations of what can be achieved, in and after school. The spotlight is there, but so is the pressure to perform well, and better than in the past.

Even so, the spotlight is an uncertain one. Keeping special educational needs to the forefront of people's minds is not easy, especially when so much else is competing for attention and resources. Special education has traditionally been marginalized and seen as an issue which is not 'my responsibility'. It is easily displaced to the bottom of the agenda or left off altogether. (For example, there is not much evidence that special educational needs were seriously considered during the drafting, or even the debates, on the 1988 Education Reform Act). It is, however, vital that everyone concerned with education is obliged to understand and work through seriously the issues concerning children with disabilities and special educational needs. A large measure of responsibility for ensuring that the needs of one in five are not ignored or glossed over will rest with special schools themselves.

Thus, special schools are faced with positive opportunities, but at the same time those opportunities are sometimes perceived as unwelcome challenges and threats. Many teachers and schools feel besieged by hostile forces, and the siege mentality can easily creep into any discussions involving a change of any kind. Tentative discussions about the future quickly give rise to rumours of closure overnight, and the inevitable mixture of angry, anxious correspondence, resolutions and meetings. Dean Acheson's famous remark, 'Britain has lost an Empire, but not yet found a role' has obvious parallels with special schools. They are leaving behind a relatively secure and safe role, which perhaps suited both the special schools themselves and the rest of the 'system'. It is not entirely clear what is to be their new role, and how that is best achieved.

Given this backcloth of uncertainty and pushing forward in response to internal and external demands and expectations, the obvious step for each special school is to carry out a careful appraisal of itself and then formulate a series of aims and objectives for the future. This is much easier said than done. Apart from the fact that it may prove enormously difficult, for practical, emotional, personal and philosophical reasons, to create a consensus, there is the obvious fact that the special school cannot act in isolation or independently of the local authority. For the school to know which direction to take, the local authority must have a clear overview and know how the individual school fits into the picture.

The 1981 Act obliges the authority to keep under review its provision for special educational needs and the recent report by the House of Commons Select Committee on the implementation of that Act concluded:

> We have observed during the course of the inquiry that a policy for special education is something in which LEAs have a particularly important role to play. The difficulties which arise are too wide ranging to be soluble by schools alone and too localised to be capable of close direction by central government. As a result, it seems clear to us that a successful implementation of the 1981 Act is very much dependent on the development by an LEA of a clear and coherent policy, arrived at in a way which enables it to command the support of *those* — parents, teachers, and voluntary organisations — who are most affected by it. (Select Committee Report, 1987).

It is to be hoped that the 1988 Education Act will not invalidate the attempts of any authority which wishes to review, and then plan a coordinated system of provision, making the best use of its mainstream schools. The capacity to plan must depend on the extent to which an authority can exercise direction and influence over its institutions. If most decision-making powers have passed to the school, including the ability to leave the authority altogether, it is difficult to see how the above recommendation can be implemented.

However, a great many authorities have carried out thorough reviews of their provision for special educational needs (or are in the process of doing so). Many of these reviews have been characterised by attempts to take a broad, long-term view of needs and trends. Rarely, if ever and contrary to common belief have they been seen as cost-cutting exercises by hard-hearted Members and officers. The idea that integration schemes, for example, are brought in to save money is laughable.

Naturally, there is great variation in the detail of these review documents, but certain common themes and conclusions stand out, which directly affect special schools. Firstly, there is the problem of definition of special needs, and linked to that, the notion of relativity. The Fish Report states unequivocally:

> Our definition of handicap is a dynamic and relative one. Disabilities and difficulties become more or less handicapping depending on the

expectation of others and on social contexts. Handicaps thus arise from the mismatch between the intellectual, physical, emotional and social behaviour and aspirations of the individual and the expectations, appropriate or otherwise of the community and society at large (ILEA, 1985b).

If it is right, as it surely must be, to move away from a deficit model of special needs, which sees the difficulties and needs as located solely in the individual child, then that presents schools and authorities with the trickier problem of trying to accurately identify and define those needs. As Professor Weddell commented to the Select Committee, 'The point at which somebody says a child has special needs is at the point when the teacher or whoever feels that they actually cannot help a child enough. That obviously varies from one teacher to another, from one school to another, and from one local authority to another.' And equally telling is Mary Warnock's comment, 'For whom are extra resources beyond the normal provision of the school necessary? The terrible danger is that we shall say "They all need extra." My love-affair with the expression 'special needs' came to an end the first time I heard someone say, "All children are special: they all have special needs."'

At a more anecdotal level, anyone, on whatever side of the special education fence involved with moderate learning difficulties or emotional and behavioural difficulties, will have experienced some puzzlement as to why some children but not others have found their way into a special school or class. The peripatetic support teacher will frequently be subjected to a long stream of inquiries (sometimes critically phrased) as to how some children have managed to 'get' support but not others. 'I could give you three or four who are worse than that one' is not unknown!

It is difficult to see the way through this dichotomy. But even accepting the fact that schools and society are not a neutral canvas against which a child's special educational needs stand out independently, there must surely be a clearer notion of what constitutes a special educational need. The circular reasoning of the 1981 Act is not helpful. Surely it cannot be right that the proportion of statemented pupils in an authority varies from 0.04 per cent of the school population to 4.2 per cent? Or that in one authority 98 per cent of statemented pupils are in special schools and in another it is 31 per cent? Even allowing for the fact that statistical returns do not always accurately mirror the actual education received by pupils, much less the quality, there are clearly wide discrepancies between and within authorities as to the range of pupils deemed to need special provision, and the nature, quality and location of that provision.

A second feature noted in most reviews is the very complex pattern of provision that now exists. It was probably fair to say in the 1950s that special education was synonymous with special schools. That is no longer the case, although that fact has not dawned on everyone. Perhaps the majority of the general public, and some professionals and politicians at local and national level, still think this way. The tendency to equate special schools with special education will be familiar to anyone who has ever had to first raise the issue of special provision with parents. The initial letter sent to the parent of a child with moderate or severe learning difficulties, following a request for a formal assessment from the medical officer at the Child Development Centre, provoked the following response:

> Andrew is my son and he is not, is not, going to a special school. You can get all the doctors you want, but my mind is made up.
>
> At the nursery a year ago they said that a normal school is better for Lincoln. Now you say special school. *No way*.
> And please don't send someone round to talk to me.

However, although some special schools and their governors may find this difficult to come to terms with, the truth is that special educational provision is not exclusively to be found in special schools. Even if one discounts the 18 per cent of pupils with special educational needs who have always been, and still are, in mainstream schools, there is still a large proportion of pupils (statemented or not) who are receiving special provision outside of that normally provided by the mainstream school.

A brief description of the provision to be found in one small outer London Borough demonstrates the range and complexity of services provided. The authority has a school population of roughly 25,000 who are multi-cultural, multi-racial and multi-lingual. Resources for special schools (staffing, not buildings) are very good, but resources for other special educational provision are less satisfactory. Around 850 children and young people are receiving some form of special provision, either on a full-time or part-time basis — that is 3.4 per cent of the total school population. This provision includes:

- five day special schools (for moderate learning difficulties; severe learning difficulties; emotional and behavioural difficulties; physical disabilities; and hearing impaired)
- one residential school which traditionally was for delicate pupils (due for closure)
- nine off-site classes or centres for secondary-aged pupils who show emotional and behavioural difficulties of one sort or another. These classes cater for suspended pupils, long-term truants, school-phobics, psychiatrically ill pupils, young people at risk
- six Opportunity classes in mainstream primary schools for pupils with learning difficulties

- three special classes in mainstream primary schools for language impaired pupils (there is also a pre-school centre for language impaired pupils)
- a number of pupils with statements attending their local schools and receive substantial teaching and ancillary support. Most common are Downs Syndrome pupils
- roughly 20 per cent of the 850 pupils attending out-borough day and residential special schools (although this number is gradually being reduced)

In addition to the above there are also various peripatetic teachers for the sensory impaired and with specific learning difficulties (mostly reading); there is a team of eight educational psychologists; there is a small advisory support team; at post-school level there are courses in the Further Education colleges for students with moderate and severe learning difficulties. Students with other disabilities are supported, to varying degrees, on mainstream courses; there are also good link arrangements between the special schools and the colleges.

All the above refers primarily to provision made by the Education Service, but significant inputs are made by the District Health Authority, mostly in the form of paramedical services to the special schools, i.e., speech, physio- and occupational therapies. Social Services provide day nurseries, respite and long-term care, support for families, social workers to the special schools, an adult training centre, and day centres for adults with physical disabilities.

It should also be noted that all of the hearing impaired pupils who are on the roll of the authority's special school for the hearing impaired, in fact, attend mainstream schools. This is also true for a third of the pupils on the roll of the school for children with physical disabilities.

Thus even in a small authority there is an extensive and complex range of provision managed by three different services. In this particular case the District Health Authority is at least co-terminous with the Local Authority but this is not the case in many parts of the country. Given the fact that one or more features of this range of provision is usually being reorganised, and that the turnover of personnel is high, it is not surprising that hardly anyone is entirely knowledgeable or familiar with exactly what is available and how to gain access to it at any one time. A common complaint of all those involved with special education is that they do not know what exists, how it is organized and managed or coordinated. Individuals get locked into their school or piece of the service and either never understand other pieces of the jigsaw, or lose touch with them.

The complexity of it all seems symbolised in the Statementing process which appears to many as a bureaucratic labyrinth designed to confuse and delay.

This complex pattern has not, unfortunately, .been planned as an organic whole. Bits and pieces have been added on, adapted, squeezed or expanded, allowed to die slowly, or force-fed to grow quickly. On the whole the schools are the older and more established and perhaps more than a little suspicious or disdainful of the younger generation of support systems and special classes linked directly to mainstream. It may appear to them that their place and position is being usurped.

A third feature of reviews of local authority provision is the focus on mainstream schools and colleges. This can be illustrated in two ways. Firstly, there is the growing concern with the needs (largely unmet) of the 18 per cent; and secondly, there is the still growing demand to maintain pupils with more complex and severe needs in a mainstream setting and to integrate those who have either been taken out of the system, or never entered it in the first place.

Although the Warnock Report did much to heighten awareness of the fact that a large number of children are likely to have difficulties of one kind or another in school and with the curriculum on offer, the 1981 Act did not address this issue in any serious way. Nor has any DES advice since. True, the Act begins with a broad generalization about the definition of special educational needs which could incorporate the one-in-five referred to in Warnock (and since taken as the gospel figure). But thereafter, the Act concerns itself solely with the processes of statementing, which is itself concerned essentially with those children who have complex and severe difficulties. Despite this omission in the Act, or perhaps because of it, there has been a growing sense of unease about the unmet needs of a large proportion of pupils in school who do not experience much, if any success with the curriculum that is on offer.

It must always have been the case that schools and the curriculum were not matched appropriately to the needs and abilities of many less able children, but in a different social and economic climate, where there were different expectations, this mismatch did not provoke too much disturbance. But the mismatch no longer hides itself. Disaffected pupils show through non-attendance or disruptive behaviour their disapproval of schooling. Society upbraids schools because so many leave after eleven and more years of education without the literacy, numeracy and social skills deemed to be essential in a modern society. Parents want to see their children achieving marketable qualifications, and increasingly expect to see additional support and help given where necessary. The advent of the GCSE will do little to improve the situation for the less able. Indeed it will sharpen the mismatch. The initial hopes for the GCSE were linked to a single exam system which would be for the great majority of pupils, and offer to them all qualifications which would be considered acceptable. But if 80 per cent of pupils take one or more GCSEs, a sizeable proportion are going to be given grades which will be considered of little value. This means that in an average six-form-entry comprehensive with a broadly balanced ability intake, between thirty-five and seventy pupils each year are going to leave school with little, in conventional terms, to show for their education. This issue, which is partly about the nature and organization of schools and the curriculum, and partly about levels of resourcing, will not go away.

The National Curriculum with its programmes of study and attainment targets will point even more forcefully to the unmet needs of those in the bottom half of the ability range. If, as is argued, testing at 7, 11 and 14 is partly designed to identify and diagnose needs, there will be a crescendo of protest arguing for the resources to tackle the under-achievement and unmet needs.

Paradoxically, at the same time as there is a growing unease about the failure of schooling to meet many of the needs of its consumers, there continues to be a growing pressure to integrate and mainstream. There cannot be an authority in the country which does not explicitly state that its policy is to integrate children, as far as possible, into ordinary schools. In some ways it does not matter that the phrase 'as far as possible' can mean all things to all men. The point is that this is now a commonplace of authority policy statements, and there are more and more examples of how this is being achieved in practice. Maybe not to the extent and speed with which many would like to see it progress, but the direction is clear. Thus, withdrawal teaching in primary and secondary schools is being replaced by in-class support; more and more special classes or resource bases are being established in mainstream schools as opposed to classes in special, segregated schools; authorities (for financial as well as educational reasons) are sending less pupils to out-borough schools and less pupils to residential schools.

Authorities are beginning to be judged by how many pupils with special educational needs are not in special schools. This obviously creates problems and tensions for special schools. It means that the pressure is on them to reintegrate those who are most successful in their setting and to watch while alternative arrangements are made for those who traditionally would have been admitted into their schools. This in turn leads, as is being increasingly recognized, to the 'rump effect' in the special schools, that is, that the most disabled pupils are left behind and those pupils have far fewer opportunities to benefit from mixing with their less disabled peers. This is difficult and distressing for both the pupils and the staff who work with them.

There are many other conclusions that emerge from local authority reviews but these are perhaps the key ones. The task therefore for the local authority is to work towards a pattern of provision for special education which has a clearer definition of what special educational needs means, allied to better screening and identification of needs. Provision must be more coordinated, better publicized and generally made more accessible and flexible without being random. Proper weight must be given to the non-special-school wing of special education, which needs to be adequately resourced, managed and supported. Much more attention and resources must be given to the 18 per cent in ordinary schools, and the trend towards including people in, rather than shutting them out, must be maintained.

Where, then, does this leave special schools? In the long term it must mean that all, or the great majority, of special schools, as we understand the term 'school', will be phased out. For those whose children are happily and successfully attending special schools now, such a statement will not be welcomed. Nor will it be welcomed by those whose working lives have been devoted to special schools. Nor will those who work in mainstream schools be over-enthusiastic about the prospect of the eventual closure of all special schools. No doubt such comments are regarded as typical of those who work in ivory towers or who merely deal in numbers and pound signs, surrounded by cups of municipal coffee. But does even the staunchest supporter of the special school believe that fifty years hence, we will still be building separate, segregated special schools on plots of land unconnected with mainstream schools? Will there be MLD and EBD schools celebrating their centenary years? I think not.

But the long term is probably a great way off. For all kinds of reasons (some good, some bad) there is little likelihood that any authority will commit itself to a firm policy of closing all its special schools. The typically British mixture of compromise, pragmatism, muddle and realism will hold good. Even when an authority genuinely attempts to plan for the future, it can really only look at the medium term, and even then planning is fraught with many dangers. Changes of political control, unforeseen economic crises, new items on the agenda, changes of personnel and the weight of public opinion can all conspire to thwart the best laid plans.

Whilst the long term may still be a long way off, that should not prevent special schools from anticipating it and evolving slowly towards it. This is asking a great deal of staff, governors and parents. To return to the Empire metaphor, they are being asked to do what Churchill refused to do: 'I have not become the King's first minister in order to preside over the liquidation of the British Empire'. But if the phrase 'making the special school ordinary' means anything, it must point to the incorporation of special schools within ordinary schools and colleges.

Essentially the special school, the local authority and mainstream schools will have to cooperate together to identify and preserve those features of special schools which are most positive, whilst trying to eliminate those features which actually work against the best interests of pupils and staff alike. It must be emphasized all the time that it is not special education and provision which is being phased out, but rather the institutional framework which has traditionally delivered it. The most obvious positive feature of special education is the generally favourable staffing ratios and the specialist equipment and resources. There is no reason why this cannot be continued in designated resource bases in mainstream schools. Although it is often argued that it is economically unviable to relocate a school in several departments spread across several schools, the increased costs are not likely to be wildly disproportionate. The main problem from a resources point of view is when an alternative model is being established and it is not possible to divert resources from the existing provision. Such problems cannot be glossed over but if a long-term view is taken, it should not be assumed too easily that a special school is automatically bound to be significantly cheaper than a more integrated model. Capital programmes will also be a source of concern for local authorities. Purpose-built facilities for the physically disabled, those who are profoundly and multiply handicapped and those with other complex needs are not easily dispensed with. But again it must be understood that there is nothing intrinsically impossible about building a suitable environment for even the most handicapped of pupils on the same site as an ordinary school. Although the degree of integration that these pupils are likely to experience is minimal, their parents, their staff, and the pupils, staff and parents of the mainstream school will find the coexistence of great value. Many parents who are fully aware that their children could not integrate into any ordinary lessons, and who would oppose such an idea if it were floated, nevertheless long for some recognition from the non-disabled community that their children exist and are part of society, and are not to be put in even the most congenial of ghettos.

As regards the individual attention, the careful attention to individualized planning, the regular reviews, and specialized teaching techniques such as the use of behaviour modification techniques or signing systems, there is no reason why this cannot take place in an ordinary school. And, of course, it already is. Special schools which have relocated units and classes in ordinary schools, or special classes established by the authority independent of any special school are already functioning, and have, in some cases, been doing so for many years.

It will not be possible to transfer lock, stock and barrel the whole ethos of a special school. And many will be worried that the hurly-burly, competitiveness, cruelty and general size of mainstream schools will be detrimental. This will be especially true for children with learning difficulties who were failing and experiencing unhappiness in ordinary schools. For example, one parent wrote:

> For two years I remained a convert to the cause of integration. But as she grew older, signs of strain began to show. Her friends always eventually outgrew her, leaving a trail of heartbreak. Finally we sent her to a special school for children with moderate learning difficulties. She has now been there two years. No longer does she tremble in the playground. No longer is she dominated by a sense of failure in her achievements or dogged by her difference from other children. The abstract ideology of integration seems paper-thin beside the palpable reality of her happiness in school.

It will not be easy trying to transfer that sense of security and acceptance which usually (but not always) characterizes a special school, whilst at the same time ensuring that pupils are not over-protected and under-exposed to the rigours of normality.

As attempts are made to ensure that all the positive features of special schools are carried through, or as many as possible, thought must be given as to how the negative features will be eliminated. Simply educating pupils with special needs on the same campus or in the same building as other pupils does not guarantee a better quality of education and life for them. Putting different groups of staff and pupils together in close proximity does not automatically mean that the problems of isolation, restricted peer group (for staff as well as pupils), stigma, narrow curriculum and limited opportunities for growth and development disappear. There are many examples in the country of locational integration, or even (in theory, at least) of social and functional integration where there is little purposeful interaction between the 'unit' and the rest of the school.

A strategy and an outlook which seeks to preserve the best features of special schools whilst eliminating their worst and capitalizing on the opportunities available in mainstream schools, will have the following features:

Firstly, special schools (and that must first of all mean their headteachers and deputies) must have a vision for the future which is broadly based, open to new ideas, and willing to be experimental and exploratory. Schools which cannot see further than the existing staff, or next year, or who see problems and difficulties with every new suggestion, other than that of adding more staff to the existing set-up, will be doing themselves and their pupils a disservice. Pursuing a narrow, almost sectarian line will in the long run be counter-productive. It is all too easy for special schools, or any school, to want to fight to preserve their existence, territory or sphere of influence.

Instead, special schools should be looking for connections and mutual exchange of interests and information as much as possible. That means creating some sort of common identity amongst all those schools, services and special classes which form the special education system, and not seeing different parts as rivals. It is surprising how often those in one sector of special education see themselves as quite different to another sector. Anxieties and defences about 'expertise' manifest themselves just as much within special as they do between special and mainstream. The truth is that the common ground between all these sectors is very great. The broad view will be one which recognises that the school is only the means to an end, and not the end itself. Maintaining a unique identity may not be the best way of providing high-quality education.

Secondly, special schools should be energetic lobbyists and pro-active agents on behalf of special education in general and their pupils in particular. Despite the higher profile, there is still a great deal of ignorance and misunderstanding about the nature of special needs and special education. There is a constant campaign to be waged of informing, persuading, enthusing and soliciting all and sundry in the cause of special education, especially when it comes to promoting the ideas of closer association and integration into the mainstream of education. Rather than responding to other people's pressures or resisting the current, special schools should be the ones who are the initiators. The lobbying and the public relations must not be geared to narrow self-preservation. If there is a collective and cooperative approach which is aimed at pressing Members, officers, schools and colleges to take the legitimate aspirations and expectations of children with special needs seriously then the moral and political strength of the argument will be greater. At the same time, schools must seek to reassure parents and others who may be alarmed at some of the more far-reaching ideas which are being mooted. Almost certainly they will have the trust and confidence of most of their parents in a way which bureaucrats and politicians do not.

Part of that task of lobbying and informing is to demolish some of the myths about pupils with special needs. Teachers, governors, parents, advisers and politicians need to be told that there is no great gulf between 'our' pupils and 'your' pupils. Nothing dramatic happens on the day the statement is finally signed. There is a great tendency to speak in hushed tones about the expertise that is to be found in special schools and their staff, as opposed to the 'humdrum' skills of mainstream staff. By and large this is a myth. In a sense both sides of the divide need to preserve it. Mainstream needs it because then it can argue that pupils are far better off where they are with staff who have the expertise. That can be a convenient justification for not accepting pupils or justifying their departure. But special schools also need to hold onto the myth, otherwise it might be difficult to justify their role and existence. Undoubtedly there are some aspects of the curriculum and teaching approaches which do demand a high level of training and substantial experience. But most special school staff learn most things like everyone else in life, by doing the real job in a real situation. At the risk of being simplistic, the characteristics of high-quality teaching in special schools are characteristic of high-quality teaching anywhere. There is nothing of a mystery religion about careful and detailed preparation, content closely matched to pupils' abilities and interests, good record-keeping, flexibility and a willingness to learn new content and skills, ability to work in a team, or a structured approach.

Another myth which needs to be dissolved is that some children will always need to be in special schools. The truth is that there is no group of special needs pupils who are not being integrated, in one way or another, in some part of the world. It may be that neither attitudes nor resources will be sufficient for many years for some groups of pupils in some authorities to be brought closer to mainstream. But this is not so much a reflection of the specialness of the pupils themselves as the failure of imagination or enterprise or will on the part of the non-disabled community.

Thirdly, special schools must put some real substance behind the phrase 'special schools as resource centres'. It is an attractive, positive idea, but developing the school along these lines is a risky business which may lead to some uncomfortable conclusions. Essentially it means providing ideas, staff experience and skills, materials, equipment and facilities which are going to help staff in other schools (mainstream and special) as well as other professionals and parents in their work with children with similar needs. Credibility is the name of the game and if the school cannot provide high-quality in-service and advice which counts in real situations, the special school will not become a resource centre. Staff have to have a good understanding, not only of how pupils progress best in the special school situation, but how they will make progress in mainstream. Primary class teachers, or secondary teachers with 100–150 pupils to see each week, will not welcome advice and guidance exclusively based on teaching a small group of ten pupils most of the week. Special school teachers need to find opportunities for spending significant amounts of time with mainstream colleagues and in their schools, as well as in other special schools so that they can become familiar with those situations and develop in-service accordingly. This can be achieved by encouraging personal and institutional links between individuals and schools for regular meetings through structured visits, regular meetings, joint in-service and teacher-exchanges. Such exchanges must be the best and cheapest form of in-service training there is. To develop as a resource centre, the special school has to promote itself and to some extent market itself. But again, this should be done, if at all possible, in conjunction with other special schools, or services, or curriculum support groups in the authority. Ideally they would act as a consortium offering a range of packages including, for example, video libraries, special lectures and seminars, consultancy work, in-house courses, learning materials and equipment. To develop in this way they will have to persuade the local authority to support and finance them — although some of it could be self-financing, especially as schools begin to budget for their own in-service needs. One main measure of success will be the degree to which other schools cease referring children with more complex needs onto the special schools. This will be particularly true for MLD schools, who, if they are effective, will be 'drying up' the supply of pupils to them.

The fourth, and most critical and difficult item to be included in a long-term strategy, is the creation of formal links with mainstream schools with a view to integrating pupils in the ordinary school. Circumstances vary from locality to locality, and a scheme which is eminently successful for hearing impaired pupils in an urban situation cannot be replicated for pupils with severe learning difficulties in a sparsely populated rural area. However there is no special school which could not, on a good day with a following wind, think of ways in which all or most of its pupils could be part, in some way or another, of an ordinary school. It would make an enormous difference to the possibility of integration if the whole of the special school community — staff, governors, parents and pupils — is actively arguing for integration. There are now very many different schemes and settings for the integration of pupils with special needs. Lessons can be learned both from the successes and failures of those schemes. It will be important to avoid the rhetoric and the over-reliance on the moral and emotional dimension to integration. Developing a scheme and making it work demands a high degree of practical thinking and first-rate management skills. Goodwill and enthusiasm will only go so far, and even the necessary physical and human resources are only part of the story. Inevitably any scheme for placing children with special needs in mainstream will lead to dual management and a sharing of roles. That will lead to positive benefits but it will also lead to conflicts over the use of staff, the appropriate curriculum, the extent to which the mainstream schools modifies itself to accomodate its new intake, and many other points. Who sorts out transport? Who decides on accommodation? Who is first point of contact for parents? Which roll are the pupils on? How is capitation organized? What happens when one of the original headteachers is replaced by someone with a different approach? What if a parent does not want that particular mainstream school to be the one for her child, even if it is a designated resource base? What are the lines of communication and the structures for review and open debate on the scheme? These and many other questions have to be sorted out before and during the operation of a scheme, and it will not all be sweetness and light.

There are two main groups of pupils to be considered when developing integration schemes. Firstly there are those pupils already in the special school, who need to be given some first-hand experience of an ordinary school setting, either on a part-time or full-time basis. Secondly there are those pupils who have not been admitted to a special school but for whom a period of assessment or long-term placement in a special setting is considered appropriate. In some ways, it is easier to develop a scheme for the second group of pupils, but then whatever provision is made is likely to have a looser connection with the special school. It is sensible for the local authority to designate a number of mainstream schools as specialist centres or resource bases for particular kinds of special needs. It will help matters if special schools have already been cultivating links with the most likely mainstream schools in order to smoothe the way. Although it is common for special schools to retain a high degree of responsibility for the staff and pupils in the integration scheme, the logical and right thing in the long term will be for mainstream schools to assume full responsibility for all the pupils attending their school, but properly supported and advised by specialist staff, from within and outside the school. In time, therefore, there will be an external and hopefully unified special education service, supporting all pupils and staff working in mainstream schools. It will be the responsibility of the authority (if it is allowed to exercise it) to ensure that checks and safeguards are built into its procedures so that pupils with special needs and their staff continue to have a special place in the school and in the allocation of resources of all kinds.

The response to the invitation and challenge to special schools should be neither one of pulling up the drawbridge to prepare for a long-drawn-out siege, nor one of enthusiastically putting up the 'For Sale' signs. So as not to put at risk those pupils who are already in the system, and so as to avoid alienating the various constituencies which must be drawn together in a positive framework for change and development, there must be careful, patient building of bridges and planting of seedlings. This is not the same as foot-dragging, but an approach which is realistic and ultimately likely to be most effective. Although the times, the budget, the location of schools and the current agenda will never be exactly right for proposing and implementing a phased programme of development, significant progress will be possible if there is an energetic and far-sighted lead given by special schools.

Chapter 15

The Paradox of the Special School
Tony Dessent

THE INITIAL PARADOX

There are some amazingly good special schools about at the moment. Within those special schools which I know well, and with which I have had the privilege of working closely, I see much good practice and any amount of dedicated care and attention being given to meet the needs of children and their families. I see few, if any, instances of bad practice, and certainly no more examples than could be seen within a range of mainstream schools. I see many children whose confidence and self-esteem have been affected by experiences of failure within mainstream schools. I see many of these children being effectively helped to make educational progress, and helped to re-develop a sense of self-worth with skilled and patient attention from teachers within special schools. I see staff and head teachers within many special schools adapting and responding creatively to the constantly changing context which surrounds them. In the best of our special schools, I see teachers eager to anticipate and predict future needs, and preparing themselves to respond to them.

Paradoxically, all this is occurring at a time when special schools are under threat — at a time when many special school teachers feel uncertain about their professional future, and often undervalued and 'de-skilled' within what must seem an increasingly hostile educational/social environment. This book, in part at least, has been an attempt to examine and understand this central paradox. It is one paradox amongst many. The field of special education is beset by conflicting aims, contradictory outcomes and mixed messages. The paradoxes which surround the idea and practice of special schooling will provide the focus for this chapter. Understanding these paradoxes is, I believe, of some considerable importance. They reveal the tensions, difficulties and changes which our system of special education is currently undergoing. The paradoxes of special schooling demonstrate the fundamental difficulties of operating a dual system — *special and ordinary*. Ultimately, if the 'Special School Is To Be Made Ordinary' this distinction must disappear...

THE SUCCESS PARADOX — 'IT DOESN'T PAY TO BE A SUCCESSFUL SPECIAL SCHOOL'

When it comes to making a success of the way a special school functions, headteachers and their staff are faced with some interesting double-binds. Consider for example the case of headteacher A. Headteacher A is a 38 year-old, newly appointed head of a mixed special school for children with so-called 'moderate learning difficulties' in the heart of a Shire County. The school roll has been dropping over a number of years. The majority of the teaching staff have worked in the school for ten years or more and little curriculum development has occurred in the recent past. Staff morale is low. The LEA is looking for a 'new broom'. The priorities for the LEA are the development of supportive links with mainstream schools in order to maintain children with special needs within ordinary classes. Rejuvenation of the school's curriculum and, more importantly, changes in the school's image within the local community are of similar importance. In comes head-teacher A like a knight in shining armour! Headteacher A has all the right credentials — extensive experience of working in mainstream and special schools — committed to the idea of integration for children with special needs — convinced too of the need for high-quality special schools when integration is not possible. Last but not least headteacher A comes to the post from a background of recent successful management experience as a deputy headteacher of a Special School where a number of innovative changes have occurred. Progressively (and sometime painfully) the change process ensues. Old staff leave and new staff join the school. Curriculum working groups are set up. A senior management team is formed to develop future policy and practices. The development of a mainstream 'support service' arises from the empty coffee cups of numerous after-school staff meetings. A number of children are gradually reintegrated into local mainstream classes. The school joins the local TVEI consortium and the local INSET cluster. 'Networking' within the local community of schools is underway. Headteacher A is invited to contribute to in-service courses in order to talk about the 'changing role of the special school'. The school itself becomes a base for in-service activities within the area.

What are the consequences of all these changes? Many (hopefully most) will be positive. Some, paradoxically, could be regarded as negative. If the school is increasingly successful in helping ordinary schools to support children with special needs, if more and more children are successfully integrated back into mainstream classes — what then will be the final scenario? A recent applicant for the headship of a special school asked the LEA interviewing panel exactly this question. His question was a simple one. 'If within five years I am able to return pupils back to ordinary schools to support them there, and thereby reduce the number of pupils on roll from 110 to 10, would that be regarded as success? What would the LEA then do about the school's staffing?' These questions proved difficult to answer! This applicant's questions pinpointed one of the central paradoxes which confront many special schools at the present time. Those special schools which respond successfully to the current needs of the education service have a high probability of shooting themselves in the proverbial foot! Special schools have for a number of years been aware of some of the negative consequences of their own success. Every time one of the more able youngsters from a special school is returned to a mainstream setting the special school is arguably the poorer because of the move. The special school probably loses one of the pupils who contributed most positively to the curriculum, to the peer group and to the climate within the special school. As support links between special schools and mainstream schools become more and more commonplace (Jowett, Hegarty and Moses, 1988) other negative consequences can ensue. Headteachers of special schools may feel that the practice of releasing able members of their staff to visit and support local mainstream schools impoverishes the educational input for pupils within the special school. Headteachers face a genuine dilemma when deciding between the priority to be given to work 'outside' special schools, and the priority to be given to work 'inside' the special school (Dessent, 1984).

Of course the ultimate negative consequence for a special school which is successful within the integrationist philosophy of the late 1980s is to bring about its own closure. No doubt somewhere in Great Britain this has already happened to at least a few special schools. Is this what special schools should be aiming to do — to do away with themselves? Ultimately of course they should. What other aim could make logical sense? Nobody surely wants more handicapped children? Do we not all want less disability rather than more? Does anyone want more children with special needs? These questions are not rhetorical — they actually need to be answered! Sometimes the vested interests which we all have in our own professional territory can lead to some intriguing twists in our logic. The notion that 'doing themselves out of a job' is a quite reasonable aim for special schools is also true of many, if not all, of those involved in our special education system. It applies to special education advisers, to advisory teachers, to educational psychologists, etc. Our collective aim should be to 'do ourselves out of a job'. We have no automatic right to exist. We exist by default. We exist because of the lack of resources, the lack of expertise and knowledge, perhaps even the lack of sympathy and appropriate attitudes within the ordinary education system. Living with and understanding the paradoxical aim of 'doing ourselves out of a job' is fundamental to the future work of special schools.

THE INTEGRATION PARADOX — 'INTEGRATION BEGETS SEGREGATION'

Let us return to our mythical, newly-appointed special school headteacher. Let us suggest an alternative scenario to the changes which have been introduced by our new head. Let us suggest that as a result of the new direction the school takes in developing an 'integration' service for mainstream schools — in attempting to reintegrate their own pupils back into ordinary schools and in developing expertise as an in-service training base for local teachers — the school roll rockets! This is at least as likely a scenario as that of the headteacher leading the school towards its eventual closure. Thus, we have another paradox. A special school can be genuinely committed to promoting a more integrated approach to meeting special educational needs, be genuinely committed to emptying itself, and yet end up with an increasing waiting list of pupils. The reasons are to some extent obvious. Parents of children with special needs are more likely to find the image of our restructured and rejuvenated school attractive for their child. The fact that the special school is linked into, and intent upon returning children back into, mainstream classes, holds out for the parents the possibility of hope for the future. Similarly the school, by becoming increasingly 'open' to mainstream schools, and perhaps other individuals such as social workers and paramedical staff, can inadvertently attract more customers. Perhaps for the first time local mainstream teachers actually get a chance to meet teachers within the special school. Perhaps they get a chance to visit and see what is on offer at the special school. What is on offer for children are smaller classes, more adult attention, good teaching resources, a calm and peaceful atmosphere. A veritable educational Utopia! Not at all difficult for any mainstream teacher to 'find' a few children who would quite reasonably benefit from what is on offer in a special school and which is not on offer in their mainstream classes.

This paradox — promoting segregation by increasing our efforts towards integration — was referred to rather aptly by a colleague as the 'Bridge Over the River Kwai' phenomenon. It is a phenomenon which is not restricted to the workings of special schools. Many of the developments and changes which have ensued in special education since Warnock and the 1981 Act have had similar unintended consequences. Newly developed 'Awareness Courses' in special educational needs for mainstream teachers can inadvertently lead to more segregation in terms of attitude and perception rather than less. I can well remember the example of the mainstream infant school where the staff wrote into the LEA listing 'their 20 per cent' following an Awareness Course and also asking what the LEA would be doing about them! Similarly, there are examples where the work of advisory support services, which have been developed to support children with special needs in ordinary classes, seem to have been linked to an increase in the number of children with special needs being placed in special school settings (Goodwin, 1983). Less obvious examples occur when mainstream schools are in receipt of additional teaching resources in order to meet special educational needs. Depending upon the policy which a particular school adopts, the additional resources can lead to an increase in both the number of children who are segregated from the ordinary curriculum and an increase in the amount of time during which pupils are removed from the activities which go on within ordinary classrooms.

At the root of this paradox is the problem of providing something special for children in an ordinary way. Our separate special educational system is not in tune with this purpose and the special school is the example *par excellence* of this separation.

THE CAREER PARADOX — 'GETTING ON MEANS GETTING OUT'

To return once more to headteacher A. This time the purpose is to glance quickly at our mythical headteacher's curriculum vitae. Headteacher A's teaching career began in mainstream education, teaching within the Humanities department of a large secondary school. For a number of years our future headteacher's timetable included some sessions teaching a remedial class of first and second years as well as what was described as a 'challenging' final year, non-examination group. Success in dealing with these latter groups combined with a developing interest in working with pupils who exhibited learning difficulties, led headteacher A inevitably along the special needs career path. Three years on, and a full time 'remedial' post falls vacant. Success in this post was followed again within a few years by a transfer to a neighbouring school which could boast a Head of Remedial Department, albeit on a lowly scale. Nevertheless, so far so good. Successful teaching experience — recognition — some career advancement. Our mythical headteacher is able, hard-working, well-qualified, ambitious and committed to working with less able pupils. What next? Where are the future promotion prospects for this teacher? Answer — within special schools. In terms of career advancement, mainstream education has not traditionally provided an extensive promotional path for teachers interested in working in the field of special educational needs. In order to 'get on' teachers have had to 'get out'. They have had to get out of the mainstream system and into the segregated special school system. Special education has been (and perhaps still is) largely associated with the work of special schools. Special education teachers have been mainly perceived as those teachers who work in special schools. Career prospects have, to a large extent, followed these perceptions. If it were possible to gather together all of the headteachers of mainstream secondary schools in Great Britain who have had extensive previous experience of working with children with special educational needs, they would probably constitute a relatively small and exclusive gathering! This, of course, is not surprising, particularly when one considers that 'remedial education' has, in the past, been a Cinderella area within mainstream schools. Historically, within primary schools, special needs teaching has been mainly undertaken by part-time, unqualified teachers on unpromoted posts. Within secondary schools 'remedial' or special needs departments, if they existed at all, rarely attracted the kind of status and significance of other curriculum/subject departments. This is now, of course, changing dramatically. The status, training and credibility of special needs teachers within mainstream schools have increased substantially within recent years. However, there is still the career question, 'Where does the head of special needs go next?' Do all routes still lead to the segregated sector?

There is another dimension to the career paradox. This concerns the career prospects of those teachers who have moved into special schools and currently work within them. Some would argue that in the current climate they themselves are confronted with an identical dilemma — viz. 'getting on means getting out'. The ubiquitous special schools' allowance or additional incentive allowance — a seductive 'extra' upon entry to special schools — can be a financial impediment to those considering moving back into mainstream teaching. A far bigger problem is the 'career trap' which can confront those teachers who move outside of the mainstream system into special schools or off-site units. Consider the following comments from senior staff within mainstream primary and secondary schools who are considering applicants for special needs posts:

- 'I am not sure how a special school teacher would cope with the hurly-burly of a mainstream secondary school.'

- 'I am not sure that a special school teacher would really be up-to-date enough in terms of modern primary methods.'
- 'How would a special school teacher cope with large classes?'.

Sometimes it seems that special school teachers can be perceived as professionals who acquire some of the same needs (e.g. 'for a protected environment') as the pupils they teach!

In terms of career development, the field of special educational needs is in a state of flux. Senior management posts have historically been invested within the segregated system — within special schools. To some extent this is still the case. Recruitment of Advisory and Inspectorial posts within special education seems largely still to be from the ranks of ex-head teachers of special schools. Perhaps in the future, the changes currently in evidence will go further. Perhaps in ten years' time the numbers of head teachers of secondary schools who have a substantial background of experience in meeting special educational needs will be somewhat higher than the 2 per cent revealed by some recent NFER research (Weindling and Earley, 1986).

The career paradox is yet another reflection of the dual system — special and ordinary. Career prospects for special needs teachers within mainstream education will always be limited, whilst special education is perceived primarily as something which occurs outside the ordinary schools. Facilitating the transfer of teachers between the two systems is an important priority for the future, in order to correct some of the mutual misconceptions which currently arise.

THE PARADOX OF POSITIVE DISCRIMINATION — 'HELPING KIDS CAN HARM THEM'

Special education is first and foremost about helping children who have difficulties. Educational sociologists, and others, may argue that it fulfils many other, perhaps more cynical, functions. Both viewpoints have validity. Clearly, one of the historical origins of special education, and particularly special schooling, lies in the pursuit of the humanitarian ideal of providing positive discrimination for children who are handicapped, disabled or disadvantaged in some way. Special schools have traditionally been the main vehicle for ensuring that this positive discrimination occurs. Special education is about providing something 'extra', something additional, something 'special' to 'some' children. Educating children with special needs is demonstrably more expensive, more labour-intensive, and costs more in terms of equipment/materials and support staff than probably any other area of the education service. Some information on the relative costs of special education were given in evidence to the House of Commons Select

Committee on the Implementation of the 1981 Education Act. Derbyshire LEA reported that approximately 7 per cent of the authority's educational expenditure was attributed to meeting the special educational needs of some 2.5 per cent of the authority's child population (House of Commons, 1987).

Why, then, if special education is about helping children, about providing extra resources and support, do so many parents (and sometimes children) seek to avoid it like the Plague?! This is the paradox of positive discrimination. It indicates that some forms of positive discrimination are not perceived as such and, indeed, can be seen as forms of negative discrimination.

Some examples may shed light on this point. Recently I heard that a well-respected colleague, an educational psychologist, had retired from his post. In the twilight years of his career he had apparently grown somewhat disillusioned with his work and his role. Prior to retirement he had given some 'tongue in cheek' advice to the schools which he served — 'Please don't refer children to me — I am worried about the harm that will be done to them!'. Many will understand his sentiments. They relate to the close historical link which educational psychologists have had with special education, with segregated provisions and the inevitable stigma and anxieties that this entails. The negative aspects of special education are also seen clearly in the case of children from ethnic minority groups. Negative feelings are frequently expressed by the parents of children from ethnic minority groups when special educational provision is recommended. This has been most in evidence in the case of parents of Afro-Caribbean children in the ILEA (ILEA, 1985b). The same phenomenon is observed by most ordinary schools when they are discussing with parents their child's difficulties and the need for 'referral', 'assessment', and the 'statementing' of their child. Having 'extra help' can itself be seen as stigmatizing no matter how that extra help is provided. How much greater the anxieties for parents when getting extra help involves formal procedures, referral and the threat of the removal of their child from that which is 'ordinarily available'. 'Statementing' can be perceived by parents as very similar to the idea of 'certification'.

The special school often lies at the end of this path of anxiety and stigma. It exists to help children in need, it exists to provide the something extra and the something special which many children so obviously require. Yet as it is a form of positive discrimination which is structurally, organisationally and managerially separate from that which is 'ordinary', its work is disadvantaged from the outset. We talk of protecting children with special educational needs, we talk of the protection of a statement, we talk of protecting resources and provision for children with special needs. Special schools represent the ultimate in terms of protected resources. Again, paradoxically, as soon as a child enters the special school environment the teaching staff have to make conscious efforts to guard against the negative consequences of such protection – namely 'over-protection' of the individual child! Helping children can harm them. Moreover, special education and special schooling certainly come to fulfil functions in our society other than the simple and straightforward one of attempting to help an individual child. At one level, the special school functions to help those children who remain in the ordinary school, whose education is seen to have been hindered by the presence of pupils with special educational needs.

Resolving the paradox of positive discrimination is not easy. The notion that 'helping children can harm them' is certainly not a recommendation that we should stop helping children with special needs. If anything, we should be aiming to give more help to more children. Our problem again is to find ways of helping children, of finding ways of positively discriminating in favour of those who are educationally disadvantaged, of providing special help in an ordinary way.

THE PARENT PARADOX — 'FIGHTING AGAINST AND FOR SPECIAL SCHOOLS'

The parent paradox is concerned with the attitudes of parents towards special schools. While scientific knowledge of how attitudes are formed and changed is still rudimentary, there are a few things which are known. We know that human beings abhor incongruity, inconsistency and imbalance between their beliefs, attitudes and behaviours. A person who holds one belief which is totally inconsistent with another belief or behaviour is a person likely to experience a degree of psychological discomfort or tension. Such a person is likely also to either change their belief, change their attitudes or alter aspects of their behaviour in order to achieve consistency. Many parents of children with special needs are forced into this position. Some parents will struggle against the notion that their child has special educational needs. Several more will express anxiety and strong reservation about the idea of their child going to a special school. Their attitude towards special schools could reasonably be described as 'defensive' if not 'negative'. Some will openly express their intention to 'fight against the idea of special schooling'.

Over time, a sizable number of these parents are likely to eventually accept the idea of special school placement. Some will continue to have reservations and negative attitudes towards their child's special school. Perhaps, however, the majority will change their attitudes. Those parents who initially fight against the idea of special schooling can later become the parents most vocal in their defence! This 'parent paradox' is not an unusual occurrence. Such dramatic changes in attitude result, no doubt, from a number of factors. Many parents will change their attitude towards special schools because they see evident changes in their child's educational progress, their child's happiness, their child's self-esteem, and their child's willingness to go to school following special school placement.

This, however, is not the whole story. Parents are under considerable pressure to reconcile their attitudes (views about special education and special schools) with their behaviour (agreeing to special school placement). These attitudinal changes demonstrate clearly that parents too experience difficulties in coming to terms with the problems and inconsistencies of our dual system of special and ordinary education.

THE ADMINISTRATIVE PARADOX — 'SEGREGATING CHILDREN IS REWARDING'

Consider the workings of the 1981 Education Act from the perspective of a hard-pressed LEA administrator. Often the administrator is the final arbiter and decision-maker with regard to special educational provision for individual children. What are the choices — local mainstream school? — special unit? — special school? What are the factors that will influence the decision — parental preference? professional advice? finance and the availability of resources?

There is also a less evident factor which will powerfully influence the choices being made. It is known as the 'hassle factor'. It relates, of course, to the amount of 'hassle' the administrator will *personally experience* as a result of the decision which is made in any one case. On occasions, the 'hassle' which ensues from proffering a special school placement to reluctant, vocal and articulate parents can be considerable. In such cases a mainstream option, although perhaps considered more expensive and more complex to establish, may still be the chosen course of action. I would however, suggest that this is often not the case. The special school option frequently provides the easiest, 'hassle-free' route for the administrator or decision-maker to follow. A decision to go for a segregated special school placement can in fact be enormously rewarding to an LEA decision maker. Looked at behaviourally, segregation, as an administrative act, can be a relatively easy and straight-forward option, notably lacking in any 'punishing consequences'. Integra-tion, on the other hand, holds many administrative pitfalls and can result in a number of 'punishing consequences'. Why does the administrative paradox occur? My suggestion would be that our system of special schooling provides the 'Holy Grail' which any administrative system seeks in the field of special educational needs. The special school system provides the answer to all of the most complex definitional, resourcing and organisational questions which administrators have to answer. Some examples:

> Which children in our school system have got special educational needs?.....Those children who attend special schools.

> Which children should get extra resources?.....Those children who attend special schools.

> Which teachers should receive salary enhancements for working with children with special educational needs?......Those teachers who work in special schools.

Special schools represent a neat and tidy administrative solution to the problem of assigning both resources and professional responsibility for managing children with special educational needs. One of the great strengths of segregated special schools lies in their administrative and financial simplicity. Each time a decision is made to provide for a child with special needs within the ordinary school system a whole host of issues, questions and uncertainties arise which are less likely to arise if, instead, a special school placement is made. Again, some examples:

> 'Will the child's class teacher have the right attitudes and be prepared to teach the child?'

> 'Will the building be able to accommodate the child?'

> 'How should the placement be resourced? What level of provision should be made?'

> 'If additional staffing is involved, to whom will the staff be responsible?'

> 'Will the teaching staff be able to respond adequately to parental concerns and anxieties?'

> 'What will happen in the future? Who will monitor future needs?'

> 'Will the resources allocated to the mainstream school be properly used and focused in order to meet the needs of this child?'

There are unlikely to be any clear answers to such questions. It is very likely that with children placed in mainstream settings LEA administrators and members of the LEA support services will need to have much greater involvement, often over extended periods of time. In contrast, placement within special schools seems to require considerably less involvement from such external agencies. Looked at administratively, special school placements can be relatively hassle-free! Children who have special needs who are placed *within* their ordinary schools are placed *outside* of the system which has been designed, organised, resourced and structured to meet their needs.

THE PARADOX OF THE SPECIAL SCHOOL TEACHER — 'SPECIAL SCHOOL TEACHERS HAVE SPECIAL NEEDS'

Some time ago I was made acutely aware of the fact that special school teachers themselves have special needs. A special school teacher involved in a discussion group along with a wide range of teachers from mainstream and special education displayed to the group all of the signs and symptoms of someone under considerable professional stress. An able teacher, a dedicated teacher, a professionally sound teacher but nevertheless a teacher feeling under pressure — a teacher feeling under threat. A defensive attitude would be displayed by this teacher immediately either special schools or special school teachers were mentioned. Few discussions got far without this particular teacher mounting an argument, both defending and spelling out in no uncertain terms the enormous advantages of a separate special school system. What this particular teacher found perplexing was why fewer rather than more children now seemed to be going to special schools!

How typical were this teacher's reactions? How many special school teachers across the country are feeling confused, devalued and under threat as professional educators? How many feel the need to justify to others their work in the special school setting, to extol the advantages of a special school system, to cast a cynical eye on attempts to integrate 'their children'? What seems certain is that few LEAs have come to grips with the consequences for special school teachers of the changes which are now occurring in the field of special education. Little or no attention has been paid to meeting the special needs of special school teachers. Training opportunities for special school staff are important but are not the only response required. There is a need for greater involvement and discussion between teachers and headteachers within special schools and those concerned with planning and provision in the LEA. There is a need for greater 'openness' and frank discussion about the issues which currently impinge upon the special school, the role of the special school teacher and the pressures which LEAs are confronting and will need to confront in the future. There is a need to give time and money to facilitating the career development of special school teachers, whether within special schools or within mainstream schools. More than anything there is a need to ensure that special teachers feel that their work is valued and of importance. Teachers feeling devalued and under threat are unlikely to respond flexibly and openly to the challenges which will confront many special school teachers in the future.

THE FINAL PARADOX — 'MAKING THE SPECIAL SCHOOL ORDINARY'

If the special school is to be made ordinary then the positive aspects, the positive qualities and characteristics of special schools, the positive discrimination which special schooling attempts to provide, must be incorporated into our system of ordinary education. In the process, many of the paradoxes, inconsistencies and contradictory outcomes associated with special schooling should disappear. *Making the Special School Ordinary* is in fact part and parcel of *Making the Ordinary School Special* (Dessent, 1987). Paradoxically, the aim of making the ordinary school special is unlikely ever to be fully achieved as long as establishments like special schools continue to exist in glorious isolation from our ordinary school system. Eliminating the paradoxes which surround special schools and special education requires the progressive development of a unified, fully comprehensive system of education. A system in which the distinctions between 'special' and 'ordinary' are gradually eroded. A system in which the 'ownership' of special education is no longer invested solely with the 'special educators'. A system in which both the responsibility and the resources for meeting special educational needs are devolved to, and 'owned' by ordinary schools themselves. A unified rather than a dual system.

Within this unified model the special school of the future will be fundamentally incorporated into the structure, organization and management of mainstream education. The building, the equipment and the staffing would become part of that structure. This model will have some perceived losses for the special school as we know it today. There will be the loss of an autonomous self-contained unit and the loss of an autonomous headteacher. The special school will become a small part of a larger whole. 'Special children' will join with the community and continuum of children in their area and 'special teachers' will join with the community of teachers in their locality. Within such a model there is likely still to be a need for groupings of children which provide a different/modified environment for some, or indeed, a substantial part, of the school day for some pupils.

This model will never be viable unless the crucial aspects of our present separate system of special education can be successfully transferred to the mainstream. Of central importance is the issue of positive discrimination which lies at the heart of special education. If positive discrimination towards children who are handicapped, disabled or relatively disadvantaged in relation to their peers cannot be incorporated into the mainstream system, then there will be a continuing need to protect children with special needs outside of ordinary schools. This, in my view, will be to everyone's loss. It will be to the loss of the 'special' child and the loss of the 'ordinary' child. It will also be to the loss of the 'special' teacher and to the loss of the 'ordinary' teacher. Ultimately the real excitement and potential of special education lies in the aim of taking the special out of special education. To make what we now consider special to be normal.

Concluding Remarks to Volume 1
Derek Baker and Keith Bovair

This book was written in order to ensure that sufficient information was available regarding the developing role of special schools at a time of rapid and radical change following a period during which the demise of the special school seemed a possibility.

At all times the authors have adopted a positive view as to the actual and potential contribution of special schools in services dedicated to meeting children's special educational needs. They acknowledge that there should and will come a point in time when both special and ordinary schools become a unified service eliminating the disadvantages and divisive nature of the existing dual system. The challenge for us all is to harness the best of recent good practice from both special and ordinary schools in the interest of the children for whom we all work. They only have one chance. It is our responsibility to ensure that all available resources are used for their maximum benefit.

The aim of this volume has been to highlight key areas which will need close attention if an effective special needs service is to be developed and maintained for all children. In the areas of setting, curriculum, professionals, parents, leadership and policy we must take positive steps forward to ensure the continued development of practice.

Volume 2 provides further examples of innovative practice drawn from a wider range of professional expertise and concentrating almost exclusively on school-based developments which may be replicated and enhanced to meet the needs of children in other settings.

Notes on Contributors

Derek Baker is currently headteacher of Moselle School (MLD) in the London Borough of Haringey. His teaching experience includes comprehensive schools, a residential special school (EBD), and day special schools (PhH). He also taught in Canada at an elementary school and on undergraduate education courses. Following teacher training at St. Luke's College Exeter he read for his M.Ed (Educational Administration) at the University of Alberta, and has the Advanced Diploma (Special Needs) of the University of London.

His interests include the management of change, and the use of microcomputers in special education as both a learning and administrative tool. He has contributed to a number of conferences and Special Needs courses and for the last two years has been a tutor at the Cambridge Special Education Summer School. In recent years he has visited Sweden and the United States to give presentations and to observe their 'special provision' in action.

He is currently completing work on *Invent the Future: Managing Change in Schools* which will be published in 1989.

Keith Bovair, born Detroit, Michigan, 1949; graduate of the University of Michigan, BSc. Special Education Distinction, 1975; taught children with emotional and behavioural difficulties, Ferndale High School, Ferndale, Michigan (received a Community Mental Health Award for programme); moved to England in 1977; teacher in charge, Intermediate Treatment Unit, Sheffield, 1977–1980; headteacher, residential school for emotionally and behaviourally impaired, Tyne and Wear, 1980–1984; presently headteacher, the Lady Adrian School, Cambridge, for children with moderate learning difficulties. The school received the Schools Curriculum Award for 1987.

Mel Ainscow is a Tutor in Special Educational Needs at the Cambridge Institute of Education. He is also Honorary Lecturer at the University of East

Anglia. Previously he has been a headteacher and a local authority adviser. He has published widely in the special needs field and is well-known as a speaker at courses and conferences. Prior to taking up his post at Cambridge, Mel was co-director of the Special Needs Action Programme (SNAP), a major in-service training initiative about meeting special needs in ordinary schools. His latest book, *Encouraging Classroom Success*, was published by Fulton in June 1988. Currently he is working on a new book with Jim Muncey about meeting individual needs in primary schools.

Maggie Balshaw is currently an Area Coordinator for Special Educational Needs in Cambridgeshire. Her teaching experience encompasses mainstream primary schools, an all-age special school for moderate learning difficulties, and more recently an all-age special school (MLD) which over a period of years developed links with its local mainstream primary and secondary schools.

She has considerable in-service training provision experience with special school teachers, support teachers in both primary and secondary schools, 'named' teachers (special needs coordinators) in primary schools, and with assistants working with children with special needs in mainstream primary and secondary schools and a range of special schools.

She has an Advanced Diploma in Special Educational Needs (London Institute) and has recently successfully completed a piece of research at the Cambridge Institute of Education resulting in becoming a Research Associate.

Barry Carpenter is currently headteacher of Blythe Special School in Warwickshire. Following initial training at Westminster College Oxford he entered special education in 1976 taking up a post in an MLD school. From there he entered the SLD field specialising in curriculum development and augmentative communication. He completed postgraduate studies in special needs at Avery Hill College, and the University of Nottingham. He is currently a course tutor to the B. Phil (Ed)(Special Needs) at the University of Warwick. In addition he is a tutor for the British Institute of Mental Handicap and a teacher-supervisor for school's experience from Westhill College Birmingham. He contributes extensively to in-service training of teachers throughout the UK, particularly regarding the education of children with profound and multiple learning difficulties. In 1986 he undertook a lecture tour of Australia. He has published several articles and papers.

Allan Day is head of Southall School, which is an all-age special school for children with moderate learning difficulties in Telford, Shropshire. Having gained a modern language degree at Cambridge University, he began his teaching career teaching French to remedial and ESL pupils, followed by

Russian to Oxbridge entrants, before sidestepping into special education in a multi-ethnic Inner London special school. He subsequently took charge of a secondary school MLD unit before moving back into the special school sector, and has experience of both mainstream learning support and MLD schools at teaching and management levels. He gained his M.Ed. in the Social Psychology of Special Education at Liverpool University in 1980. He contributed to the Schools Council Programme 4, The Curriculum in Special Schools, and has lectured on curricular matters to practising mainstream and special school teachers, and students at Crewe and Alsager College. A term's Associateship at Crewe and Alsagar College in 1987 led to a report on links between special and ordinary schools, and his chapter draws on some of that material.

Tony Dessent is Area Educational Psychologist in Cambridgeshire. He has wide-ranging interests in the field of special educational needs and related services, and writes regularly on matters relating to integration, support services, working with parents, and the needs of pre-school pupils. He has contributed to *Reconstructing Educational Psychology* (ed. B. Gillan, 1978), to *Integrating Special Education* (eds. Booth and Potts, 1983), to *Management and the Special Schools* (ed. Bowers, 1984) to *Management and the Psychology of Schooling* (eds Jones and Sayer, 1988), and has recently written *Making the Ordinary School Special* (Falmer Press, 1987). He trained as a teacher working in middle schools in Norfolk before going on to train in educational psychology. In 1986, he was seconded to London University Institute of Education to carry out a special investigation into policy, provision and resourcing in relation to special educational needs in the ordinary schools.

Ian Galletley BA, MEd and B.Ed. (Hons), is the Principal of Britain's first Vocational College for 14–19 year olds. He has been the headteacher of three Special Schools and most recently Special Needs Advisor at Newcastle upon Tyne. Ian's earlier experience included mainstream teaching in a Leicestershire Community College and an inner city school in Wolverhampton. He has published many books and articles over the years.

Andrew Hinchcliff, B.Ed. University of Durham is presently deputy headteacher of a day special school for MLD. He has had previous experience in a Support Unit for Disruptive Pupils and was a teacher at a residential school for children with emotional and behavioural difficulties. He has lectured on various areas of special needs and has recently been involved in organising in-service courses for Welfare Assistants.

Ann Lewis is currently a lecturer in Education at the University of Warwick and joint editor of *Education 3–13*. She has had a wide variety of teaching experience including work in a special school, a special unit, and mainstream primary schools. She has been heavily involved in the development of curriculum-based assessment for children with learning difficulties, early identification procedures, and strategies to promote integration. She has published work on the professional and academic aspects of curricula for children with special needs, and is currently carrying out research into discourse strategies used by young non-handicapped children with peers with severe learning difficulties.

Jim Muncey is currently Adviser in Coventry where he is responsible for the SNAP programme. After a brief period of teaching in secondary modern schools Jim Muncey obtained a degree in experimental psychology from Cambridge University. He then taught in a grammar school and a residential school for pupils with emotional and behavioural difficulties. After completing professional training in educational psychology he worked as a psychologist in Norfolk and Coventry. He has written a number of articles on teaching approaches and in-service training and has contributed to books on special education.

Catherine Pearce took a degree in English at Oxford, and after a year's teaching fellowship at the University of Michigan, studied for a PGCE at the London Institute of Education, when James Britton and Nancy Martin were in charge of the work in English. She has been involved in Initial Training since 1958, with some years out while her children were small, and a second spell of work in school. She was an Open University tutor and counsellor for seven years, and was involved in the adult literacy programme. Her post at Homerton is her fourth in Colleges of Education; she has been there since 1977, and is now head of the English Department. She helped to edit *Short Stories of Today* (Barnes, 1963) and *Presenting Poetry* (Blackburn 1966), and wrote a book for Japanese readers: *Women in England Today* (1979).

Tom Peryer read History and English at York University prior to teacher training at Southampton. He taught for 10 years at comprehensive schools in the ILEA before moving into educational administration in 1984; he was Assistant Education Officer (Special Education) in the London Borough of Haringey from 1984–1988.

He is an education adviser to the Industrial Society, and has published *English in the Making* (1985) Cambridge University Press.

At present he is working as Development Officer for the Urban Studies Centre, an independent trust based in the East End of London.

Carmen Renwick, Cert. Ed., Adv. Dip. Ed. is currently completing an MA in Special Needs, University of East Anglia. Teaching experience has been as Head of Art and Design in a comprehensive and presently Assistant Head at day Special School for MLD. From September 1988, she will be a deputy headteacher of a Residential School for children with emotional and behavioural problems. She has had experience as a Youth Leader and Adult Tutor in various FE and local educational institutions.

Morag Styles, is presently Senior Lecturer and coordinator of Language Education at Homerton College Cambridge. Her initial training was at the University of Edinburgh and Homerton College. She has been extensively involved in in-service training on poetry and childrens' literature, has run poetry workshops and courses, and has written and edited numerous anthologies and poetry books including *I Like That Stuff* (1984).

Eileen Tombs, M.Ed is currently Adviser Special Educational Needs in Hertfordshire. Her career has included teaching in secondary schools, particularly regarding ROSLA, following which she worked for 18 months in the USA with inner-city children. In the early 1970s she entered special education and was later Acting Headteacher of an MLD school in London. This was followed by the headship of a school for children with complex learning difficulties, emotional, speech and language difficulties. She has undertaken research into record-keeping strategies for modified curriculum, and curriculum modifications and death education for children with terminal illness. At present she is particularly concerned with school-focused INSET developments.

Sheila Wolfendale is Tutor to the MSc Educational Psychology Course, Psychology Department, North East London Polytechnic. She has contributed extensively to journals and other publications on issues relating to parent involvement in schools, with multi-cultural education, on learning difficulties, and with early child education. She has co-authored *Identification of Learning Difficulties: A Model for Intervention* (1979), and *Word Play* (1986), and co-edited *Parental Involvement in Children's Reading* (1985). She has written *Parental Participation in Children's Development and Education* (1983), and *Primary Schools and Special Educational Needs; Policy, Planning and Provision* (1987). She has been a primary school and remedial teacher, worked as a Lecturer at Nottingham College of Education, and has been employed as an educational psychologist in Hull, Nottingham and Croydon LEA. It was in Croydon she worked on the Croydon Screening Procedures. From 1980–1981 she was research associate at Homerton College, Cambridge, investigating the whole area of parental involvement. She has been Guest Editor for the journals *Early Child Development and Care* and *Remedial Education* and is a member of the Advisory Board of the journal *Support for Learning* (NARE). During 1988 she was awarded the title of Professor in the Psychology department, North East London Polytechnic.

Mike Wright, Dip. Ed., M. Ed., is currently Senior Advisor, Special Educational Needs, Humberside. He previously was a headteacher of a day Special School and a deputy headteacher in two residential schools for ESN (M) and Maladjusted. He was a Lecturer Fellow at Sheffield Polytechnic, seconded for two years to be Lecturer at Sheffield Polytechnic, and a Consultant Special Needs Lecturer, Bretton Hall College. Over the years, he has contributed to numerous Department of Education and Science courses.

Bibliography

ADAMS, F. (Ed.) (1986) *Special Education*, Harlow, Longman.

AINSCOW, M.(Ed.) (1984) 'Curriculum management in special school: The role of management', in BOWERS, T. (Ed.) *Management and the Special School*, Beckenham, Croom Helm.

AINSCOW, M., and MUNCEY, J. (1983) 'Launching SNAP in Coventry', *Special Education: Forward Trends*, 10, 3, 8–12.

AINSCOW, M., and TWEDDLE, D.A. (1979) *Preventing Classroom Failure: An Objectives Approach*, Chichester, Wiley.

AINSCOW, M., and TWEDDLE, D.A. (1988) *Encouraging Classroom Success*, London, Fulton.

ALFONSO, R.J., FIRTH, G.R., and NEVILLE, R. (1975) *Instructional Supervision*, Boston, Allyn and Bacon.

ARMSTRONG, S.P. (1986) *A Comparative Study of Outreach Support Services from Schools for Children with Moderate Learning Difficulties*, unpublished M.A. thesis, University of London Institute of Education.

ATKINSON, E. (1984) 'Thirty years on: A study of former pupils of a Special School', *Special Education, Forward Trends*, December.

BAKER, D.S. (1970) *Personnel Utilisation*, unpublished Master's thesis, University of Alberta.

BAKER, D.S. (1989, in preparation) *Invent the Future: Managing Change in Schools*, Lewes, Falmer Press.

BALSHAW, M.H., (1987) 'Mainstream support work — What *is* it all about?', in BOWERS, T. (Ed.) *Special Educational Needs and Human Resource Management*, London, Croom Helm.

BALSHAW, M.H. (1988) *It's not what you do: it's the way that you do it: A case study of a group of schools working co-operatively*, unpublished dissertation for Research Associateship, Cambridge Institute of Education.

BASTIANI, J. (Ed.) (1987) *Parents and Teacher 1: Perspectives on Home—School Relations*, Windsor, NFER-Nelson.

BEATTIE, N. (1985) *Professional Parents*, Lewes, Falmer Press.

BECKER, W., and ENGLEMANN, S., (1977) *The Oregon Direct Institution Model. Comparative Results in Project Follow Through. A summary of Nine Years of Work*, Eugene, Oregon, University of Oregon Project Follow Through.

BENNIS, W.G., BENNE, K.D., CHIN, R., and COREY, K.E. (1975) *The Planning of Change*, New York, Holt, Rinehart and Winston.

BINES, H. (1986) *Redefining Remedial Education*, London, Croom Helm.

BLANCHARD, K., ZIGAMI, P., and ZIGAMI, D. (1986) *Leadership and the One Minute Manager*, Glasgow, Collins.

BLOOM, B. (1979) *Alterable Variables: The New Direction in Educational Research*, Edinburgh, Scottish Council for Research in Education.

BLYTHE SCHOOL (staff) (1986) *Working with Makaton*, Surrey, Makaton Vocabulary Development Project.

BOND, J., and LEWIS, A. (1982) 'Reversing a sentence for life', *Special Education: Forward Trends*, 9, 4, 11–13.

BOND, J., and SHARROCK, C. (1984) 'Castle School lends support', *British Journal of Special Education*, 11, 4.

BOOTH, T. (1987) *Integration. A Framework of Support*, Centre for Studies on Integration in Education, The Spastic Society.

BOOTH, T., POTTS, P. and SWANN, W. (1987) *Preventing Difficulties in Learning*, Oxford, Basil Blackwell/Open University Press.

BOWERS, T. (Ed.) (1984) *Management and the Special School*, Beckenham, Croom Helm.

BOWERS, T. (1987) *Special Educational Needs and Human Resource Management*, London, Croom Helm.

BRAY, E. (1986) in LLOYD-JONES, R. and BRAY, E. *et al.*, (Eds) *Assessment: From Principles to Action*, Basingstoke, Macmillans.

BRENNAN, W.K. (1979) *Curricular Needs of Slow Learners*, London, Evans/Methuen.

BRENNAN, W. (1985) *Curriculum for Special Needs*, Milton Keynes, Open University.

BROADFOOT, P. (Ed.) (1986) *Profiles and Records of Achievement*, London, Holt Education.

BROWDER, D. (1983) 'Guidelines for in-service planning', *Exceptional Children*, 49, 3, 300–306.

BRUDENELL, P. (1986) *The Other Side of Profound Handicap*, Basingstoke, Macmillan Educational.

BRUNER, J. (1966) *The Process of Education*, Harvard University Press.

BUCKLEY, S. (1985) 'Teaching parents to teach reading to teach language: A project with Down's Syndrome children and their parents' in TOPPING, K. and WOLFENDALE, S. (Eds), *Parental Involvement in Children's Reading*, Beckenham, Croom Helm.

BUCKLEY, S., EMSLIE, M., HASLEGRAVE, G., and LEPREVOST, P. (1986) *The Development of Language and Reading Skills in Children with Down's Syndrome*, Portsmouth Polytechnic.

BUNNELL, S. (1987) opinion in *Teachers Weekly*, 30/11.

CAMERON, R.J. (Ed.) (1986) *Portage: Pre-schoolers, Parents and Professionals*, Windsor, NFER-Nelson.

CAMPBELL, R.J. (1985) *Developing the Primary Curriculum*, Eastbourne, Holt, Rinehart and Winston.

CARPENTER, B. (1984) 'Curriculum development using the skills analysis model: A practitioner's viewpoint', *Mental Handicap*, 12, 58–59.

CARPENTER, B. (1987) 'Curriculum planning for children with profound and multiple learning difficulties', *Early Child Development and Care*, 28, 2, 149–162.

CARPENTER, B., LEWIS, A., and MOORE, J. (1986) 'Integration: A project involving young children with severe learning difficulties and first school children', *Mental Handicap*, 14, 4, 152–157.

CARR, J. (1980) *Helping your Handicapped Child*, Harmondsworth, Penguin.

CAVE, C. and MADDISON, P. (1978) *A Survey of Recent Research in Special Education*, Slough, NFER.

CENTRE FOR STUDIES ON INTEGRATION IN EDUCATION *see* CSIE.

CHILDREN'S LEGAL CENTRE (1985) *The Flaws in the 1981 Act*, paper given at the International Congress on Special Education, Nottingham.

CLARK, D., LOTTO, L., and ASTUTO, T., (1984) 'Effective schools and school improvement: A comparative analysis of two lines of enquiry', *Educational Administration Quarterly*, 20, 3, 41–68.

CLERKIN, C. (1987) 'Preparing job descriptions: The Head's role', in CRAIG, I. (Ed.) *Primary School Management in Action*, Harlow, Longman.

CLUNIES-ROSS, L., and WIMHURST, S. (1983) *The Right Balance*, Windsor, NFER-Nelson.

COHEN, A., and COHEN, L. (1986) *SEN in the Ordinary School*, London, Harper and Row.

CORNWELL, N. (1987) *Statementing and the 1981 Education Act*, Cranefield, Cranefield Press.

COUPE, J. and PORTER, J. (Eds) (1986) *The Education of Children with Severe Learning Difficulties: Bridging the Gap between Theory and Practice*, Beckenham, Croom Helm.

CPRA (1987) *A Guide for Schools*, University of Cambridge Local Examination Syndicate, Cambridgeshire County Council.

CRAFT, M., RAYNOR, J., and COHEN, L. (Eds) (1980) *Linking Home and School, A New Review*, 3rd ed., London, Harper and Row.

CRAIG, I. (Ed.) (1987) *Primary School Management in Action*, Harlow, Longman.

CROLL, P., and MOSES, D. (1985) *One in Five — The Assessment and Incidence of Special Educational Needs*, London, Routledge and Kegan Paul.

CROYDON EDUCATION AUTHORITY (1985) *Primary Education in Croydon: A Guide for Parents*, Croydon, Croydon Education Authority and the Voluntary School Authorities in Croydon.

CSIE (Centre for Studies on Integration in Education) (1986) *Caught in the Act: What LEAs Tell Parents under the 1981 Education Act*, Croydon, The Spastics Society.

CULLINGFORD, C. (Ed.) (1985) *Parents, Teachers and Schools*, London, Robert Royce.

CUNNINGHAM, C. (1985) 'Training and education approaches for parents of children with special needs', in DAVIS, H., and BUTCHER, P. (Eds.) *Sharing Psychological Skills*, Leicester, The British Psychological Society.

CUNNINGHAM, C. and DAVIS, H. (1985) *Working with Parents: Frameworks for Collaboration*, Milton Keynes, Open University Press.

DALE, N. (1986) 'Parents as partners: What does this mean to parents of children with special needs?', *Educational and Child Psychology*, 3, 13.

DAY, C., JOHNSTON, D., and WHITAKER, P. (1985) *Managing Primary Schools: A Professional Development Approach*, London, Harper and Row.

DES (1974) *In-Service Education and Training* (Advisory Committee on the Supply and training of teachers), London, HMSO.

DES (1978) *Special Educational Needs* (The Warnock Report), London, HMSO.

DES (1980) *Special Educational Needs* (White Paper), London, HMSO.

DES (1981a) *Education Act*, London, HMSO.

DES (1981b) *The School Curriculum*, London, HMSO.

DES (1983) *Assessments and Statements of Special Educational Needs* (Circular 1/83), London, DES/HMSO.

DES (1984) *From Coping to Confidence*, London, DES.

DES (1985a) *Better Schools*, London, HMSO.

DES (1985b) *The Curriculum for 5–16* (Curriculum Matters 2. An HMI Series), London, HMSO.

DES (1987a) *The National Curriculum 5-16: A Consultation Document*, London, DES.

DES (1987b) *Task Group on Assessment and Testing, A Report*, London, DES.

DEPARTMENT OF HEALTH AND SOCIAL WELFARE (1987) *Mental Handicap: Patterns for Living*, Milton Keynes, Open University.

DESSENT, T. (1984) 'Special schools and the mainstream — The resource stretch', in Bowers, T. (Ed.) *Management and the Special School*, London, Croom Helm.

DESSENT, T. (1987) *Making the Ordinary School Special*, Lewes, Falmer.

ESP, D. (1987) 'Employer/employee relationships: A chief education officer's viewpoint', in CRAIG, I. (Ed.) *Primary School Management in Action*, Harlow, Longman.

EVANS, J. (1987) *Decision-making for Special Needs*, pilot edition, Institute of Education, University of London.

EVANS, K. (1965) *Attitudes and Interests in Education*, London, Routledge and Kegan Paul.

EVANS, L., FORDER, A., WARD, L., and CLARKE, I. (1986) *Working with Parents of Handicapped Children*, London, Bedford Square Press/NCVO.

EVANS, P., and WARE, J. (1987) *Special Care Provision: The Education of Children with Profound and Multiple Learning Difficulties*, Windsor, NFER/Nelson.

FAMILY FOCUS (1983) 'Parents: Underrated but undeterred?', *Special Education, Forward Trends*, 10, 4, 27–28.

FISH, J. (1984) *Special Education: The Way Ahead*, Milton Keynes, Open University.

FISH, J. (1985) *Educational Opportunities for All?*, London, ILEA.

FLANDERS, N.A. (1970) *Analyzing Teacher Behaviour*, Reading, Addison-Wesley.

FULLAN, M. (1982) *The Meaning of Educational Change*, New York, Teachers College Press.

GALLETLEY, I. (1984) 'Shared leadership in the school', in BOWERS, T. (Ed.) *Management and the Special School*, Beckenham, Croom Helm.

GALLOWAY, D., and GOODWIN, C. (1987) *The Education of Disturbing Children*, London, Longman.

GARDNER, J., MURPHY, J., and CRAWFORD, N. (1983) *The Skills Analysis Model*, Kidderminster, British Institute of Mental Handicap.

GEORGIADES, N.J., and PHILLIMORE, L. (1975) 'The myth of the hero innovator and alternative strategies for organisational change' in KIERNAN, C., and WOODFORD, F. *Behaviour Modification for the Severely Retarded*, Oxford, Association of Scientific Publishers.

GIPPS, C., GROSS, H., and GOLDSTEIN, H. (1987) *Warnock's Eighteen Percent*, Lewes, Falmer Press.

GLEIDMAN, J., and ROTH, W. (1981) 'Parents and professionals' in SWANN, W. (Ed.) *The Practice of Special Education*, Oxford, Basil Blackwell and Open University Press.

GOODWIN, C. (1983) 'The contribution of support services to integration policy' in BOOTH, T., and POTTS, T. (Eds.) *Integrating Special Education*, Oxford, Blackwell.

GRAY, J. (1979) 'Reading progress in infant schools: Some problems emerging from a study of teacher effectiveness', *British Education Research Journal*, Vol. 5, No. 2.

GROSS, H., and GIPPS, C. (1987) *Supporting Warnock's Eighteen Percent*, Lewes, Falmer Press.

GULLIFORD, R. (1971) *Special Educational Needs*, London, Routledge and Kegan Paul.

GULLIFORD, R. (1985) *Teaching Children with Learning Difficulties*, Windsor, NFER-Nelson.

HALLMARK, N. (1983) 'A Support Service to Primary Schools', in BOOTH, T., and POTTS, P. (Eds) *Integrating Special Education*, Oxford, Blackwell.

HALLMARK, N., and DESSENT, T. (1982) 'A special education service centre', *British Journal of Special Education*, 9, 1.

HANKO, G. (1986) *Special Needs in Ordinary Classrooms — An Approach to Teacher Support and Pupil Care*, 2nd ed., Oxford, Blackwell.

HARING, N.G., LOVITT, T.C., EATON, M.D. and HANSEN, C.L. (1978) *The Fourth R: Research in the Classroom*, Columbus, Merrill.

HARING, N.J., STERN, G.G. and CRUICKSHANK, W.M. (1958) *Attitudes of Educators Toward Exceptional Children*, Syracuse (NY), Syracuse University Press.

HARINGEY, LONDON BOROUGH OF (1987) *A Review of Special Educational Needs*, London, Borough of Haringey.

HART, S. (1986) 'Evaluating support teaching', *Gnosis*, No. 9, Sept. 1986, ILEA SPS.

HATCH, S., and HINTON, T. (1986) *Self-Help in Practice — A Study of Contact-a-Family, Community Work and Family Support*, Joint Unit for Social Services Research, Sheffield University and Community Care.

HAVELOCK, R.G. (1973) *The Change Agent's Guide to Innovation in Education*, New Jersey, Educational Technology Publications.

HEDDERLEY, R. and JENNINGS, K. (Eds.) (1987) *Extending and Developing Portage*, Windsor, NFER-Nelson.

HERBERT, M. (1985) *Caring for your Children: a Practical Guide*, Oxford, Basil Blackwell.

HOGG, J., and SEBBA, J. (1986) *Profound Retardation and Multiple Impairment, Volume II*, Beckenham, Croom Helm.

HOLDAWAY, E.A. (1978) *Teacher Satisfaction with Working Conditions*, Edmonton, University of Alberta.

HOPKINS, D. (1985) *A Teacher's Guide to Classroom Research*, Milton Keynes, Open University Press.

HOPKINS, D. (1987) *Improving the Quality of Schooling*, Lewes, Falmer Press.

HOUSE OF COMMONS (1987) *see* Select Committee Report (1987).

HULL UNIVERSITY (1986) *Aspects of Education*, Hull University.

ILEA (1985a) *Improving Primary Schools*, London, ILEA.

ILEA (1985b) *Educational Opportunities for All?* (Fish Report), London, ILEA.

IMISON, T. (1985) 'How to get a Head', *Education*, 18/1/85.

INDEPENDENT DEVELOPMENT COUNCIL (1985) *Living Like Other People: Next Steps in Day Services for People with a Mental Handicap*, London, IDC.

JOHNSON, D.W., and JOHNSON, R.T. (1986) 'Mainstreaming and co-operative learning strategies', *Exceptional Children*, 52 (6), 553–561.

JOHNSON, V.R., and WERNER, R. (1980) *A Step by Step Learning Guide for Older Retarded Children*, London, Constable.

JONES, K. (1985) *The Special Education Consultant Teacher*, paper presented at International Special Education Congress, University of Nottingham.

JOWETT, S., HEGARTY, S., and MOSES, D. (1988) *Joining Forces: A Story of Links Between Special and Ordinary Schools*, Windsor, NFER-Nelson.

KITSUSE, J.I. (1962) 'Societal reaction to deviant behaviour', in BECKER, H.S. (Ed.) (1964) *The Other Side: Perspectives on Deviance*, New York, Free Press.

KRAMER, J. (1987) 'Special educational needs and the voluntary groups, a report on the conultative process', *European Journal of Special Needs Education*, Vol. 2, No. 1, 53–62.

LEWIS, A. (1987) 'Modification of discourse strategies by mainstream six to seven year olds towards peers with severe learning difficulties', *Proceedings of the Child Language Seminar*, University of York.

LEWIS, A. and LEWIS, V. (1987) 'The attitudes of young children towards peers with severe learning difficulties', *British Journal of Developmental Psychology*, 5, 287–292.

LEWIS, A. and LEWIS, V. (in preparation) 'The attitudes of young children towards peers with severe learning difficulties: A follow-up study'.

LOMBANA, J. (1983) *Home-School Partnerships, Guidelines and Strategies for Educators*, Grune and Stratton, London.

McCONACHIE, H. (1986) *Parents and Young Mentally Handicapped Children: A Review of Research Issues*, Beckenham, Croom Helm.

McCONKEY, R. and McCORMACK, B. (1983) *Breaking Barriers: Educating People about Disability*, London, Souvenir Press.

McCONKEY, R., McCORMACK, B. and NAUGHTON, M. (1983) *CARA Project — Information Pack*, St Michael's House Research/Health Education Bureau.

McPHERSON, R.R., CROWSON, N. and PITNER (1986) *Managing Uncertainty: Administrative Theory and Practice in Education*, Hemel Hempstead, Prentice-Hall.

MAR MOLINERO, C. and GARD, G.F. (1987) 'Distribution of special educational (Moderate) needs in Southampton', *British Education Research Journal*, Vol. 13, No. 2, 147–158.

MASLOW, A.H. (1965) *Eupsychian Management*, Homewood, IL., Irwin.

MASON, A. (1987) 'The Headteacher's role in the development of staff' in CRAIG, I. (Ed.) *Primary School Management in Action*, Harlow, Longmans.

MENCAP *A London Directory of Services*, London, MENCAP.

MIKLOS, E., BOURGETTE, P. and COWLEY, S. (1972) *Perspectives on Educational Planning*, Edmonton, Human Resources Research Council.

MILLARD, D. (1984) *Daily Living with a Handicapped Child*, Beckenham, Croom Helm.

MITTLER, P. and McCONACHIE, H. (Eds) (1983) *Parents, Professionals and Mentally Handicapped People*, Beckenham, Croom Helm.

MOORE, J., CARPENTER, B. and LEWIS, A. (1987) '"He can do it really" — Integration in a first school', *Education 3–13*, 15 (2), 37–43.

MORGAN, C., HALL, V. and MACKAY, H. (1984) *A Handbook for Selecting Senior Staff for Schools*, Open University Press.

MULLINS, S. (1982) *A Study of the Role of the Support Teacher in Relation to Children with Special Educational Needs in Mainstream Primary Schools in Sheffield*, unpublished M.Ed. dissertation, University of Sheffield.

MUNCEY, J. and WINTERINGHAM, D. (1987) *Special Needs in the Secondary School; A workshop for School Governors*, Coventry LEA.

NAGM (National Association of Governors and Managers) *Governors and Special Educational Needs, Paper No. 5*, Sheffield, NAGM.

NEWALL, P. (1985) 'Backlash — Don't gag the professionals', *British Journal of Special Education*, 12, 1, 9.

NEWSON, E., and HIPGRAVE, T. (1982) *Getting through to your Handicapped child*, Cambridge University Press.

ORTON, C. (1986) *Integration in Practice*, London, Spastics Society.

OUVRY, C. (1986) 'Integrating pupils with profound and multiple handicaps', *Mental Handicap*, 14, 157–160.

OUVRY, C. (1987) *Educating Children with Profound Handicaps*, Kidderminster, British Institute of Mental Handicap.

OWENS, R.G. (1970) *Organisational Behaviour in Schools*, New Jersey, Prentice-Hall.

POWERS, D.Q. (1983) 'Mainstreaming and the in-service education of teachers', *Exceptional Children*, 49, 5, 432–439.

PUGH, G. (1981) *Parents as Partners*, London, National Children's Bureau.

RECTORY PADDOCK (STAFF) (1983) *In Search of a Curriculum*, Kent, Robin Wren Publications.

REED, J. (1986) 'Managing change in the primary school: what we have learned about the role of external support', *School Organisation*, 6, 3, 339–345.

ROBSON, C., *et al.* (1987) *In-Service Training and Special Educational Needs*, Manchester University Press.

RUSSELL, P. (1986) 'Parents as partners: The changing scene', in COUPE, J. and PORTER, J. (Eds.) *The Education of Children with Severe Learning Difficulties*, Beckenham, Croom Helm.

SANDOW, S., STAFFORD, D. and STAFFORD, P. (1987) *An Agreed Understanding? Parent-professional Communication and the 1981 Education Act*, Windsor, NFER–Nelson.

SANDBROOK, I. (1987) 'Appraisal — the system in one primary school', in CRAIG, I. (Ed.) *Primary School Management in Action*, Harlow, Longman.

SCHEIN, E.H. (1970) *Organisational Psychology*, New Jersey, Prentice-Hall.

SCULLEY, J. (1987) *Odyssey*, New York, Harper and Row.

SELECT COMMITTEE REPORT (1987) *Special Educational Needs: Implementation of the Education Act 1981*, Third Report from the Education, Science and Arts Committee of the House of Commons, London, HMSO.

SERGIOVANNI, T.J. and CARVER, F.E. (1973) *The New School Executive*, Toronto, Dodd and Mead.

SHEARER, A. (1983) *Integration: A New Partnership*, London, ACE/Spastics Society.

SHEARS, B., and WOOD, S. (1987) *Teaching Children with Severe Learning Difficulties: A Radical Reappraisal*, Beckenham, Croom Helm.

SMITH, C.J. (1985) *New Directions in Remedial Education*, Lewes, Falmer Press.

SMITH, D. (1986) 'Participating parents: promise and practice', *Educational and Child Psychology*, 3, 3.

SOLITY, J. and BULL, S. (1987) *Bridging the Curriculum Gap*, Milton Keynes, Open University Press.

STAINBACK, W. and STAINBACK, S. (1984) 'A rationale for the merger of special and regular education', *Exceptional Children*, 51, 2, 102–111.

STENHOUSE, L. (1975) *An Introduction to Curriculum Research and Development*, London, Heinemann.

STONE, K. (1987) *The Statementing Process, Professional Power and Parental Interests (Social Work Monograph 51)*, Norwich, University of East Anglia.

STUBBS, M. and DELAMONT, S. (1976) *Explorations in Classroom Observation*, London, John Wiley.

SWANN, W. (1985) 'Is the integration of children with special needs happening?: An analysis of recent statistics of pupils in special schools', *Oxford Review of Education*, 11, 1.

SWANN, W. (1987) 'The educational consequences of Mr Baker', *Special Children*, 13, 18–19.

TASK GROUP ON ASSESSMENT AND TESTING, *see* DES (1987b).

THOMAS, G. (1985) 'Integrating personnel in order to integrate children', *Support for Learning*, 1, 1, 19–26.

TOMLINSON, S. (1982) *A Sociology of Special Education*, London, Routledge and Kegan Paul.

TOMLINSON, S. (1983) 'Why assess — and who benefits?', *Special Education, Forward Trends*, 10, 4, 10–12.

TOPPING, K. (1986) *Parents as Educators*, Beckenham, Croom Helm.

TOPPING, K. (1988) 'Parents as reading tutors for children with special needs' in JONES, N. (Ed.) *Special Educational Needs Yearbook*, London, Woburn Press.

TOPPING, K. and WOLFENDALE, S. (Eds.) (1985) *Parental Involvement in Children's Reading*, Beckenham, Croom Helm.

TOWFIQUEY-HOOSHYAR, N. and ZINGLE, H.W. (1984) 'Regular class students' attitudes toward integrated multiply handicapped peers', *American Journal of Mental Deficiency*, 88 (6), 630–637.

TURNER, P. (1984) 'Headship: Aspects of the role', in Bowers, T. (Ed.) *Management and the Special School*, Beckenham, Croom Helm.

WALKER, M. (1978) 'The Makaton Vocabulary', in TEBBS, T. (Ed.) *Ways and Means*, Basingstoke, Globe Education.

WEBSTER, A. (1986) *Deafness, Development and Literacy*, London, Methuen.

WEINDLING, D., and EARLEY, P. (1986) *Secondary Headship: The First Years*, Windsor, NFER-Nelson.

WELLER, K. (1985) 'A chart of the New World Examinations', *Education*, 165 (22), 485–490.

WESTMACOTT, E.V.S., and CAMERON, R.J. (1981) *Behaviour Can Change*, Basingstoke, Globe Education.

WILLIAMS, T. (1980) Unpublished presentation to the 1980 NCSE Conference.

WOLFENDALE, S. (1983) *Parental Participation in Children's Development and Education*, London, Gordon and Breach.

WOLFENDALE, S. (1986) 'Parental contribution to Section 5 (Education Act 1981) assessment procedures', *Early Child Development and Care*, 25, 3 and 4.

WOLFENDALE, S. (1987a) 'Parents and professionals in cooperation: Workshop on developing skills for successful co-working', *Educational and Child Psychology*, 4, 3 and 4.

WOLFENDALE, S. (1987b) 'Involving parents in behaviour management: a whole-school approach', in HINSON, M. (Ed.) *Teachers and Special Educational Needs*, Harlow, Longman and NARE.

WOLFENDALE, S. (1987c) *Primary Schools and Special Needs: Policy, Planning and Provision*, London, Cassell.

WOLFENDALE, S. (1988a) *The Parental Contribution to Assessment* (Developing Horizons No. 10), Stratford upon Avon, National Council for Special Education.

WOLFENDALE, S. (1988b) *Records of Achievement and Pupil Profiling: the Parental Dimension*, unpublished report, North East London Polytechnic Psychology Department.

WOLFENDALE, S. (1989, in preparation) *Dimensions of Parental Involvement: a book of readings*, London, Cassell.

WOLFENSBERGER, W. (1972) *The Principle of Normalisation in Human Services*, Toronto, National Institute on Mental Retardation.

YOUNG, LADY (1981) in *The Guardian*, 20/2/81.

Index